TRUMAN CAPOTE

A *Study of the Short Fiction*

Also available in Twayne's Studies in Short Fiction Series

Twayne's Studies in Short Fiction

Gordon Weaver, General Editor
Oklahoma State University

TRUMAN CAPOTE
Photograph courtesy of the National Archives, Washington, D.C.

TRUMAN CAPOTE

A Study of the Short Fiction

Helen S. Garson
George Mason University

TWAYNE PUBLISHERS • _NEW YORK_
Maxwell Macmillan Canada • _Toronto_
Maxwell Macmillan International • _New York Oxford Singapore Sydney_

Twayne's Studies in Short Fiction Series, No. 36

Twayne Publishers
Macmillan Publishing Company
866 Third Avenue
New York, New York 10022

Maxwell Macmillan Canada, Inc.
1200 Eglinton Avenue East
Suite 200
Don Mills, Ontario M3C 3N1

Macmillan Publishing Company is part of the Maxwell Communication Group of Companies.

Library of Congress Cataloging-in-Publication Data

Garson, Helen S.
    Truman Capote : a study of the short fiction / Helen S. Garson.
        p.   cm. — (Twayne's studies in short fiction : no. 36)
    Includes bibliographical references and index.
    ISBN 0-8057-0851-0
    1. Capote, Truman, 1924–   —Criticism and interpretation.
    2. Short story. I. Title. II. Series.
    PS3505.A59Z6553   1992
    813′.54—dc20   92-10836
                                                                        CIP

The paper used in this publication meets the minimum requirements of American National Standard for Information Sciences—Permanence of Paper for Printed Library Materials. ANSI Z3948-1984.∞™

10 9 8 7 6 5 4 3 2 1

Printed in the United States of America

For Neil

Contents

Preface

Truman Capote was a man of many faces. Like the ringmaster at a circus, he led us from one dazzling act to another. He wrote short stories, novels, novellas, a "nonfiction novel," plays, film scripts, and a variety of journalistic pieces. Although not a prolific writer, he seemed to want to explore every type of writing.

Despite success with many forms, Capote came closest to achieving descriptive, formal, and imaginative perfection in his short fictions. The short stories and novellas bring us closest to Capote the writer and the man. Perhaps that is because he was an autobiographical writer, who—from first to last—fictionalized the key experiences of his life. He was very personal in both style and subject matter. He often made himself a player in his stories and called his reader's attention to the identity between writer and character by giving the person a name or initials like his own. He sometimes even stated flatly that he was himself a particular child or adult character.

But it is easy to be misled by Capote into believing that something is "true," or nonfictional; for whatever reasons he thought important at the time, he attached such labels to a number of works, both fictional and nominally nonfictional. *Handcarved Coffins* should serve as a warning to those tempted to read all Capote's fiction as a form of autobiography. Published more than a decade after the enormously successful *In Cold Blood*, it was Capote's attempt to recover from both personal and professional devastation. He had been unprepared for the adverse reaction of critics and friends to a group of gossipy tales published in *Esquire* in the seventies. He responded to these attacks by creating what purports to be another "nonfiction" piece about a criminal to show he was still a master writer in control of his art. A close reading of the story, however, tells us that, once again, Capote was manipulating terminology; indeed, *Handcarved Coffins* is really a fictional hoax on reviewers who had questioned the authenticity of *In Cold Blood*.

In interviews he granted and essays he wrote, Capote suggested that art transforms reality, and that as a consequence, in a sense, true stories are actually false to the facts that underlie them. Most writers would agree with that observation, and also with his assertion that the artist is obligated to nobody and nothing but his art. However, friends, interviewers, and biographers have often noted that Capote used terms such as "truth" and "facts" to suit himself. He was equally cavalier about labeling his stories. For purposes of publication, or publicity, or even for effect, he altered descriptions. At various times he labeled *Breakfast at Tiffany's* a short story, a novella, and a novel. Apparently to maximize his earnings for *One Christmas*, a slim work of 41 pages, it was published in book form, thus suggesting that this short story was a novel or at least a novella. He used the term "novel" to describe the unconnected stories that were to comprise *Answered Prayers*. And he claimed that *Handcarved Coffins*, clearly an imaginative work, was "nonfiction." Thus we cannot take Capote's classifications for his work as authoritative.

In the first two decades of Capote's professional life critics talked of the extremes in his work, using such images as daylight and darkness to suggest the Janus-like characteristics of the fiction. A number of his short stories belong to the mode of his first novel, *Other Voices, Other Rooms*, in their marked affiliation with the southern gothic style. The fact that some of these stories are set outside the South does not alter the categorization, for most of the pieces in the collection *A Tree of Night and Other Stories* fit the definition of new gothic. They are stories of fear, terror, and horror, of loneliness, psychological doubling, and disintegration. Some are about betrayal, some are about schizophrenia, and some are about both. Although Capote never returned to the dreamlike, nightmare world, part reality and part fantasy, that distinguishes "Master Misery," "Miriam," "A Tree of Night," "The Headless Hawk" and "Shut a Final Door," he never lost interest in the kinds of characters who inhabited that world. In one guise or another, similar characters would appear in various later essays, fiction, and purported nonfiction.

The works most celebrated by his readers—apart from his widely acclaimed "novel," *In Cold Blood*—are total opposites of the early gothic stories. Other fictions he wrote, "Children on Their Birthdays," *Breakfast at Tiffany's*, *The Grass Harp*, and *A Christmas Memory* are gentle, tender, funny stories tinged with a soft-hued melancholy and a yearning for the past, for the lost world of childhood when it seemed everything was possible, and for the joy of beginnings, of being young, of starting out. Capote's later stories, even those that focus on childhood, hold little of the happiness and hopefulness that shine out from "Children on Their Birthdays," *Breakfast at Tiffany's*, *The Grass Harp*, and *A Christmas Memory*. *The Thanksgiving Visitor*, clearly intended to capitalize on the phenomenal success of *A Christmas Memory* (it uses some of the same cast of characters), speaks more of the harsh lessons of childhood than of its pleasures. And the story "Dazzle," which appeared at the end of the seventies, which also goes back to childhood, is written in the confessional mode the author adopted earlier in that decade.

Although most of Capote's stories share resemblances to other stories, in 1960 he wrote a one-of-a-kind piece called "Among the Paths to Eden." Realistic, unsentimental, with an unusual setting and a unique Capote protagonist, it lacks any of the hallmarks of the writer. When it appeared, at least one critic believed Capote was moving into another type of short fiction. William Nance postulated a link between the research Capote was doing for *In Cold Blood* and "Among the Paths to Eden." He noted that the story "shows signs of the new strength and freedom he feels he derived from his work on the nonfiction novel. One of his principle aims in that project was to enlarge the range of characters he could portray sympathetically. In this story he does precisely that."[1] Nance's statement proved to be partly prophetic. Capote's stories did change, but not in the manner Nance predicted. The later stories have an air of fatigue, and the characters are harshly drawn.

The writer had sent out signals for some time that he was interested in turning gossip into art, but nobody was prepared for the type of stories that were intended to be part of the picaresque, and as it turned out, unfinished, novel, *Answered Prayers*. The night before his death Capote announced to a friend, at whose home he was staying, that he had just completed the work, but all we have of it are three of the same four stories that had already appeared in *Esquire* in 1975 and 1976: "La Côte Basque," "Unspoiled Monsters," and "Kate McCloud." "Mojave," the first of the four *Esquire* stories, was originally projected as part of the novel, but was printed instead in *Music for Chameleons*. These stories, long and rambling, in questionable taste, and revelatory of a writer who had lost his finely honed sense of style and form, nevertheless have important biographical significance. They provide insight into both Capote and his art.

In spite of the critical view that Capote had written his best work long before his death, his distinctinction as a writer of short fiction remains undisputed. From the moment he first appeared on the scene in the 1940s he was regarded as an innovator, different from earlier writers in both subject matter and technique. In one form or another, all his work remains in print. Much of it has been translated into other languages. Many reference books concerned with modern American fiction contain articles about Capote. Although in Capote's lifetime some people confused the celebrity, the "star," with the writer, the writer was dedicated to his craft, and his best work will surely become part of America's literary treasury.

I wish to thank my students for sharing their insights with me, and to express my gratitude to Professor Roger Lathbury of George Mason University, Professor Jan Nordby Gretlund of Odense University, Professor Melvin Friedman of the University of Wisconsin, and Mrs. Florence Feiler, literary agent for the Rungstedlund Foundation, for their special help.

Note

1. William L. Nance, *The Worlds of Truman Capote* (New York: Stein and Day, 1973), 83.

Acknowledgments

Blake Allmendinger, "The Room Was Locked, with the Key on the Inside: Female Influence in Truman Capote's 'My Side of the Matter.'" *Studies in Short Fiction* 24 (Summer 1987): 279–88. Reprinted with permission of *Studies in Short Fiction* at Newberry College.

Karen Blixen (Isak Dinesen), "Introduction" to *Holly* (*Breakfast at Tiffany's*)," trans. Jan Nordby Gretlund (Denmark: Gyldendal, 1960). Printed with permission of the Rungstedlund Foundation.

Melvin J. Friedman, "Towards an Aesthetic: Truman Capote's Other Voices." In *Truman Capote's 'In Cold Blood': A Critical Handbook*, ed. Irving Malin (Belmont, Calif.: Wadsworth, 1968), 163–76. Reprinted with permission of the author.

Peter Hays, *The Limping Hero* (New York: New York University Press, 1971), 42–44, 88–89. Reprinted with permission of the author.

Michael J. Larsen, "Capote's 'Miriam' and the Literature of the Double." *International Fiction Review* 7, no.1 (1980): 53–54. Reprinted with permission of the author.

Paul Levine, "Truman Capote: The Revelation of the Broken Image." *Virginia Quarterly Review* 34 (Autumn 1958): 600–617. Reprinted with permission of *Virginia Quarterly Review*.

Robert Siegle, "Capote's *Handcarved Coffins* and the Nonfiction Novel." *Contemporary Literature* 25, no. 4 (Winter 1984): 437–51. ©1984 by the Board of Regents of the University of Wisconsin System. Reprinted with permission of the editor.

Photograph courtesy of the National Archives, Washington, D.C.

Part 1

THE SHORT FICTION

The Gothic World

"A Tree of Night"

Of the eight stories that comprise Capote's first published collection of short fiction, *A Tree of Night and Other Stories* (1949), five are dark pieces in the new gothic mode with which the author had been identified since the appearance of his first novel, *Other Voices, Other Rooms*. Like the novel, "A Tree of Night," "Miriam," "The Headless Hawk," "Master Misery," and "Shut a Final Door" offer shadowy and elusive mixtures of reality, dreams, and fantasy. The gender and ages of the principal characters, the setting, and other incidental features may vary from one story to the next, but those differences do not alter the underlying relationship of the pieces.

Like traditional gothic fiction, new gothic has a strong element of terror, but the terror is usually brought about by internal weakness and character flaws rather than by some external force. New gothic characters are flat and stylized, narcissistic and obsessive, weak and anxiety-ridden. Southern gothic stories frequently include characters who are cripples, homosexuals, freaks, or dwarfs. In the new gothic, family plays an important negative role; in many stories of this type the family is responsible for the disintegration of the protagonist. The parent is never kind, thoughtful, or concerned for the welfare of the child. Instead, he or she is a destroyer of self-esteem, hope, and identity. Communication has long since broken down or never existed, and often the protagonist seems to live in a world of silence.

The forces set loose by the family or environment lead to splintering. The character's secret or hidden life can no longer be controlled, and it erupts to take over, or at least to threaten, the public persona. Dreams—often Freudian in nature—provide clues to the horrors and fears of this hidden life. In stories that seem dreamlike order breaks down, chronology becomes confused, and the real and the imaginary blur. Multiple symbols and images suggest the nightmare world. Reflections, rooms, and journeys are distinguishing marks of the new gothic. The character, confronted with unbearable knowledge, tries to flee his or her own inner room, that is, the hidden self, by embarking on a journey or series of journeys. But flight always fails to secure peace. Escape is no more possible for new gothic figures than for those in absurdist literature.

Capote's characters are anxiety-ridden, obsessive, and narcissistic. They live in their own new gothic environment: an encapsulated and terrifying internal world from which they long to escape but cannot break out. Each of them fears self-revelation, knowledge of the buried self whom they have tried to flee. This hidden self often appears to the haunted protagonist as a vision in the mirror, reflection in the window, voice on the telephone, or meeting with a strangely familiar "other." They have sleeping and waking nightmares that reveal them to be alone defenseless, naked.[1]

Surely, in his youth, Capote knew nothing of the psychological literature on narcissism, yet his characters might serve as case studies. These are people without a center, symbolized by recurring images of wavering reflections; whatever their chronological age, Capote's characters remain captives of their unvanquished childhood fears and longings. And everywhere in the dark stories we find reminders of the landscape of death: images of freezing, the heat of the underworld, green death, white death, death by drowning, death through being buried alive, self-destruction, or destruction by the "other."

"A Tree of Night," one of the earliest of these nightmare stories,[2] traces an eerie journey taken by a young woman returning to college by train after attending the funeral of her uncle. Even before Kay boards the train, the reader is led to expect bizarre and inexplicable events. There is a menacing sound in the unembellished three-word opening line: "It was winter."[3] As is typical of Capote's stories, realistic details are juxtaposed with the fantastic. As Kay stands on the platform, holding her dead uncle's green guitar, all is chill, the atmosphere forbidding; like monstrous teeth, icicles hang over the deserted station. The approaching train itself seems a kind of monster, rumbling and glaring as it halts for the lone passenger to board. Decay, rotting food, a leaking fountain, and the noxious smells on the train convey an atmosphere of death. With its gloomy interior, the train is prophetic of the surrealistic voyage ahead. Images of enclosure suggest the train as a metaphoric coffin; later, other coffin images are introduced, suggesting that Kay's journey is one in which the destination will be the country of death.

Weary-looking people, indifferent to everything, have filled all the seats but the one that Kay must take, located in an area isolated from the other passengers. This physical isolation quickly becomes total as Kay is made virtually a prisoner by the freakish man and woman she now encounters. The couple are and remain nameless, identified by the author only as "the woman" and "the man." Their namelessness adds to the reader's mounting sense of unease, especially since they know who Kay is—her pocketbook announces her name in large brass letters—and their knowledge of her name and her ignorance of their names seems to give them power over her. But the fact that she knows nothing about her strange companions is less important than her ignorance about herself. Kay's lack of self-knowledge enables the weird couple to maneuver Kay into helplessness and eventually to do with her as they want.

The problem of knowing one's identity underlies the surface events of the story. That Kay owns a pocketbook that publicly declares her name initially seems to suggest that the owner of the pocketbook knows who she is. However, Capote soon implies that personal identity is precisely what is at issue. Kay has not confronted her inner self. When it becomes necessary for her to discover that hidden self, she fails, becoming a victim of the grotesque partners.

Kay is almost 20,[4] and a college student, but she has little understanding of life. Perhaps the college world, like her earlier home and school worlds, still shelters her and prevents her from growing up. The strange woman scornfully informs Kay that college is useless: "I'm plenty educated and I never saw the inside of no college" ("Tree," 23). Viewed superficially, Kay should be the person in control, for by most measures she is superior to the older woman. In appearance Kay is tall, attractive, and well dressed, whereas the older woman is very short, disproportionately built, and shabbily clothed. Capote makes it clear that Kay is a product of money and comfort, while the woman and her companion are poor. However, nothing in Kay's life has prepared her for this encounter. Not knowing how to cope, she finds herself unable to resist the demands the couple make of her.

The contrast between Kay and the woman extends to more than age, appearance, education, social status, or wealth. The woman has had many experiences that include familiarity with the occult. She was once a fortune teller in the city from which, by dark coincidence, Kay comes. She has some mysterious potency that enables her to frighten Kay so that her dominance over the girl is complete. Soon after Kay sits down, the woman begins to complain about the difficulties the pair have in living on the "take" from their vaudeville show. She decides that Kay is very rich, and announces this insight pointedly to her companion.

Whether the man understands what he is told about Kay is never clear, for he is a deaf-mute. Everything about him makes Kay uncomfortable: his clouded, marblelike eyes,[5] the remote and blank look on his face, his cheap, sickening perfume. It is not long before Kay recognizes that the grotesque pair want her money, but she becomes even more alarmed when the man makes disturbing sexual overtures to her. He caresses her cheek, and offers to sell her a love charm, a peach pit that he strokes lewdly and which she refuses to buy. Through him two elements that at first appear unrelated, money and sex, become connected. When Kay rejects the charm, the woman pointedly asks: "Where could you get love cheaper, honey?" ("Tree," 29). The woman knows Kay is frightened. But there are other terrors functioning here as well: Kay is afraid of sexual violation and death. Although Capote does not allow Kay to think directly about such things, the episodes of the story and the symbols he uses make Kay's deeper fears clear to the reader.

Capote establishes an obvious link between money, sex, and death. The woman reveals that she and her companion make their living by putting on a burial show: she plays the role of mourner, and he the person buried alive in the coffin.[6] Here the early symbolic suggestion of the train as coffin becomes real. Curiously, the mock corpse wears a bridegroom's suit, not a shroud, during the burial show. The man's stage name is Lazarus, a reminder of the biblical figure who returned from the dead. With the articulation of the deaf-mute's stage name, death becomes the central link to money (the income from the show) and sex (the marriage suit). Furthermore, although the first association with the name is biblical, we cannot overlook the intrusion of bits and pieces of both the Persephone and Orpheus myths. The parts are shuffled, altered, even reversed in their meaning, but they are present in the form of a pretty young girl, a journey into the realm of death, a Hades figure, and a musical instrument.[7]

Fear leads Kay to relive the funeral she has recently attended. Suddenly, the deaf-mute appears to resemble her dead uncle. Next he begins to remind her of someone far more frightening, the wizard man of her childhood nightmares, the demon who brings danger and even death to the child who wanders from home. She recalls "a memory, a childhood memory of terrors that once, long ago, had hovered above her like haunted limbs on a tree of night. Aunts, cooks, strangers—each eager to spin a tale or teach a rhyme of spooks and death, omens, spirits, demons. And always there had been the unfailing threat of the wizard man: stay close to the house, child, else the wizard man'll snatch you and eat you alive! He lived everywhere, the wizard man, and everywhere was danger. At night, in bed, hear him tapping at the window? Listen!" ("Tree," 30). Unconscious terrors coalesce: childhood fear of abandonment, of being lost and unprotected, fear of the dark, fear of strangers, fear of violence, fear of the demon that will snatch little children. These reawakened childhood fears unite with a more adult fear, conscious or unconscious fear of rape.

Kay's ultimately futile effort to hold on to her purse represents more than an attempt to safeguard her money. A purse, as any Freudian would point out, is a symbol of the vagina, and thus, a symbol of Kay's sexuality. By tightly clutching her closed purse Kay tries to prevent her own violation. She makes three efforts to escape the ever more terrifying pair, but each fails. The first time, the woman uses physical force to stop Kay; the second, Kay tries to speak to the conductor but finds herself inexplicably incoherent; in her last attempt, she manages to flee to the observation platform, but she is followed by the man, who, with a wave of his hand, directs her to return to the isolated alcove. Totally defeated, she obeys.

By the end of the story Kay's terror leads her to believe that she is traveling to the country of death. Earlier, at the time of her second try for freedom, the warning implicit in the woman's description of the burial act and in the handbill with the yellowed appearance of something "centuries old" had meant nothing to her. Neither did a second omen, in the form of a train with "golden windows" (an image of light, suggesting life) passing in the opposite direction, with its bells sounding wildly in warning.[8] As the light-filled train passes, all momentarily becomes dark on Kay's train, which is passing through country she has never seen before. She is aware of darkness, mist, and enclosing trees, of a peculiar landscape that blends the familiar with the strange.

When Kay reenters the train after her last aborted effort to rid herself of the evil pair, she wants to cry out but does not: she fears that she will discover all her fellow passengers are dead. In her terror, Kay seeks to strike a bargain with the woman. She will buy the love charm if that is what the woman wants. But it is too late. Perhaps it was too late for Kay from the moment she boarded the train. The woman smiles at the man when Kay makes her offer, and then takes away Kay's pocketbook and arranges the raincoat over the girl's head, in the manner of a shroud, as Kay sinks into unconsciousness. The last thing Kay sees is the face of "Lazarus."

The pointed descriptions of the removal of Kay's purse and of the raincoat shroud bring together sex and death images, and serve to emphasize the symbolic implications of the final episode. The language of the concluding passage subtly suggests a rape: "As Kay watched, the man's face seemed to change form and recede before her like a moon-shaped rock sliding downward under a surface of water. A warm laziness relaxed her. She was dimly conscious of it when the woman took away her purse and when she gently pulled the raincoat above her head" ("Tree," 31). Even though the words appear to describe somnolence, the images are actually those of sexual violation. The deaf-mute, he who is buried alive, he who wears a bridgegroom's suit in a coffin, he who is Lazarus or Hades or both, no longer has to sell his love charm. The wizard man no longer has to tap outside at the window. He is inside now and he has gained his bride.

"Miriam"

"Miriam," first published by *Mademoiselle*,[9] was the first Capote story to attract serious attention. It appears to be a serious exploration of psychological aberration, and may readily be interpreted as a study of schizophrenia. Yet the author said on a number of occasions that it was one of his least favorite pieces; indeed, Capote dismissed it as "a good stunt and nothing more."[10]

"Miriam" and "A Tree of Night" were created during the same period of Capote's development as a writer and share numerous resemblances. Kay and Mrs. Miller, the protagonist in "Miriam," are both isolated females, uncertain about themselves, and fearful of many things. The ordinary predictability of their lives is disturbed, time and space are altered, their surface identities become blurred, and their long-dormant hidden identities assert themselves and take over. Structurally, the two stories are marked by three transitions as the protagonist becomes progressively entrapped by the incomprehensible figure of the antagonist. By story's end, each woman is overcome by that which she fears most, losing herself to the overwhelming force of the "other."

The season in both pieces is winter, the landscape dark and

deathlike. Although the basic situations seem to be rooted in reality, the events and descriptions soon take on a surrealistic air. The two stories function almost like textbook examples of the new gothic. There is a dreamlike atmosphere which is also the essence of nightmares. Actual dreams or fantasies exist side by side with realistic events and details. Yet the outer world has little relationship to the inner fears of the protagonist, an anxiety-ridden narcissist. The terror in each case is provoked by secret tensions, suggested by images of darkness, disorder, and death. Reflections waver; eyes, windows, mirrors, and light alter perceptions. The train journey in "A Tree of Night" and the short trips in "Miriam" inevitably end in failure. There is no exit in any of Capote's gothic tales.

The opening paragraph of "Miriam" focuses on the emptiness of Mrs. H. T. Miller's life: "Her interests were narrow, she had no friends to speak of, and she rarely journeyed farther than the grocery store."[11] That she is first identified by her late husband's initials immediately suggests a person without an identity of her own. Sixty-one-years old, Mrs. Miller lives a sterile existence, cleaning her small apartment, feeding herself and her canary, carrying out other invariable daily acts to fill her empty life. She is so isolated from real life that none of her neighbors know her.

Then Mrs. Miller's world is altered forever. Foreshadowed by symbols and images, the change begins one snowy, winter night. Mrs. Miller, described as resembling a mole in its obliviousness as she struggles against the weather, goes to a neighborhood theater, a place of fantasy and escape. There she is approached by an unusual little girl who asks Mrs. Miller to buy a ticket for her. Everything about the child is exquisite and elegant. The beautiful youngster might have stepped down from a Gainsborough portrait. Clad in a silk dress and a richly colored velvet coat, she presents an extreme contrast to Mrs. Miller's plainly dressed form. Mrs. Miller's grey hair is clipped and short, a sensible, practical, but unappealing style, whereas the child has long, silvery hair, the kind one might expect of a fairy princess.

The differences between the two become significant later in the story when we begin to recognize that the little girl is not an actual child at all, but the creation of an increasingly disturbed woman. Clue after clue piles up to suggest that the child is imaginary. Both Mrs. Miller and the beautiful child share the same first name, Miriam. The little girl's eyes are not childlike. Her vocabulary is adult. She seems to have no mother at home to be concerned about her.

In their first encounter the child is as passive as the older Miriam. However, the child appears twice more, and each time is more powerful. On her third appearance she takes over Mrs. Miller's life.

Following their initial meeting, Mrs. Miller's daily existence becomes even more cloistered. She is confined to her home by a week of heavy snow that changes the ordinary external landscape into a blurred and silent world. Everything outside appears unfamiliar. Even the light of day is changed so that day seems to be much like night. The curtain of snow seems to separate Mrs. Miller from recognizable space and time. The days have no separate identity or individual meaning. The one day she goes outside everything is shut and silent, so that the outside world is no different from her at-home world.

The external sense of unreality mirrors what happens to Mrs. Miller's inner life. After a week of snow, having had contact with no one, Mrs. Miller is more isolated than ever. She appears to be following her ordinary routine, cooking, going through the usual bedtime rituals, and so forth.[12] The reader begins to recognize that something has changed for Mrs. Miller. Previously a woman of strict habit, she loses her inner sense of time. The evening of the day she ventures out onto the empty, silent, cold streets she remains up long past her usual bedtime, something she has never done before. It is as if at some level she is excited, awaiting the experience to come.

And come it does, initiated by the furious ringing of the bell. The bell is actually a warning, but Mrs. Miller does not recognize it for what it is, and she opens the door to the visitor. Though it is already late at night, the unescorted little girl Miriam stands outside Mrs. Miller's apartment demanding entry.

Now Miriam's dual character becomes even more apparent. Physically she is a child, but her comments are those of an adult. With adult perception she faults the paper roses, finding imitations "sad," but then she had a childish temper tantrum and shatters the vase containing the flowers. She steals Mrs. Miller's cameo and like a demanding child insists on keeping it; yet she appears the stronger of the two by forcing Mrs. Miller into a confrontation about the jewelry. Miriam's dominance over Mrs. Miller is discernible from the moment she arrives. The child Miriam gives orders to the older Miriam, which the woman obeys, in part because she does not appear to question them and in part because she is afraid. It is as if their roles are reversed.

One might ask what Mrs. Miller fears from the dainty little girl. At this point in the story the woman remains cognizant of the many unanswered mysteries about the child: where did she come from, how did she find Mrs. Miller, why does the canary sing in Miriam's presence at night even though its cage is covered? Further, Mrs. Miller has a growing sense of her total isolation from anyone who might help her. However, even as she registers this knowledge, the images of the room become wavery, and the light begins to flutter. At the same moment reality intrudes in the form of her awareness of her absolute solitude— the changing light suggests her inability to understand the meaning of that reality. The precariousness of her hold on stability is manifested by alterations in her appearance and behavior.

During this visit the little girl presents a larger and more powerful presence than during their first meeting. She was described as very pale when she confronted Mrs. Miller at the movie theater, but when she invades Mrs. Miller's apartment her cheeks are flushed with color, an image of the greater substantiality of her existence: she has taken on life. When she eats, it is with the gusto of a hungry child, yet the unreality of Miriam's existence is imaged by the "cobweb movements" of her fingers, and her face seems a mirrored reflection of the carved ivory face on the cameo she has stolen.

After Miriam's reluctant and angry departure, Mrs. Miller takes to her bed only to dream about a little girl, obviously Miriam even though she is not identified by name. Everything about the child is wintry, from the white bridal gown she wears to her resemblance to a "frost flower." On her head is a wreath of leaves, an oddly funereal addition to a bridal gown. Recalling Capote's use of the bridegroom suit for Lazarus in "A Tree of Night," one may find a link in this use of bridal and funereal symbolism. Both stories ironically show the wedding figure as a reversal of expectation. Each is really a bringer of psychic death. In the dream Miriam is leading a "gray"—elderly, or passive, or repressed, like Mrs. Miller?—"procession" away from, not toward, a mountain top; traditionally, mountain tops represent wisdom, achievement, and understanding, but these people clearly are not being led in that positive direction. Are they following the "bride" toward death? They do not know, according to an old man at the front of the procession, nor do they appear to care. The shining brightness of the child's beauty seems to rob the group of all volition. This strange dream serves both as a reminder and as a foreshadowing of Mrs. Miller's state.

The old man of Mrs. Miller's dream seems to become real the next day. Although she awakens to a morning that promises sunshine, warmth, and blue skies, this promise turns out to be as deceptive as everything else she has recently experienced. By the end of a day that sees her compulsively, yet happily, going on a shopping spree, an action completely out of character for her, she is caught again in snow, isolation, and the final eradication of her identity.

In the course of her shopping, and following close on her sense of being absolutely isolated from everyone she passes, Mrs. Miller sees an old man, perhaps the old man of her dream. Although she does not recognize him, the reader makes the obvious connection. The two smile coldly at each other, yet Mrs. Miller otherwise refuses to acknowledge the man. She is afraid of him and his mocking actions. Once again her anxieties are revealed by means of images: "He kept quite close; from the corner of her eye she watched his reflection wavering on the shopwindows" ("Miriam," 9). Later, when the child Miriam appears for the third time, she informs Mrs. Miller that she has left the home of an old man to move in with her. Thus the old man, like the child Miriam, makes three appearances: as the old man in the dream procession, as the old man who follows Mrs. Miller, and as the old man with whom Miriam lived.

The language of the story directs us to the ending. Earlier images are repeated, images that introduced the initial visit of Miriam. As Mrs. Miller returns home from her shopping trip, the weather changes: sunshine turns to dark clouds, warmth to chill. By the time Mrs. Miller reaches her apartment house the snow has become so heavy that her footsteps are obliterated, a foreshadowing of her fate. Inside, Mrs. Miller knows immediately who it is that rings her doorbell in the late afternoon. Yet, in spite of the fact that all her purchases are intended for the visitor, she shows some reluctance to let Miriam in. But, as before, Miriam is too strong for her psychologically and takes control. In this third and last episode with Miriam, the girl's power has grown enormously.

Like a frightened child, Mrs. Miller attempts to flee, asking a neighbor for assistance. The man, of course, finds no menacing young girl in the apartment, and Mrs. Miller returns to the apartment, where at first she believes herself alone: "this was an empty room, emptier than if the furnishings and familiars were not present, lifeless and petrified as a funeral parlor" ("Miriam," 12). In the moment of recognition, when she thinks the emptiness would be more tolerable were Miriam there, the now familiar images recur: spinning, blurring, surging. For a short time Mrs. Miller imagines she has regained her old, careful existence, but she is mistaken. Loud sounds of a person's moving in give way to soft murmurs that grow in intensity until they fill the apartment, and Mrs. Miller loses her last hold on reality.

Although there are many ways to interpret "Miriam," any analysis that assumes that Miriam is an actual child would be erroneous. Capote grounds this piece so carefully in realistic detail that it sometimes misleads readers. Various interpretations have been offered: doubling, schizophrenia, hallucination. Some critics see the child Miriam as the embodiment of Mrs. Miller's lifelong desire to be what Miriam represents. Those who subscribe to the theory of schizophrenia view Mrs. Miller's mental disintegration as a textbook case. Mrs. Miller's ability to live simultaneously in both an actual and a hallucinatory world is supported by Capote's artful combination of fact, images, and symbols. One may subscribe to the particulars of any of these readings, but they all share the view that Mrs. Miller is a woman who finds her life intolerable, and who therefore creates another self, a person she simultaneously longs to be and rejects. She is destroyed by the revelation and can escape it only through madness.

"The Headless Hawk"

"The Headless Hawk," Capote's most complex short fiction, presents a male protagonist trapped in a narcissistic self from which he cannot escape. His inertia and hopelessness are symbolized by the story's circular structure, a form the writer utilized several times in different types of work. Circular stories begin at the end, return to the beginning, and then move chronologically to the point at which they started. In the sunny stories a circular plot structure works to enclose an episode, thereby preserving it as a precious memory out of the past. In the dark stories such circularity suggests the despair of the protagonist and his inability to alter the static condition of his existence. Here the effect of the circularity resembles that of an absurdist play, in which nothing can or will change.

The opening scene of "The Headless Hawk" produces a sensation of hallucination, although it is not one of the dream sequences in the story. Images of blindness and drowning are pervasive. Vincent Waters, the manager of an art gallery, leaves work at the end of a hot July day to go home to his apartment. On the darkening street he moves like a blind man, with his umbrella tapping as if it were a cane. Vincent feels as if he is underwater: everything appears to be green; the buses are like fish, and the faces of people are distorted like those behind underwater masks.

Within moments Vincent sees a young woman in a green overcoat; the color is part of an organized series of underwater images. Although he apparently expects to see the girl, the two neither greet nor speak to each other. Instead they immediately fall into a kind of pavane that appears to be a familiar pattern for them: he walks, she follows; she walks, he follows—always in total silence. Only once do they stop at the same point, as if by arrangement, in front of an antique store filled with odds and ends and discarded objects. The girl, we learn by the end of the story, is herself a discard that Vincent picked up and now cannot rid himself of. One of the pieces seen through the window symbolizes the relationship of Vincent and the girl, later identified only as D. J. This item is a revolving fan. The fan objectifies the circularity of the story. It cannot alter direction, and as the pattern of the story emerges, the fan also becomes representative of two lives that are and will be bound together, until one of the parties destroys self or other.

In the shop window Vincent sees the green and blurred image of the young woman. The wavering reflection represents Vincent's inability to see the girl, himself, or his relationships to other people with clarity. To see, to understand, and to accept reality would free him from the prison of self, from the narcissistic death implied by the series of underwater drowning images.

Vincent enters his apartment. Without warning, the story shifts back to the past, to the time when he and D. J. met at the gallery. She has come in to sell a strange painting, a self-portrait: "A headless figure in a monklike robe reclined complacently on top a tacky vaudeville trunk; in one hand she held a fuming blue candle, in the other a miniature gold cage, and her severed head lay bleeding at her feet: it was the girl's, this head, but here her hair was long, very long, and a snowball kitten with crystal spitfire eyes playfully pawed, as it would a spool of yarn, the sprawling ends. The wings of a hawk, headless, scarlet-breasted, copper-clawed, curtained the background like a nightfall sky."[13] Vincent, intrigued alike by the girl and her painting, wants to buy it, but she disappears, leaving the portrait behind.

The girl's oddities are apparent in her behavior and her conversation. Nevertheless, those very peculiarities attract Vincent, who recognizes that he has always been interested in "freaks" of some kind. Those whom he has loved invariably have had something "wrong" or "broken" in them. But he also knows his love always dies, killed by the

14

very element that captures him initially. All Vincent's love relationships have been circular. They end as they begin, with his consciousness of the abnormality of the partner. The pattern will repeat with D. J. But this time he will not be able to escape the effects of the affair as he did with earlier ones.

At their first meeting D. J. mentions Mr. Destronelli, claiming that he is a recognizable figure to young and old, and has the appearance of anyone and everyone. Clearly, Mr. Destronelli is the symbolic name of the destroyer inside us all. As the story builds, D. J.'s fear of the Destronelli element in Vincent takes form. Vincent becomes both destroyer and victim.

After D. J.'s sudden disappearance, Vincent spends much time analyzing her painting. He begins to identify with it. He sees himself in the hawk, an identification that foreshadows his bonding to D. J., who obviously visualizes herself as the headless figure in the painting. Vincent is reminded of his own failures: of his desire to be a poet, but his inability to write any poems; of his desire to be a painter, but his inability to create any pictures; of his longing to be a man totally in love, but his inability to truly love anyone.

Vincent eventually finds D. J. and she moves in with him. At first, he is filled with a sense of pleasure and pride in his masculinity. However, the instability of their relationship is symbolically suggested by the wavering light of the blue candles and "the mirrored door where uncertain light rippled their reflections" ("Hawk," 52). Without recognizing the implications of his thoughts, Vincent begins to think of the girl's mind as "a mirror" that "reflects blue space." The extreme limitations of their life together become troublesome. D. J. lives in an interior world disconnected from time and reality. Her only interest is the movies, used by the author here—as in "Miriam"—to suggest her need to escape from reality. On the last night the two spend together, D. J.'s 18th birthday, they see a film she identifies as "handcuffs" because of an incident in which a man and a woman are handcuffed together. When she speaks of the people who are "caught" and "locked together," she unknowingly refers to her own and Vincent's fate. They will never be free of each other, in spite of all his efforts to sever the relationship.

For her birthday, Vincent gives D. J. violets, which she pins to her pillow before she goes to sleep, murmuring how sad it is that the flowers must die. Because flowers in Capote's stories are often associated with partings, suffering, or death, we become aware that this particular night has special meaning. Vincent smells the scent of violets on an abandoned lover he reencounters in a terrible dream; when he awakens the fragrance of the "drying violets" on the pillow is "tawdry."

Vincent's dream takes place in a hall without exits. Here he is forced to confront his past as well as his future. From out of his past come the people he has injured and abandoned. His future is symbolized by the figure of a horrible old man, himself, who climbs on the back of his handsome young self and will not be shaken off. D. J. also has a figure on her back, a beautiful little child. She and Vincent touch: "The instant their hands meet he begins to feel the weight upon him diminish; the old Vincent is fading" ("Hawk," 57). The burden on his back might float away. When the child on D. J.'s back states that she is "heavier" than she looks, the horrible figure on Vincent's back proclaims himself "heaviest of all." Although Vincent cannot interpret his dream the reader recognizes that the dream offers Vincent the possibility of exchanging the heaviest burden of all, his narcissistic self, for the lighter burden, the beautiful, innocent child that is D. J. At the end of the dream the hawk, though headless and therefore blind, flies down and claws Vincent. He recognizes that he will never experience true freedom.

From what does Vincent wish to free himself? It becomes apparent shortly thereafter, when he wakes up, that he wishes to drop D. J., the lighter burden. And what is the hawk in his dream? It is not the same symbol he identified with in D. J.'s painting, that same failed self who longs to be something other, yet who never faces the truth about himself or has the courage to take corrective action? The blindness of the hawk replicates Vincent's refusal to see himself. When Vincent awakens to find D. J. outside in the shabby garden, she warns him to go indoors because of the presence of "him," obviously Mr. Destronelli. For the first time, Vincent allows himself to mouth the word he had avoided: "crazy." The sky is gray, the moon is setting, the dawn is aging, symbolic words that make us aware, as Vincent is, of "the death of love."

Vincent rids himself of D. J. As he puts her things outside, a butterfly comes into the apartment. Although he attempts to destroy the lovely, yellow creature, he fails, and instead stabs the hawk in the painting and cuts it into fragments. This final reminder of the identification of Vincent and the hawk is also a symbolic act of self-destruction.

The story now returns to present time. Vincent leaves his apartment to stand briefly under a streetlight. D. J. comes up to him as a rainstorm breaks. "Like a curtain of splintered glass" the rain falls between them, as they stand there, each alone, yet locked together by invisible chains.

"Master Misery"

All the dark stories are filled with symbols of death and images of dying, but the stories in which the major figures are male, that is, "The Headless Hawk" and "Shut a Final Door," are distinguished by final episodes in which a steamy, unbearably hot atmosphere suggests hell. In contrast, the stories that focus on female characters include scenes set in bitter cold, and images that suggest sterility. The story "Master Misery" seems to be encased in ice. Like "A Tree of Night" and "Miriam," "Master Misery" combines realism and surrealism in its characters and situations. The protagonist, Sylvia, is drawn realistically, but the events in which she becomes involved and the characters she meets fall into the gray area where things are not quite real, even when they are described in ways that reflect everyday life.

Sylvia, a young woman from the Midwest, has come to New York expecting to find a more exciting life than the one she left behind. For a short time she lives with a couple whom she finds boring because they remind her of small-town existence, with its petty rules and strict mores. Work also disappoints her; she is a typist for an underwear company called "Snugfare," a name that ironically evokes everything Sylvia rejects but also everything she lacks. Instead of finding a pleasurable life, Sylvia is isolated, lonely, and unhappy, absolutely lost in the cold, mechanical city.

Sundays and holidays, the bane of all those who are alone, are the worst days for Sylvia. Living with a young couple, Sylvia is aware of, and disturbed by, their sexual relationship. She takes sleeping pills to escape her misery. Then one day she overhears a man talking about selling dreams to a Mr. Revercomb, and she decides to do the same. From this point the story begins to take on dreamlike qualities even though it remains rooted in ordinary details of life. Sylvia visits Revercomb, tells him her dreams, and is paid for her effort.

Leaving Revercomb's office that first evening, Sylvia incautiously walks through the dark park, knowing she is putting herself at risk. Two boys begin to follow her "like menacing flames," and the sounds they make as they whistle and run a stick along a fence suggest "an

17

oncoming engine." This sexual image combines with another when
Sylvia briefly considers throwing down her purse, but she is able to
escape the situation when someone else walks by. Later that evening,
however, Sylvia has the sensation that her purse was actually taken,
and when she falls asleep she has sexual dreams about Mr. Revercomb.

The park sequence introduces a major theme in the story, the
division in Sylvia's desires: she wishes to be an adult but she has an
equally strong yet unconscious longing to regress to the safe world of
childhood. When Sylvia first enters the park she sees children's chalk
drawings. Then, in the gathering dusk, the two males appear; on one
level, these males are toughs and potential muggers, and thus realistic
embodiments of negative features of the urban world, but on another
level they are symbolic representations of adult sexuality. A character
named Oreilly, whom Sylvia first sees at Revercomb's office, also
throws light on the split within Sylvia. The scene during which Oreilly
first appears is strangely hazy, not quite real. Outside, darkness is
gathering. The waiting room is dimly lit: "It began to rain; melting
window reflections quivered on the walls."[14] A fire in the grate and the
ticking of a clock complete the dreamlike atmosphere in which Sylvia
feels suspended between sleep and waking. At that moment, Oreilly,
a drunken, unwelcome visitor to the office, creates a disturbance and
is thrown out, but Sylvia encounters him a second time as she leaves
the office.

Oreilly is like a child. When Sylvia leaves Revercomb's office, she
finds Oreilly bouncing a ball in the street. He skips beside her in
childlike fashion. Questioned by Sylvia, he admits to having once been
a clown. This identification is exceedingly important for her: her
childhood room was decorated like a circus, and her dolls were clown
figures. As the two walk along, Oreilly calls Sylvia "baby," and she
feels as if she is walking with a doll out of her childhood, now "grown
miraculous and capable." That Sylvia thinks of Oreilly in this way is a
clue to the split in her psyche. Oreilly warns her that Revercomb, or
"Master Misery," as he calls him, has left him with "niente" and the
same might happen to her. Sylvia does not heed the advice he offers.
Torn between her conflicting desires to be a child *and* to be an adult,
she is trapped in a place where she is neither. But her longings to
escape to the safe, happy world of childhood grow stronger as the adult
world becomes more threatening.

Sylvia disintegrates rapidly once she starts to sell her dreams. She
moves to a furnished room: "Large enough for a daybed and a splintery

old bureau with a mirror like a cataracted eye, it had one window, which looked out on a vast vacant lot" ("Misery," 83). Fired from her job, Sylvia survives by selling her dreams. She gives way to total indifference about her appearance, her health, her whole life. The vacant lot she sees outside her window is a fitting image of her existence. She sells her possessions, the most significant of which is her watch: now she lives her life outside of clock time. Caught between happy memories of childhood—remembered as springtime and flowers—and constant dreams, Sylvia cannot bear to face the fragmentation of her life.

She becomes ill, and for a brief period experiences happiness. Oreilly moves in and takes care of her. The experience is like a wonderful party. Through Oreilly, Sylvia is able to bring together her two conflicting desires, the yearning for the safe, happy world of childhood, and the need for adult love. But when she tells Oreilly she will not be afraid anymore, he warns her that fears never leave us: the things we fear are always with us. Oreilly, of course, is a frail support for Sylvia to depend on. He is one of the wild creatures, the untamed, those who live in the sky, unattached, always moving on. Before he goes off to "travel in the blue" again, however, he tries to help Sylvia regain hope and thus her grip on life by sending her to Revercomb to buy back her dreams. But it is too late. Sylvia's dreams are gone forever, "used up" by Revercomb, and she must exist without Oreilly and without dreams.

At the end of the story, when she is again followed at night by two young men, Sylvia is a different person from the young woman who walked through the park the night of her first visit to Revercomb. Now she is a woman convinced she has nothing left to live for. She has no money, no job, no friends. Further, she is bereft of love, of hope, and of dreams. The final images of the story suggest a woman adrift. Here the green, drowning images of "The Headless Hawk" become perilous icy seas, the "white waves of a white sea," representations of emptiness, frigidity, and sterility.

The significance of Mr. Revercomb, the gray invisible man, with his flat gray eyes, clinical odors, and anonymous face, remains shadowy. He seems to be a therapist of sorts. Who else would be interested in dreams, or take them away and "use them up"? Oreilly tells Sylvia that "most dreams begin because there are furies inside of us that blow open all the doors" ("Misery," 87). Both furies and dreams drive people to seek therapy. Revercomb's name carries with it a number of symbolic possibilities. The first part, "reve," apparently comes from the French word that means dream. Yet another association with "reve" is "reave," which means to despoil, or rob, to take away life, rest, or sight, words that describe Sylvia's ultimate condition.[15] Whoever Revercomb may be, both Oreilly and Sylvia fear him. And for good reason: Revercomb robs people of their dreams and thereby forces them to see their naked selves.

"Shut a Final Door"

Walter Ranney, the protagonist of "Shut a Final Door," is the most autobiographical of any of the characters in this collection.[16] What is more, Walter is a forerunner of P. B. Jones, Capote's narrator and alter ego in the unfinished collection of stories *Answered Prayers*.

"Shut a Final Door" is set in two cities Capote knew well: New York and New Orleans. Like Capote, Walter combines charm and energy with bitchiness. Walter seeks fame and publicity, as did his creator. Both enjoyed playing the role of protégé to successful men. Both loved tap dancing as a child and both use the memories of their childhood dancing world to escape from the adult world when it becomes terrifying. Mirroring Capote, Walter despises both his parents. He unconsciously fears his father, and, true to the pattern of a classic psychological case study, yearns for mothering.

The character and the author even share physical traits. Although Walter's physical appearance is not described, it probably parallels that of his friend, Irving (who briefly serves as a type of double for him): Irving is 23 (the same age as Walter), but looks 16, and he has the soft hair and the pink cheeks of a baby, details that fit the descriptions and pictures of Capote himself at that age. All three names, Truman, Walter, and Irving, have the same number of letters, a subtle underlining of the complex doubling that is so important to this story. Irving's heterosexuality is in question, and we soon learn to question Walter's heterosexuality as well. Described several times in a dismissive tone as "sweet" and "little," Irving has "more or less" a girlfriend, but cannot be a husband because "he is everyone's little brother."[17] Irving's characteristics and actions provide the earliest clues to the story's sexual theme. Not only does Irving look "like a little boy" (therefore not manly, sexual, or potent), but his behavior suggests effeminacy. When, in anger, Irving tries to strike Walter "as if he clutched a knife," the blow is unsuccessful. The suggestion of phallic impotence is unmistakable.

At this early point in the story the focus is on Irving's actions rather than Walter's. Only later do we recognize that Irving serves as a kind of double for Walter at the beginning of the study. The question of Walter's sexuality is veiled and subtle. After an acquaintance contemptuously labels him a "female. . . . a man in only one respect" ("Door," 68), the reader begins to sense that Walter's sexual identity, not Irving's, is the focus of the story. Irving is no longer mentioned, and shortly thereafter Walter becomes "involved" briefly with his employer. Walter's recognition, fear, and rejection of his homosexual nature are central to our understanding of the story.

The title itself is provocative. The "door" that shuts prevents Walter's escape from confrontation with his real being and also prohibits his return to the life in which he can pretend to be a carefree heterosexual. Knowledge comes to Walter in a variety of ways, but he cannot bear these revelations. He runs until he can run no further, and at the end attempts to retreat into an empty world, a world of wind, of "nothing things." Like Mrs. Miller in "Miriam," who finds madness preferable to reality, like Vincent in "The Headless Hawk," who avoids self-knowledge, Walter attempts to escape into a state of nothingness.

At first, Walter appears to be an ordinary young man, bent on finding a career and enjoying a busy social life. Like the other flawed protagonists of these nighttime stories, however, he has a hidden self that must surface and ultimately destroy the external facade. He creates his own hell, later symbolized by the intense August heat of New Orleans, because the angry, uncertain, defensive side will not allow the healthy, though weaker, part of his character to emerge.

Walter's compulsions drive him to do things that wound others. For a short time his charm enables him to climb the financial and social ladders. He supplants Irving in the affections of his girlfriend, Margaret. Through her he meets Kurt Kuhnhardt, who briefly makes him his protégé, and also introduces him to the wealthy society world. But Walter's serious personality flaws eventually cause him to offend everyone, and one by one his society friends break off with him. Walter wants and needs love, but he does not love anyone. He is even more hollow than Vincent, of "The Headless Hawk," who at least loves people briefly. In an eerie foreshadowing of Capote's own life decades later, Walter, afraid of betrayal, is always a betrayer.

Filled with self-pity, Walter expects forgiveness for all his misdeeds. The absolute narcissist, he is incapable of looking outward. Even more tragically, he is unable to look inward. His fears have driven all understanding of self underground. A friend's words prove to be prophetic when she warns Walter that things are never what they seem. When Walter's hypocrisies destroy all his friendships, cost him his job, and leave him without prospects, he still seems blind to the truth that he is the creator of his own problems. Although he recognizes that everything comes to zero for him, he rationalizes his situation and tries to convince himself that he has found peace in his failure, for he cannot abide uncertainties, and at least his failure is certain.[18]

Walter is wrong. There will be no more peace for him. Pandora's box has been opened. Alone in his apartment after he has been fired, he daydreams of ways of escape. Then, as if a film of the past has clicked on in his head, he is a child again, in the company of his father. He briefly dances around the room, but as the music stops his phone rings. The room alters, deadens in ways that remind us of scenes in "Miriam." And although no "person" appears, as one does in "Miriam," Walter has an encounter with "someone" who will remain with Walter, just as the child Miriam did with Mrs. Miller. The "dry and sexless" voice on the phone will not identify himself, responding to Walter's query only with the mysterious statement that Walter knows who he is. From that moment, Walter will find no escape from the voice, no matter how he attempts to flee it. He begins a series of train journeys that will end pitifully with his withdrawal from reality.

Each phase of his travels represents a symbolic movements backward in time. Since his last thoughts before the phone call were of his childhood experiences with his father in Saratoga, Walter seems compelled to return there. On the train he has a terrible dream in which people he has injured or who have injured him in the past return to him: his father, erstwhile friends, his employer and a new protégé, and even a former algebra teacher. They are all in black cars, as if in a funeral procession, while he stands alone on an empty, deserted street, naked and unprotected. When his father opens a car door as if to shelter him, Walter runs toward it, crying "Daddy," but Daddy slams the door shut on his son's hand, severing his fingers. The father laughs and throws a wreath of roses out the car window at Walter. All the other people in the black cars follow Daddy's example, opening car doors invitingly but never allowing Walter in, laughing at him in his nakedness, throwing roses covered with thorns. Then, as if the funeral has been concluded, the cars leave silently. Walter, described in images recalling a sacrificial figure, screams in despair and flings himself upon the mound of roses whose thorns rip his flesh.[19] His blood, mingled with rain, covers the leaves of the flowers.

The father, the symbolic castrator, is the leader from whom all others take their cue. The destructive father in this episode obviously connects with the theme of homosexuality. Walter's dream signals both his unconscious understanding of his sexual identity and his despair about his understanding. He is running from knowledge of his homosexual nature.

The dream episode is linked to an earlier episode in which Walter took the role his psyche assigns to his father in the dream. Having met a pleasant and intelligent man in a bookstore, Walter leads him to believe he is interested in something more intimate. After enticing the man, Walter enters a cab, slams the door, and laughs at him through the window. Before the collapse of his fragile world, when Walter tells a friend of his experience with the man, he describes it as having two parts: one is repayment for anyone who has ever injured him, but the other part "was something else." That something else is symbolically replicated through the acts of exclusion and castration in Walter's dream. However, in his dream, the father is in control, and he is not only mocking but violent as well.

After everything fails for him and the strange phone calls begin, Walter, like a hurt child, seeks mothering and finds it briefly in the attentions of a crippled woman he meets on the train to Saratoga. He spends the night in her hotel room, but manages to avoid having sex with her when his nemesis, the voice on the telephone, saves him from having to confess his sexual inability. The kind woman holds the weeping Walter in her arms, crooning to him "Poor little boy." As if he were a baby, Walter then falls asleep.

From that time on, Walter sleeps no more. Pursued by the voice on the phone, he travels south to New Orleans,[20] believing he has "traveled to the end." The end, however, paradoxically suggests the beginning in its images and symbols. Circularity is ubiquitous: wheels that turn, fans that spin endlessly, rings of trees, circles within circles—all suggest Walter's inability to alter his reality. His journey leads nowhere. It too is circular, for it only returns him to the self. The story's conclusion is filled with gothic images in which all polished surfaces, eyes, and mirrors reflect, distort, and confront Walter. Even his feet are "amputated stone," with toenails that are "ten small mirrors reflecting greenly" ("Door," 75).[21]

In a stifling hot hotel room, Walter lies in bed, terrified. He cannot bring himself to leave his room, for he fears he will be lost forever. The fan goes round and round, symbolizing the circle that goes back to the beginning. The description of the room, dark, with a window that cannot be opened, the sounds beyond the room and the silence within it, all image the womb he unconsciously seeks. Walter longs to regress to that place of safety, even though it is also a place of nonbeing. To escape the terrible voice, Walter prefers psychological death, the return to absence, to wind, to the sounds of nothingness.

Handcarved Coffins

After he had completed the stories that comprise *A Tree of Night*, Capote put aside most of the techniques he had employed in the five dark pieces, but characters like Vincent and Walter continued to preoccupy him throughout his writing career. His interest in aberrant figures remained. We see it expanded in his choice of subject matter for the nonfiction novel *In Cold Blood*, and then later in the novella *Handcarved Coffins*.

Because Capote labeled *In Cold Blood* "A Nonfiction Account of an American Crime," readers are inclined to take the writer at his word. Few of us question the designation, and even if we do, fewer still would take the time to analyze its genre identity. *Handcarved Coffins* first appeared in Andy Warhol's *Interview* magazine as part of a series Warhol called "Conversations," which was "a rather wide-ranging term to cover miscellaneous writings." The story "was the December, 1979 contribution to those 'conversations.'"[22] In 1986, when Random House published *A Capote Reader*, *Handcarved Coffins* was listed under a new heading: "Reportage." Capote had no qualms about claiming that the work was nonfiction. However, he also claimed that "nonetheless, [it was] mostly fictional" (Clarke 1988, 516). Everyone knew that the negative reviews of *In Cold Blood*, and even the favorable reviews that had taken issue with the whole concept of a "nonfiction novel," had angered Capote. He was bothered too by complaints that he never took any notes while interviewing people, and that reported conversations in the book were all suspect. Capote decided to play a joke on such complainers. Would they be as exacting about judging a piece if they believed it were a completely "true" story? They were not; Capote had much success with his joke, and took great satisfaction in having hoodwinked his critics.

With his eyewitness technique, Capote as narrator speaks with authority. The reader, unaware of manipulation, is persuaded to suspend disbelief; the writer, after all, is reporting "facts," some given to him by a friend who, according to Capote, saw the events unfold, and some he has observed firsthand. Thus, we are convinced of the truth of the tale and accept it wholly. But the story Capote tells is as improbable as any work of fiction. However, by using his reporter's style, which in itself helps to dispel any suspicion that the work might be fictional, Capote serves as interviewer in a horror story that would rival many a gothic tale.

Jake Pepper, a detective employed by an unnamed "State Bureau of Investigation," and working on a case in an unnamed small western town, allows Capote, after three years of telephone conversation, to "come there and look around" at the inquiry into a series of grotesque murders. Nowhere else in Capote's fiction do villages, towns, cities, and states go unnamed.

When Capote arrives, four murders have already been committed, and a fifth one is scheduled by someone who announces his plans in advance by sending his intended victim a tiny handcarved coffin containing a picture of the recipient. Every murder has been committed in a different way, and each shows incredible ingenuity, so much so that eventually we begin to think of some of Agatha Christie's "dinner party murders," where each act of violence is more bizarre than the last. In *Handcarved Coffins* the first terrible crime occurs when nine rattlesnakes kill a couple in their car. Eventually we learn the reason for the nine rattlesnakes: there will be nine victims, because the purported murderer, Robert Quinn, seeks vengeance on the nine members of a commission that voted to alter the flow of a river on which Quinn's property borders.

In the second crime a wire strung between two poles decapitates a man who is known to drive an open car. This victim had alerted Detective Pepper to important connections between Quinn and the rattlesnake murder, but before he is able to disclose the complete facts, he himself becomes a victim. Is truth stranger than fiction again? A third murder follows, this time with death by fire. The fourth victim, a coroner (who is also a loan shark and abortionist), dies of nicotine poisoning after the poison was "probably" added to his Maalox. Still another brutal act remains to be committed; it will occur after Capote's arrival. This crime will be the most dreadful of all from both Pepper and Capote's perspective, for the victim is Addie, the woman Pepper loves and whom Capote grows to admire. She is lured to her death by drowning in the river that fostered the initial controversy.

The gothic elements are multiple, but are less psychological than those found in the early dark stories. There, the gothicism is related to disintegration within the characters. Here, Capote employs an external and rather old-fashioned kind of gothicism: the horror of frequent and bizarre murders; the pervasive atmosphere of suspense and fear; the use of snakes and a snake seller; an old house; romance; adultery; illegitimacy; telepathy; a larger-than-life villain who also has been a religious figure; and, in a link to the first dark stories, the invocation and return of the unconscious fears of childhood.

Images reminiscent of Capote's early work appear frequently, but do not carry the same implications. The youthful portrait of Addie holding a white kitten reminds us of "The Headless Hawk." The snake figures significantly in *Other Voices, Other Rooms*. Caged canaries and snow fluttering at the window recall "Miriam." The guitar playing of the death-ridden Mrs. Quinn suggests the green guitar in "A Tree of Night," as well as the bejeweled instrument in the prison story "A Diamond Guitar." Capote's habitual stress on eyes appears in a description of a girl who has jewel-like lavender eyes and a villain whose eyes are gray and manic.

Connections to the gothicism of other Southern writers are also present in the story. Capote's vision of Quinn as a kind of bull—a kind of God?—at the end of *Handcarved Coffins* invokes the influence of O'Connor's "Greenleaf." The boyhood baptism Capote claims to have undergone recalls O'Connor's "The River." The figure of a black woman servant who seeks out an evangelical preacher and the force of that evangelical figure is in the line of Faulkner's *The Sound and the Fury* and Styron's *Lie Down in Darkness*. Typically, Capote concludes his narrative with a tableau, a scene designed to remain with the reader. The hand of the invincible Quinn raised toward the sky has fingers that seem larger and more powerful than the river behind him. Nothing will displace him; he has won.

Capote creates some brilliant poetic passages to describe characters and the landscape. The latter arouse memories of *In Cold Blood* with its snow-laced earth and gleaming wheat fields. The seasons are different at the end of the novel and novella, but the images suggest one another. October's threshed wheat fields, the ripple of color, and the cloudless sky in the last part of *Handcarved Coffins* remind us of the quiet ending of *In Cold Blood*, with May fields of wind-touched, golden wheat undulating under a large blue sky. Such images at the end of both works contain the imprint of poetry and fiction. Capote said *Handcarved Coffins* "combined the techniques of film, fiction, and nonfiction," and is "a distillation of all I know about writing: short-story writing, screenwriting, journalism—everything" (Clarke 1988, 516).

Those Were the Lovely Years

Capote's early work reveals a writer with two diametrically opposed styles. Although most of the the early stories are about children or young adults, the different techniques reflect the polarity of his vision. One pattern, baring the dark and frightening shadows of existence, characterizes his gothic stories; the other reveals the joyful Capote who created stories of bright, brief, happy days that seem to hold promise and hope for the future. In three of the best-known and most successful examples of this lighthearted fiction—"Children on Their Birthdays," *The Grass Harp*, and *Breakfast at Tiffany's*,—the themes are clear, the young protagonists captivating, the imagistic style haunting, the comedy both physical and verbal, the contrapuntal sounds of gaiety and melancholy always present. Lesser stories of this same period lack this totality; sometimes their humor is forced, the story derivative, or the protagonist uninteresting.

The primary force in most of the "daylight" stories is memory. Paradoxically, memory unites delight and sadness. The narrator's pleasure in recalling days—even years—of joyous youth is heightened by his and the reader's nostalgia for lost innocence and the recognition of unfulfilled desires. Out of his memory Capote selects moments in time that catch the shimmer of sunlit childhood, in its brief happiness, its expectations and longings. He reminds us that all children dream a fairytale world, but all are destined to awaken to painful reality. Although the stories differ in their plot particulars, their general outline is much the same: an event or an image triggers remembrance for the narrator, who then looks back to a childhood when everything seemed possible, and describes people from that period, friends, relatives, acquaintances. Eventually the person on whom the narrator focuses dies or goes away, and life thereafter is never the same.

"Children on Their Birthdays"

"Children on Their Birthdays," one of the earliest of Capote's published works, is a story both the author and the public favored. Miss

Lily Jane Bobbit, the protagonist of the piece and a forerunner of the young woman in *Breakfast at Tiffany's*, is a 10-year-old girl who arrives in a small Alabama town with her mother one late summer afternoon. Although she lives in the community only a year, she has a powerful effect on everyone who knows her; Mr. C., the narrator of the story, declares that she will never be forgotten. Like a summer's day, Miss Bobbit's time is brief. The fact that she dies at the height of her hopes and desires, unspoiled by disappointments and failures, seems to make her ageless, untouched by process. Roses are in bloom the day of her death, and no leaves fall.

Though realistic enough in multiple ways, Lily Jane Bobbit is a fantasy child, the mirror of the longings of all children. The fantasy quality is suggested immediately upon her arrival. Although she gets off the six o'clock bus, it is as if she simply materializes from another world. We learn almost nothing about her past life. Like many a creature from other worlds, she is not destined to remain long in the world of ordinary mortals. She has no intentions of lingering to grow old in this sleepy Southern town, for she has plans to move on to Hollywood as soon as possible. She intends to be a star.

In the real world of children mothers (and fathers) exert control over their activities, but Lily Jane's mother does not interfere with anything Lily Jane does. Mrs. Bobbit has a speech defect and appears to be mute. In a role reversal that many a child might desire, Lily Jane seems to be in charge of her mother: "My mother has a disorder of the tongue, so it is necessary that I speak for her," the girl announces.[23] Further, the secret longing to be parentless and free to do whatever they want that children sometimes have is reinforced thematically by the absence of the father figure.[24] Although townspeople, church leaders, and school authorities try to control Lily Jane, nobody is able to direct her. She is what all children wish to be: free of parental restraint; free from attending school or church; free to criticize anything; free to make the friends she wants; free to earn money as she chooses and spend it as she prefers; free to do whatever she wants when she wants to do it. And, unlike a real child, who dreams impossible dreams but does nothing to achieve them, Miss Bobbit employs all her considerable energy to make her dreams reality.

She will not be diverted from her objectives in any way. From the moment of her arrival, when she interrupts Billy Bob's birthday party, everything she does is directed toward the fulfillment of her dream. However, this extraordinary child also has a practical side, the polar opposite of her romantic, dreamer side. She refuses to eat ice cream and cake because they are not good for the figure. The very night of her arrival, though she has good reason to rest after her long bus trip, she carries on with her dance practice. Although the adolescent boys fall in love with her, and the girls in their jealousy mock her, Miss Bobbit is indifferent to such behavior. Ordinary girls are silly and unkind, and ordinary boys are foolish and immature, but Lily Jane is practical, efficient, logical, and businesslike. She concentrates on her goal of achieving stardom. She will not go to school because it would be a waste of her time; school will not teach her what she needs to learn. Church too would be a waste of time, for God would be no use to her career plans. She needs the help of the devil, who is on her side, the side of dancing.

All the boys are happy to work on her behalf in any scheme she devises, but her one true friend is Rosealba, a black girl she rescued from the sexual bullying of these same white boys. Child-woman that Miss Bobbit is, a combination of innocence and worldliness, untouched by sexual stirrings and yet strangely knowing, she is totally different from all other girls. Undeterred by Billy Bob's mother, she gives Billy Bob a "refreshing" massage when he is ill; she rejects the boys' declaration of affection, but finds them entertaining; she shocks the local audience the night she wins the prize in a talent show when she sings a wicked little ditty and displays her blue-lace-covered bottom.

Most of the humor in the story is associated with Miss Bobbit's personality and character, but Capote enlivens his tale with other kinds of humor that in time became Capote trademarks. There are funny scenes associated with animals: when Miss Bobbit is disturbed at night by the howling of dogs, she and Rosealba stalk the offenders. They carry "a flower basket filled with rocks; whenever they saw a dog they paused while Miss Bobbit scrutinized him. Sometimes she would shake her head, but more often she said, 'Yes, that's one of them, Sister Rosealba,' and Sister Rosealba, with ferocious aim, would take a rock from her basket and crack the dog between the eyes" ("Children," 98). The narrator notes that Miss Bobbit's landlady has a memorial sundial dedicated to a dog who met his end by lapping up paint. There is the comedy of exaggeration in the actions of the boys, particularly those of Preacher Star, who in spite of his name is the antithesis of a churchly child. There is the comedy of bizarrely inappropriate names. Rosealba Cat, for example, is neither a white rose nor a child of catlike grace—she is more like the "baby elephant" Mr.

C. calls her. While Rosealba's name comically contradicts her appearance, Manny Fox's name emblemizes his personality. Fox is a sly con man so persuasive that a local woman gives him the money she had intended to use to buy an angel tombstone. Capote plays with language, as in the expression "Merci you kindly." Even food becomes a vehicle for fun; ordinary mortals eat boiled ham and deviled eggs, but Miss Bobbit will eat no meat, and only raw foods, including raw eggs. The humor of the tall tale, so popular with southern and western writers, and a device Capote employed frequently, appears here through such depictions as the old drunken boarder who has a toilet-paper phobia and the vengeance Miss Bobbit and Rosealba take on him for his behavior. Many of the girls' actions fall under the tall-tale category.

Capote gains maximum effect from humor, but the comedy, while very important to the story, is not the author's major concern. He always brings us back to the primary motif, the sweet and sad lost moments of childhood, days that can only be recaptured in idealized memory.

The imaginary and the nostalgic are brought together through the title, which comes from a statement made by Miss Bobbit, who is searching for a world where everything and everyone dances and is pretty, a special, lovely world "like children on their birthdays." Adults know that such a world does not exist, but Lily Jane is one of the creatures who lives in the sky, different from all others. She is the child who will never grow up. We have seen such a character in Oreilly, the clown who also lives in the sky, in "Master Misery," and that same metaphor is used later with Holly Golightly in *Breakfast at Tiffany's*. The child or childlike creature never remains with us for long. Oreilly disappears, Holly leaves forever, and Miss Bobbit dies.

Early or late, childhood and childhood's dreams fade. The images of William Blake's *Songs of Innocence* come to mind as we look at Capote's ephemeral characters: the children who want to continue playing are watched by adults who know how short the time is, who see the darkening green all around them. Experience must come, changing, shattering, completely destroying innocence and illusions. But this will not happen to Lily Jane Bobbit, who dies in her white communionlike dress, in summer, while the air is heavy with the fragrance of wisteria and roses, the rain soft against a rainbowed sky.

Also like Blake, Capote is a colorist, and throughout "Children on Their Birthdays" he makes yellow the major hue. Miss Bobbit is first seen in a lemon-colored dress; her eyes are the yellow of sunflowers; yellow roses are given to her in tribute, twice. The faces of the boys who bring her flowers look like "yellow moons." But the boys with their roses bring about Miss Bobbit's death as she runs toward them: "That is when the six o'clock bus ran over her" ("Children," 106). The yellow of flowers, of moons, of summer thus becomes associated with death in a gentle, melancholy, and nostalgic tone much like the one describing the yellow leaves of autumn Capote was to use in *The Grass Harp* and *Breakfast at Tiffany's*.[25]

The reader knows from the first that Miss Bobbit must die, for her death is announced by an opening line that has the same quiet finality as the conclusion: "Yesterday afternoon the six o'clock bus ran over Miss Bobbit." Death in general, and the death of Miss Bobbit in particular, is an inescapable fact for Capote and his readers. Even while spinning out the story with all its humor, the author uses delicate and transient images of summer, of mutable nature, to underscore the unalterable reality that the little girl will soon be gone, like the music heard from afar, the fireflies that swoop through the early evening, the brief blooming irises. Dressed in white and glitter soon after her arrival, the child is shown dancing just before the fall of darkness, illuminating the evening before night sets in. Fantasies, hopes, and dreams must end for those left behind, for those who must grow up. But the memory of summer and a magical child is caught and preserved forever.

The Grass Harp

The Grass Harp, a novella published in 1951, has many of the characteristics Capote favored in the forties, techniques seen in "Children on Their Birthdays," as well as in the 1958 novella *Breakfast at Tiffany's*, and as late as 1966, in *A Christmas Memory*. Although almost 20 years separate the earliest from the last of these four works, the stories not only seem part of a whole in multiple ways, but also fall into pairs: "Children on Their Birthdays" with *Breakfast at Tiffany's*, *The Grass Harp* with *A Christmas Memory*. All four have a young male narrator, easily identified with Capote; each has one or more major symbols that appear and reappear to bind the work together; the four feature recurring character types; each has a circular plot structure; all employ various forms of humor, from the very gentle to the physically vaudevillian; all create a sense of nostalgia for the past; in each, the most lasting impression is the combined sense of sadness and sweetness for the irretrievably lost world of childhood.

Capote turned *The Grass Harp* into a play a year after publication of the novella, but it was a failure with both the critics and the public. Although the novella is more effective than the play, the seeds of the play's failure are already present in the novella's overt message and its sentimentality; sentimentality exists in other Capote works, but he controls it more. He conveys the delicate, magical quality of memory quite successfully in the written words of the novella, but this key feature of the novella was lost when he embodied his story with characters and actions on stage.

The major symbol in *The Grass Harp* is the Indian grass found in the meadow just below the town cemetery. The grass harp, the narrator is informed by his cousin Dolly, is a teller of tales, and this is precisely the function the narrator takes on when he reaches manhood. He becomes the bard, like the harpist of ancient times. Introduced in the very first part of the story, the special grass is mentioned several times throughout the years that pass. The final revelation comes at the end when the narrator, still a boy and about to leave his home forever, goes with an elderly friend to visit the cemetery and the meadow below it, where the September grass glows in all its fall colors. As the two stand in the field, the narrator tells the old man of the ability of the grass to sing the stories of the lives of those who are now gone. At that moment we recognize the relationship of the grass and the human storyteller, as well as the circularity of the story. The story we read is the one the narrator himself tells, the one we have just heard, of a past he has relived through the retelling.

At the beginning of *The Grass Harp* the narrator suggests that everything that follows is filtered through memory. A segment of the past is revisited, but now, because it can never be relived and experienced as it actually was, it takes on new coloration and tone because the insignificant details of daily life are forgotten and meaningful episodes are highlighted. In language similar to that of several other Capote stories, the narrator reminds us that memory is selective. The narrator, Collin Fenwick, asks, "When was it . . . ?"[26] and a little later uses words like "long before." Soon he begins to tell us a story of "the lovely years" from the time of his arrival, an orphan, at age 11, to the day of his leavetaking, several years later.

After the death of his parents, Collin is taken in by his father's cousins, two spinsters, Verena and Dolly Talbo. Also living in the household is Dolly's dearest friend and constant companion, Catherine. Catherine is a dark-skinned woman who calls herself an indian, but the rest of the community call her a Negro and treat her as inferior. Dolly becomes Collin's closest ally and mentor, and he grows up in her and Catherine's constant company. Verena is the money-maker, the businesswoman of the family, whose greed and selfishness lead to the death of her sister, Dolly, and to the end of Collin's innocence.

Before Dolly's death, however, life follows a quiet, predictable pattern. Dolly is as much a child as Collin. She likes children's play and games, has the pink room of a little girl, and prefers sweets to any other food. She does not have to pretend to enter into the childhood stage Collin is in, for she seems to have been always caught there. Only in the last few months of her life does she become an independent, self-assured woman.

Dolly makes, and sells a tonic to alleviate dropsy. Similar to the format of the later story, *A Christmas Memory*, with its seasonal trips into the woods to collect the ingredients for fruitcake, *The Grass Harp* presents making the dropsy medicine as the focal point of the week for Dolly, Catherine, and Collin. On Saturdays they take to the woods to search out the herbs, the roots, the bark, and the leaves that go into the secret remedy. Because of the sales of her medicine, Dolly has contact through the mail with customers outside her immediate circle. These letters are her only connection with other people because she is shy and timid. The money she earns from the sales provides the three companions with games, puzzles, lessons, and whatever advertised items catch their fancy.

This happy time ends when Collin is 16. Verena decides that real money can be made from the production and sale of the medicine. Verena, unable to allow her sister anything of her own, brings in an adviser from Chicago, which, in the xenophobic South of those years, represents sin city.[27] The townspeople tag Dr. Morris Ritz as a foreigner and a troublemaker, and they are right. With Ritz's advice, Verena prepares to go into large-scale production of the dropsy cure. But the plan never comes to fruition because Dolly refuses to yield to Verena.

Ritz is a con man drawn in the mold of the earlier Manny Fox, from "Children on Their Birthdays."[28] Both are sly and manipulative. Fox is "greasy and leering" as he tells off-color jokes; Ritz winks suggestively as he speaks to Collin of sexual opportunities in Chicago. Fox, the vaudeville showmaster, claps his hands; Dr. Ritz, of unknown profession, snaps his fingers as if he were in a vaudeville show. The townspeople's suspicions, Dolly's fears, and Catherine's hostility to Ritz prove well-founded, for Ritz eventually takes off with Verena's money and leaves her a broken, disappointed woman.

The turning point in the story occurs on the night Verena forces a showdown with Dolly about the dropsy cure. Not only does Verena berate her; she also blames her for the lonely life she has been forced to live because she has been ashamed of Dolly and the "gurgling fool," Catherine. Now Dolly feels she can no longer live with her sister. Although Verena tells her she has no other place to go, Dolly leaves home. Dolly, joined by Catherine and Collin, walks through the sleeping town; together they pass through the Indian grass, the grass that is the harp. As the sun rises they reach the China tree where they will live until the beginning of October.

Although the first part of the novella has a childlike, magical quality, the second segment, which describes life in the treehouse, is even closer to a fairy tale, but one with strong didactic elements. Here, Dolly and Collin grow up, with Dolly discovering her strength of character as well as her womanhood. They find friendships, and they and some of the people who become their friends learn about love. Typical of a fairy tale, they must undergo a test and be physically and emotionally challenged by various forces.

When Dolly, Catherine, and Collin take up life in the treehouse—surely the dream of many a child—they find happiness for a short time. Many people seek them out. A young man, Riley Henderson, and an old man, Judge Cool, join them as allies in the ensuing battles between the forces of conservatism and the forces of change. The handsome daredevil Riley becomes Collin's much admired friend; Judge Cool and Dolly fall in love. Each fulfills the needs of the other. For Dolly, the Judge becomes the admirer she has never had, one who approves of all she is and accepts her totally. For the Judge, Dolly becomes the beloved to whom all may be told.

The people in the treehouse learn lessons, about the world, about other people, and about the self. Uncertain men change to lovers and heroes. In old age, Dolly comes of age, becomes a woman who stands tall and assured because of love. But the treedwellers also learn that there is no escape from responsibilities. Eventually each must return to face the issues and problems he or she left behind. Dolly chooses to go back to her sister, who needs her. The Judge must also resolve his family problems. Riley will no longer behave like an irresponsible, uncontrollable boy, and Collin will move toward self-sufficient man-hood.

The story's underlying didacticism is mitigated by the liveliness of Capote's humor. The humor in the first part is more gentle, more verbal than that in the second: Catherine abandons French lessons after she learns how to say she is tired in French, for example, and she invents a version of history that suits her theories of race. The comedy of the second segment involves mock battle scenes and numerous farcical characters, some of whose names identify their personalities. Most of the interlopers suggest Gilbert and Sullivan figures. Capote mocks traditional religious figures and their attitudes, not only through their behavior, but also by creating a highly comic and sympathetic evangelist named Sister Ida Honey, who has an enormous brood of children, most of them illegitimate, but all loved. The tall-tale element is prevalent throughout this part of the story, as when Sister Ida recounts her various romances and ensuing pregnancies, or a meal intended for 5 is expanded to serve 16, or in the manner by which the good defeat the wicked invaders.

Comedic episodes dominate the middle section of the story, but the reader is never allowed to forget that nothing good lasts. With the departure of most of the people at the end of the battle, decisions about the future must be made. Dolly cannot resist Verena's pleas to return home. Just as Verena's claim seems to stand between Dolly and a new life, so too does the season, with its melancholy turn in the weather. As Dolly hesitates, attempting to choose, the rain seems to separate her from the Judge. The rain here, like the rain described as a curtain of glass in "The Headless Hawk," suggests a barrier that cannot be breeched. With the rain also comes the dissolution of cozy living in the treehouse. Everything falls, spills, or is washed away. The group leaves and takes nothing with them. What remains will be covered over by winter.

The warning of the winter to come has been present from the moment Dolly decided to leave home. From that point on in the story, the reader has a growing awareness of the swift passage of time. Before Dolly even tells Collin of her plans to go live in the treehouse with Catherine, Collin is lying in bed thinking of dead fathers—Dolly's and his own—and of the Indian grass and its stories of the dead. As Dolly agrees to permit Collin to join her in flight, a clock tolls the hour. Even in the idyllic setting of the treehouse, the Judge's gold watch is often mentioned, ticking away; although Dolly, in a magnanimous gesture, gives the watch to Sister Ida to help her and her children on their journey, time cannot be stopped. The clock is running down for Dolly, who becomes ill soon after returning home. The night of her death, just before she goes up to the attic with Collin in search of some decorations, he becomes aware of the striking of the town clock. Later, as she shows him her childhood treasures, Collin describes her face as looking like a moth's next to a lamp, so delicate is she, so brief her remaining time. Before the clock strikes again, Dolly tells Collin of the important knowledge she has gained from the Judge: "love is a chain of love. . . . Because when you can love one thing . . . you can love another, and that is owning, that is something to live with" (*Grass Harp*, 223).

Soon the sound of the clock is heard again. Moments afterward, as Dolly is dancing around the attic, she collapses. Her death at sunrise is known to Collin even before he is told, for a breeze flutters through the veil of Dolly's traveling hat, the hat she wore when they left for the treehouse, in River Woods, near the cemetery and the meadow of Indian grass. Although Dolly's death is really the end of the story, the aftermath of the lives of her friends and family are briefly summarized. Everything and everyone changes when she is gone. For Collin, childhood and the lovely years are over; he leaves home with no expectation of ever returning again.

Breakfast at Tiffany's

From the day of its publication in 1958 *Breakfast at Tiffany's* has been a much-loved book. More than 30 years after its appearance, book reviewers continue to compare female characters to Holly Golightly, Capote's unforgettable heroine.

Numerous conflicting stories have been told about the model for Capote's portrait. An actual person sparked the fictional creation, but who that person was remains a topic of debate. Typically, Capote embroidered and embellished the truth, telling different versions of the origin of Holly Golightly to interviewers over the years, and also to his biographer. All of these statements are at odds with novelist James Michener's recollections of the original "starlet-singer-actress-raconteur" he knew to be Holly.[29]

Although an actual person may have provided the mold for the heroine, Holly is yet another fantasy creature, a beautiful, captivating, elusive, lovable, and haunting young woman, a mixture of the romantic and the tragic. Generally regarded by critics as an expanded, older version of the adolescent Lily Jane Bobbit of "Children on Their Birthdays," Holly has many of the same personality traits: wisdom beyond her chronological age, brashness, courage, a longing for something that proves unattainable, and a separateness which makes her different from earthbound human beings. We respond affectionately to both Lily Jane and Holly, laughing at and with them, and mourning their loss. However, because *Breakfast at Tiffany's* is the longer, more complex fiction in which the major character is more fully drawn, the minor characters funnier, and the setting more completely realized, it is the more memorable work.

Mr. C., the narrator of "Children," has an expanded role in the novella. Though he has no name except the one Holly gives him briefly, he is obviously meant to be the young Capote, starting out as a writer in New York; even the birthdays are the same, September 30.[30] In *Breakfast at Tiffany's*, however, the Capote figure is more than an observer. He is an involved participant who falls in love with Holly and helps her whenever she has problems. He is friend, listener, defender, brother, and ultimately biographer of this captivating creature.

This story, resembling other Capote pieces in its mixture of tenderness, melancholy, and humor, is enclosed and protected in a frame of memory, inviolable, like figures carved on an urn, caught in a moment of time past. As in many of Capote's stories, time is the silent yet relentless figure in the background. In reality, autumn and winter must eventually succeed spring and summer; the church clock must toll the hours, signifying the passage of time and time-bound life. But memory, misted over with all its happy and unhappy moments, remains. The narrator's recollections are stirred by a phone call and a visit to a barman named Joe Bell. Returning to a neighborhood he knew well 15 years earlier, he learns that Joe has obtained a recent photo of a sculpted African head and that this head bears an uncanny resemblance to a much-loved person out of the past, Holly Golightly. After the bartender relates what little information he has concerning the background of the photo, the narrator walks through the neighborhood streets, back to the brownstone where he first met Holly.

It was wartime when the hopeful young writer met Holly, who lived in the same building as he. Holly, not quite 19, was a young woman who lived on "powder room money," a girl who looked like a breakfast cereal ad, but lived solely for fun and excitement. The larky atmosphere, the casual encounters, the easy money, the nightclubs, the dancing in the streets and partying with service officers—all speak of a wartime philosophy. The whole world seems young. Champagne bubbles up in glasses, in spite of or because of the war, but the war is very far away, even for Holly, whose beloved brother is at the front. When he is killed, however, her one tie with the past and normal life is destroyed.

Holly's card vaguely identifies her occupation as "traveling." The word is apt for the way she lives. Holly never stays anywhere for very long. She is a person searching for love, for a home, for a happy and safe life—all symbolized in her mind by Tiffany's. Orphaned early, the then Lulamae Barnes married Doc Golightly when she was only a child. Although she loves him—he was like a kind old father to her—she ran away. From that moment she has had a series of fantasy lives. In Hollywood, where for a time she concentrated on improving herself, Lulamae became Holly; she lost her hillbilly accent, learned a little French, became a starlet, and gained enough sophistication to realize she could not become a star. She then headed for New York to try for another kind of fame and fortune as a New York socialite. The elusive Holly is depicted as someone balanced between childhood and womanhood. In spite of her numerous lovers, she appears untouched by sordidness, and is surprisingly naive in many ways. Having had no childhood, she creates a child's world where she makes up the rules. Her girlish enthusiasm is contagious, so that all men feel more alive in her company.

In New York, although fortune eludes her, she does find fame, that is, notoriety, when she unwittingly becomes a courier for a mobster named Sally Tomato. This experience ends her only "non-rat" romance, when her skittish lover abandons her. The publicity also causes her to flee the country to avoid the courts and keep from betraying Sally, for she is an advocate of the honest heart in all circumstances. The streetwise side of Holly recognizes that her "career" in New York has been blemished and part of her life is over. Because of this mishap, once again Holly becomes a traveler. After sending a single postcard to the narrator, she fades into the soft haze of the past, a past revisited briefly when Joe Bell sends for the narrator.

All of Holly's fantasizing has a melancholy side, however, for it is really only a dream. Beneath the surface of gaiety lies the knowledge that nothing lasts. There is loneliness at the core of the dreamer. Though always surrounded by people, Holly gives the impression of being alone, still the little girl, Lulamae Barnes, still running, still searching for a home never to be hers. She knows she is one of those wild creatures who live in the sky, always an empty place; her favorite song tells plaintively of traveling "through the pastures of the sky." At times Holly confesses to the narrator her awareness of transiency, and in a sorrowful moment of revelation tells him we do not even recognize the wonder of lovely days until they are gone. Then it is too late to bring them back. For the narrator, however, they can be recalled, though only in memory.

Holly may seem like Miss Bobbit in her unchanging hope for something better, something more, but there is a far greater strain of melancholy in Holly. Holly, unlike Miss Bobbit, seems to know, at least at a subliminal level, that life will never give what it seems to promise children. Miss Bobbit dies before knowledge dims her radiance. Holly, however, even as a child, never had the kind of innocence Lily Jane has. There is a depth of sadness in her unknown to the younger girl. In spite of Holly's determination to be happy and have everything possible, she has been battered by existence and has endured poverty, hunger, loss, and abandonment.

An authority on abandonment, Holly has learned to face the world with style, even if it is veneer. When the narrator tries to tell her gently about the defection of her lover, Jose, Holly first puts on her makeup, her perfume, her earrings, and her dark glasses before she reads Jose's letter, in which he informs her that he will not marry her. A young woman who has built her personality partly on dissemblance and make-believe, partly playful, partly defensive, Holly has her own kind of armor to protect her from the harsh world. This is what leads her former Hollywood agent, O. J. Berman, to call her "a phony," but also to note that "She isn't a phony because she is a *real* phony. She believes all this crap she believes."[31]

Berman also predicts that Holly one day will finish "at the bottom of a bottle of Seconals." Although Holly battles frequently with fear and depression, in the tenderness of the narrator's memory, however, she is always young and unchanged. Still, the images associated with Holly lend themselves to both visions, Berman's and the narrator's: a birdcage she presents to the young writer, given with the admonition that he must never put anything in it; the cast-off cat she takes in, refuses to name, and then abandons when she flees New York; the yellow roses she loves (reminding the reader of the death of Miss Bobbit in "Children on Their Birthdays"); the flowers Joe Bell attempts to give her when she is leaving, flowers that fall to the floor (again reminiscent of the flowers Miss Bobbit never gets in the last scene in the short story). The downpour of rain as Holly flees New York carries with it the wind of desolation, an ache not obviated when the narrator discovers the cat at a later time ensconced in a lace-curtained window in Harlem. He hopes then that Holly too will find a place where she belongs, but that hope, the reader recognizes, may be as ephemeral as her promise to keep in touch.

Although both the short story and the novella end with a sense of loss in their images of mist and rain, a much more powerful minor key runs through the conclusion of the later work, for summer is still in the air in "Children on Their Birthdays." The rainbow that crosses the sky preserves the feeling of childlike hope, but in *Breakfast at Tiffany's* the autumnal season of heavy rain and yellowed leaves suggests only the winter to come.

However, *Breakfast at Tiffany's*, like "Children on Their Birthdays," is also lighthearted in many ways. Once again, Capote's humor is found in characters, dialogue, and events. He plays with names: Joe Bell takes phone messages; Rusty Trawler is a much-married man who has been involved in sex scandals.[32] Runyonesque characters from New York and Hollywood fill the novella. There is a chase scene with horses. And the star of the story herself provides slapstick and bawdy humor. *Breakfast at Tiffany's* shows Capote at his best, in total control as humorist, stylist, symbolist, imagist, and tone painter, characteristics that marked his fiction and nonfiction prose of the fifties and sixties.

Searching for Home: Holiday Stories

"Jug of Silver"

"Jug of Silver" is primarily a holiday story, with all the ingredients of the type. Covering only a brief period, from mid-October to Christmas Eve, a time concentrated on the excitement leading up to Christmas, the story is a warm celebration of the good things that can happen to the deserving. Bright, folksy, and pleasantly sentimental without becoming maudlin, "Jug of Silver" has none of the melancholy of the later masterpiece, *A Christmas Memory*, nor the didacticism of *The Thanksgiving Visitor*, nor the bitterness of Capote's last holiday story, *One Christmas*.

Myth, magic, and mystery combine to create what is essentially a fairy tale. Yet the magical narrative is set in a small, rather ordinary Southern community. It is the kind of town that would become familiar to Capote readers, with its central square and its clock that tolls from the courthouse steeple. The period is the 1930s, the era of the Great Depression. On Saturdays and holidays farmers come into town with their families in horse-drawn wagons or Model-T cars; the vanilla extract–perfumed girls who work in the silk mills also seek the thrills of town whenever they are free. In "Jug of Silver" the particular excitement that draws everyone is a game of chance in which a single winner will take the entire prize. This game, seemingly dependent on guesswork, is the frame on which the story is hung.

The owner of what had been the only drugstore in town decides to hold a contest to attract customers when a new drugstore opens and threatens to take away most of his business. By spending 25¢, anyone may have a try at guessing the value of the silver coins in a large jug set out on his counter. Not even the drugstore owner knows how much money it contains. Although he calls it his jug of silver, his close friend and constant companion goes further, labeling it "the pot at the end of the rainbow."

The idea of the rainbow, beautiful but mysterious, unexpected and ephemeral, becomes an important symbol in the story. Rainbows had a special significance to the young Capote, because he used them several times in his early work. Everyone muses about the rainbow: at the end of it, over it, somewhere near it, dreams will come true. "Jug of Silver" relates that dream's fulfillment for a strange little boy. But before he is introduced, the narrator describes the magical atmosphere that exists in the drugstore. Though the drugstore realistically resembles the old-fashioned soda fountains, its roots in reality do not diminish the sense of enchantment associated with the large, cool, dark shop: "When you sat on the high, delicate stools and looked across the fountain you could see yourself reflected softly, as though by candlelight, in a row of ancient, mahogany-framed mirrors."[33] Adding to the sense of the extraordinary is the name of the shop, the Valhalla, the mythical hall to which souls of slain heroes go. And, while the owner of the shop is rather prosaic, his close friend is very unusual. Hamurabi, an Egyptian with a name suggesting an ancient king of Babylon, is a man of heroic stature. Once again a name carries with it the association of the unusual, here the sense of wonder, of a person out of a distant and unknown world.

Soon after the contest begins, another figure appears, one whose name offers a further suggestion of myth. He is a boy called Appleseed; the name invokes one of the great figures of American folklore. This Appleseed, however, bears no resemblance to the famed hero, except for his sudden and mysterious appearance in the town and his disappearance some years later, after his mission has been completed. Appleseed is an unusual child. He claims to have only the one name, declares himself to be 12, although his sister states that he is only 8, and announces he can see things others cannot because he was born with a caul on his head. He also asserts that a witch put a curse on his mother when she would not relinquish the boy to her.

Special powers or not, which only he and his sister believe in, after weeks of intense concentration on the jar of coins, Appleseed gives the exact answer to the amount of silver in the jug and wins all the money. His purpose is completed, for he will be able to get his sister the false teeth she needs to become a star in "the picture shows."

As in several other Capote stories, "Children on Their Birthdays" in particular, the childhood dream of stardom is both funny and sad. It is also not achievable, as the adult world that does not believe in miracles well knows. However, Appleseed does what he is destined to do, by winning the money. In a sense, it is he who becomes the star, for the proprietor of the drugstore tells the magical story of Appleseed every year at Christmas. Even after the death of the proprietor, Appleseed remains a legendary figure. Reality, age, and time do not alter him, for he has long since left the little town. Heroes and heroines of fairy tales cannot linger, because if they did cold reality would destroy the brief happiness that belongs to children. Nobody knows what becomes of the wise child who once found the pot at the end of the rainbow.

A Christmas Memory

Recollections of boyhood holidays served as the impetus for a number of Capote pieces. One holiday story has become probably his most famous work. In interview after interview, Capote proclaimed *A Christmas Memory* his favorite piece of writing. It is not surprising to discover it is also a favorite of many people, including high school English teachers who prefer "this Capote" to the dark and difficult one of the gothic stories.

A Christmas Memory is autobiographical in multiple ways. The boy in the story, seven-year-old "Buddy," is a fictionalized version of Capote, and Buddy's "friend," his cousin, an unnamed woman in her 60s, is a romanticized version of Miss Sook Faulk, the relative young Capote loved more than anyone else. The country setting, the large house, the hostility and anger of the unnamed "others" in the house, surely based on other members of the Faulk family, are part of the autobiographical memory. Once again, the idea of memory, with all its sweet and sad nuances, a motif used with great effect in *Breakfast at Tiffany's* and *The Grass Harp*, is underscored at various points. Buddy's name has been given to him by his cousin in memory of another boy, another best friend, who lives only in her memory. Certain things are fixed in time, never to be altered.

This is yet another story with the magical qualities of a fairy tale. Capote establishes the feeling with his very first word: "Imagine." For most of the story the world he depicts is a joyful one that seems almost perfect, except for the wicked somebodies who appear now and then to spoil the fun and return "the children" to the world of reality. Buddy's friend is as much a child as he, and sometimes even more innocent. However, she is also like a fairy or a benevolent witch, for she is not one of the ordinary people. She can do extraordinary things, such as taming hummingbirds, and has magical cures for the ailments of humans. Their shared child's universe is one of intense pleasure, of spontaneity, of being at one with nature and in harmony with the seasons. Adult life, which intrudes periodically, is sober, somber, judgmental, and harsh.

Although with his opening the author invites us inside the visionary scenes of an ideal and idealized boyhood, he almost simultaneously reminds us that such a joyful and innocent period has boundaries. It must end. Thus in his second sentence he introduces the dreaded reality of time. He quietly notes that everything he is about to relate happened 20 years earlier. Having made that point, he tells his story as if it were happening at this very moment, never thereafter dropping the present tense. Nevertheless, on the last page of his reminiscence, without altering tense, he returns to the point that joy is brief; what has seemed a fairy tale does not have a happy ending; time takes all away.

As if to underscore the relentless presence of time, Capote uses seasons metaphorically. While it is true one could not set a Christmas story in spring, the seasons of late autumn and winter serve the writer's poetic purpose. This is the season of endings, of harvesting, followed by the chill of loss. Although there are a few passing references to spring and summer, they are so brief as to seem nonexistent.[34] The focus on the final weeks of the year ultimately heightens both the sense of delight and the sense of melancholy.

The story opens in late fall, "fruitcake weather," the season for nut gathering, for buying ingredients that go into the cakes, for obtaining illegal whiskey—perhaps Prohibition is still in effect, or perhaps legal liquor is unavailable because this is the dry, Bible-Belt South. Baking must be done and then decisions must be made about which people are to be the recipients of the wonderful cakes. Unlike practical grownups, the "children" bake their 31 cakes for people they hardly know or have never met. The entire process is one of absolute pleasure. During the seven years of Buddy's childhood the ritual has always been the same. Perhaps it is this very element of ritual—warm, stable, and rooted— that so attracts the readers of *A Christmas Memory*. Every year the joyous announcement is made; the same hat is worn; Buddy's same old baby carriage is hauled out for service. Capote deftly portrays the two friends and their terrier dog, Queenie, out of doors on the nut-gathering expedition, capturing with a word or a phrase the sense of late autumn. When he depicts the indoor scenes, they are filled with the sounds and smells and tastes of the baking.

The pre-Christmas segment of the story is filled with light and happiness and comedy. The humor comes in many varieties and flavors. Indeed, the story is undeniably the funniest of Capote's short fictions. He uses all the senses for comedic effect in most of the story, and at the end calls on those same senses to achieve the powerful and moving conclusion. Buddy tells of a "Fun and Freak Museum" the two friends ran briefly, where the main feature was a deformed baby chick, but the museum had to close "due to the decease of the main attraction."[35] Because Capote is an extremely visual writer, he paints one funny scene after another: for example, the elderly woman's nut-gathering apparel includes "a straw cartwheel corsaged with velvet roses" now faded. He exaggerates language and combines it with the visual for comic effect. Each year Buddy and his cousin begin "a Fruitcake Fund," consisting mainly of pennies earned in highly imaginative enterprises, such as the summer job when "others in the house contracted to pay us a penny for every twenty-five flies we killed. Oh, the carnage of August: the flies that flew to heaven! Yet it was not work in which we took pride" (*Memory*, 152). Buddy notes that he and his cousin keep their "moneys . . . hidden in an ancient bead purse under a loose board under the floor under a chamber pot under my friend's bed" (*Memory*, 151). The lack of any punctuation within this sentence increases our laughter with each repetition of the word "under."

There is aural humor as well: we hear the tremor of their voices as the old woman and the little boy call on the bootlegger, Mr. Haha Jones, in a situation which lends itself to another familiar comedic touch, playful naming: Mr. Haha is not one to laugh or smile. After their visit to Jones and the baking of the cakes, Capote further broadens the wit of Jones's query—"Which one of you is a drinking man?" (*Memory*, 153)—by having both Buddy and his cousin "taste," that is, finish off the whiskey, but so too does the dog, Queenie. The scene then shifts into slapstick comedy.

Soon after the description of fruitcake rituals, the sparkling humor yields to another sound, one that might be compared to music. Melodically the tone becomes a high, sweet note, telling of intense joy, then changes to a single, fading line of grief, as the beauty, harmony, and remembrances of the lost past grow stronger. As the season advances toward Christmas, there is an iteration of the pattern followed in the nut gathering. The narrator describes each step in decorating and making gifts. However, detail accumulates and expands in the chronicling of the Christmas tree expedition; the particularization combined with a change of tone foreshadows future loss, and this journey is converted by memory into a type of pilgrimage.

Proportionate to the lengthier passages, the poetic quality increases when the narrator recalls the hunt for the tree. Never has there been a more perfect day, with its frosted grass, its orange sun, and silvered woods. The boy and his elderly cousin pass "lemony" pools and hear birds singing "an ecstasy of shrillings" as trout stir the waters of the stream. It seems as if winter will never come. The tree they find and cut is also perfect, one of a kind, as they are, as everyone is, says Buddy's simple yet wise cousin. That day, among all the holidays that have gone before, will be the one he remembers, although as he lives it he does not realize that it is the beginning of the end of the time the two companions have together. As the narrative moves toward its conclusion, the lyrical quality of the story becomes intense. That potency, however, is offset by the practicality of the preparations for the big day, the making of decorations and wrapping of gifts.

Finally, the holiday arrives. Presents are exchanged and opened. The serious, critical adults give practical, boring things, but the two friends give each other magical gifts. Never mind that they have given each other the same thing year after year. Their gifts, paper kites, are beautiful and fragile, almost too ephemeral to hold. Their delicacy represents the days of childhood. A warm wind, good for kite flying, blows as the two of them head for the pasture. But now the narrator interjects a chilling note. The pasture is the place "where, a winter hence, Queenie will be buried" (*Memory*, 160). Because of this statement, the reader intuits that this soft wind and weather are different from the wind and weather to come in the final passages as the story moves to its elegiac ending. On their last Christmas of kite flying, sunshine, waist-high grass, and gentle clouds, Buddy's friend speaks of her belief that God shows himself in those very elements.

Then, abruptly, the fairy tale is over, and everything changes. Winter becomes leafless, birdless, joyless. At the conclusion of the story the kites take on a weight of symbolic meaning we do not see earlier. Not only are they connected with the brief golden days of childhood, but also with the happiness that once was and is no more. We are reminded again of time. Hearts are broken by events. Like kites, our brief moments of childhood joy are carried off, as if by the wind, into the winter sky.

The Thanksgiving Visitor

The Thanksgiving Visitor, published two years after *A Christmas Memory*, is set in the same early Great Depression years of the thirties, in the same small Alabama town of Capote's boyhood, and reintroduces most of the people of the earlier story. Once again, Truman is known as Buddy, but his dear "friend" of *A Christmas Memory* is given her true name, Miss Sook, in the later piece. She and her two unnamed spinster sisters, true to the facts of Capote's life, live with their bachelor brother, now called Uncle B. The dog, Queenie, also appears as the companion of Miss Sook and Buddy.

In spite of similarity of many details, the later story is actually quite different from *A Christmas Memory*. An intrusive reality enters this story in ways that eliminate the lovely fairy-tale quality of the earlier holiday story, as well as its timelessness. Actual dates are provided in *The Thanksgiving Visitor*: dates when the story takes place, specific ages, dates when Buddy last saw people, dates of the death of an old aunt and of Miss Sook. While the first story pits children against the harsh adult world, *The Thanksgiving Visitor* has no such division. Instead eight-year-old Buddy must face his bullying 12-year-old schoolmate, Odd Henderson.

Buddy's Uncle B. is depicted as a quiet, kind person. Two of Buddy's spinster cousins are hardly mentioned, except for a word about their somewhat masculine qualities and business activities. Miss Sook, his other cousin, continues to have many of the childish and innocent qualities she had in *A Christmas Memory*, but here she is adult and responsible enough to manage the entire household, cooking, cleaning, laundering, and mending clothing. Indeed, her family depends on her in ways impossible to envision for her earlier incarnation in *A Christmas Memory*. In some ways, Miss Sook is another version of Dolly Talbo of *The Grass Harp*. At times, the images associated with Sook are akin to those of Dolly: both are shy and afraid of company; both appear to be frail, yet are spiritually strong women; both have unusually beautiful eyes; and both, though poorly educated, are interested in the things the boy studies.

Although Miss Sook is still described as simple, unschooled, gentle, and thoughtful, Capote changes her in significant ways. In the earlier story, she had a child's sense of fun and a child's rebelliousness, but now she is depicted as a person concerned with right behavior. Because of her distinct awareness of societal rules and proper actions, Miss Sook now seems more an adult and less a child, in spite of the author's declaration that she is as much a child as Buddy. He announces, once again, that she is Buddy's closest friend, and even less worldly than he, a woman who can scarcely read or write, and whose knowledge of the world comes from her understanding of "the Bible and its Hero."

Because Buddy regards Miss Sook as his contemporary, expecting her to share his feelings, likes, and dislikes—which she ordinarily does—he experiences an overwhelming sense of betrayal when she protects Odd, whom he regards as his most fearsome enemy. Buddy, spying on Odd at the Thanksgiving dinner Miss Sook has insisted on inviting him to, sees him steal a brooch. But when the little boy announces the theft at the party, expecting to be applauded for his cleverness, the plan backfires, and Buddy suffers humiliation for his efforts. Capote succeeds in capturing the boy's anguish and underpins it with both psychological understanding and humor. As Buddy dramatically contemplates escape, suicide, and vengeance against the adult world for what he feels is unfair treatment, Capote shows him as foolish, yet funny, and very much like all eight year olds.

The story becomes extremely didactic, however, when Miss Sook, kind and loving in her lesson, tries to teach Buddy the difference between inadvertent harm and planned injury. The child does not want to accept that idea, but the story itself shows the effect the good Miss Sook has on the naughty Odd, who turns out rather well after all.

One of the most attractive aspects of the story is its use of the southern background. The rural South of the thirties was populated by numerous families consisting of maiden sisters and bachelor brothers who lived together throughout their lives. Some people still rode horses for transportation, as Uncle B. did, and others still traveled by horsedrawn wagon, as some of Buddy's relatives did. Kin mattered and kept in touch, even if they lived in remote areas, and holidays brought them together in large numbers. Southern hospitality made for the inclusion of strangers for holiday celebrations, where the ladies smelled of lilac water and the men of tobacco. Bootlegging, cotton growing, and other kinds of farming were a way of life, just as religion and churchgoing were.

Descriptions of food also add to the southernness of the story, with fried everything: chicken, pork chops, catfish, squirrel. Other food includes eggs and grits, collards, blackeyed peas, cornbread, biscuits, jams and jellies. The narrator speaks of the "nostalgic hunger" he still has for such meals: "These breakfasts, served promptly at 5:30 A.M., were regular stomach swellers."[36] The only food that tasted as good was the Thanksgiving repast where everybody brought a special dish, the same one year after year.

This is a world long gone. Yet, in contrast to much of his writing, *The Thanksgiving Visitor* does not emphasize nostalgia, nor Capote's feelings about the unstoppable passage of time. Nevertheless, shortly before the end of the story, a suggestion of brevity and fragility is introduced. Sook reminds young Buddy that nobody can live forever. The images of the last lines of the story serve to emphasize the swift onset of winter and death, as Odd Henderson takes away with him a gift from Sook, the chrysanthemums of autumn, flowers that burn and growl and roar "against a greenly lowering dusk."

One Christmas

One Christmas is both the last of the holiday stories and the last story Capote wrote. Although again some of the characters from the earlier pieces appear, this story is brief and somewhat thin, relying on timeworn material and lacking most of the qualities that made *A Christmas Memory* so pleasurable.[37] Another change from the earlier holiday stories is the setting, which shifts from rural Alabama to New Orleans. For the second time the author's father, Arch Persons, is introduced (Capote spoke of him once before, in "Dazzle," in 1979), though he is only referred to as "my father." Capote's mother, as a young woman, is depicted pitilessly. Such undisguised autobiography allows no distancing between the author and his tale, and only weakens the story.

The setting, the French Quarter of New Orleans, had an important symbolic role in the early dark stories. In "A Tree of Night," New Orleans is both the birthplace of the terrified young woman and also the city where the older woman once practiced fortune telling. It is the city where Walter Ranney (the author's early double and forerunner of the last double, P. B. Jones of *Answered Prayers*), in "Shut a Final Door," has his final breakdown. In the unhappy, late autobiographical "Dazzle," New Orleans again provides the setting. Clearly, Capote associated that city with fear, disappointment, and betrayal.

Capote tells of a visit he made to his father as a very young boy, one Christmas holiday. We learn that Buddy is a frightened and anxious child. He does not want to see his father, whom he scarcely knows or remembers. However, Cousin Sook, childlike though she is, uses two very adult means of persuading him to go: the first is the admonition that we must all follow God's will; the other is the suggestion that Buddy might see snow in New Orleans. With its magical, fantasy quality, snow holds a promise never fulfilled. Buddy never gets to see the snow, so it serves as a metaphor of the unattainable.

The old, unsettled conflict between father and son is the theme of *One Christmas*. Yet, for all the animosity expressed toward his father by Capote throughout his lifetime, the man portrayed in the story is merely weak and foolish rather than monstrous. Further, whether the author recognized it or not, he shows a man who longs for the love of his son and tries to win it however he can, at least for the brief time they are together. Perhaps it was his father's unscrupulous manipulation that Truman Capote resented all his life.[38]

The father is a fair-weather friend, a charmer who expects love and thinks he can buy it with gifts for his son. After all, he allows older women to buy his affection with their money. Because of the man's eager desire for the boy's regard, Buddy is able to engineer his father into purchasing a very expensive toy airplane for him. However, the maneuver backfires later, when, on Buddy's departure for Alabama, his angry, drunk father, determined to reveal truth to him, tells the six year old that neither God nor Santa Claus exists.

Home again with his dearest friend Sook, the boy is comforted, led once more into belief. Convinced he has had a message from God, he writes his first loving card to "Pop," a card later found among his father's possessions after his death. That the father saved the little note for more than 50 years softens the ugly portrait of Arch Capote kept embellishing throughout his lifetime. At the end of the story, this intimate touch—carefully disclosed by the author—implies the father's love, episodic though it apparently was. Such instances of affection combined with the rancorous nature of their relationship, details of which were discussed openly for years and written symbolically into his dark stories, reveal the ambivalence the writer never was able to reconcile.

In *One Christmas* unresolved emotions are directed not only at the father but at the author's mother. Bitterness comes to the fore every time she is mentioned. Shown to be even more avaricious than her former husband, the mother is decribed by the author not from the point of view of the child who put her photograph under the Christmas tree, but from the perspective of the still wounded almost 60-year-old man he has become. He speaks of a visit paid him in boarding school by his pearl-bedecked and sable-clad mother. Although remarried to a wealthy man, she flies into a tantrum at the mention of Truman's father, and spares the boy nothing: "All the while she talked (and I tried not to listen, because by telling me my birth had destroyed her, *she* was destroying me)."[39] Thirty years after his mother's suicide on the "Seconal road," he remains that unwanted child of an Alabama magnolia who abandoned him to go to New York in search of the rich husband and elegant life she soon found. A moving and somewhat familiar note is heard as he remembers himself: the unloved, discarded boy trying to escape from the raging voice of his mother by singing tunes in his head.

The episode suggests still another connection with Walter Ranney, whose first attempt to avoid confrontation with his failures comes when, after everything has collapsed for him, he returns to his apartment and begins to dance to music on the record player. But the episode also helps to explain the numerous orphans in other Capote stories. Capote, like Dickens, whom he much admired, symbolically kills off the parental figures that are the source of the agonies of childhood. However, in the autobiographical *One Christmas*, he can only try to shut out their voices.

The last line of the story contains a final poignant phrase as the author repeats the words he had written to his father after the Christmas holiday. It is a phrase that provides a link to Capote's early masterpieces. On the card the child reports he is learning to pedal the plane his father gave him and that soon he "will be in the sky." Those words take us back to the sad clown, Oreilly, of "Master Misery," and to the lovely but lost Holly Golightly of *Breakfast at Tiffany's*, to the company of people who live in that lonely place, the great wide and empty blue sky.

The Questions of Love

"My Side of the Matter"

"My Side of the Matter," unlike most of the first-person narratives Capote wrote, is about a narrator who bears little resemblance to Capote. Here, a 16-year-old married "man" reconstructs the story of what he considers mistreatment by his wife and her relatives.

A slight, almost nonexistent plot serves Capote for experimentation with humor of various types, some of which the author was to use again within a decade and some of which he would not revive until his last cycle of writing in the seventies and eighties. In this early story he tried out understatement and overstatement, physical and vaudevillian buffoonery, verbal jabs, incongruities, and insults. Characters are one-dimensional and rather flat, whereas their actions are as exaggerated as those in a comic stage skit.

The young narrator, who reluctantly returns with his wife to her home in a minuscule town in Alabama after they discover she is pregnant, finds himself in a world entirely female, consisting of his teenage wife, her two elderly spinster aunts, and their maid. Although his wife declares to her aunts that she has married for love, she soon joins the cabal against him. Feeling unwanted and betrayed, he decides to set the record straight, although it becomes apparent almost immediately that his version of the matter is without merit.

The dramatic monologue runs true to form in its revelation of things the narrator does not know he is telling, providing a close look at himself that is totally unflattering. In defending himself against the criticism of others—who eventually number the entire population of the town, some 300 people—he reveals a nature that is petty, cruel, malicious, lazy, and gossipy. Everything he says works against him, and he gains no sympathy for his plight from the reader. Certain he is superior to everyone he meets in his wife's household, the narrator feels he has made sacrifices to come and stay with them. His pique is so great that he informs us three times of the "perfectly swell" job he had to give up as a clerk for the Cash 'n' Carry store. The humor of his self-importance and self-concern develops with the story as he describes the ways in which he must protect himself physically and emotionally from the people with whom he lives.

The author tries out forms of humor that become more subtle and ultimately funnier in the later work. The two maiden aunts are too much alike to be differentiated in "My Side of the Matter," even though the narrator insists they are. However, in the novella *The Grass Harp*, written several years later, Capote again introduces spinster sisters who are absolutely unlike, and he does not have to direct the reader to see their uniformity. He does, nevertheless, continue to use some of the same physical characteristics.

The ironic use of names, a hallmark in much of the fiction, appears even in the earliest stories. Bluebell, the black maid in "My Side of the Matter," becomes Rosealba Cat in a more subtle use of flower names in "Children on Their Birthdays." Black girls and women have humorous roles in these two stories and even more significantly in *The Grass Harp*. Although the role of the black female is more significant in "Children on Their Birthdays," only in *The Grass Harp* does the author show the black woman as both funny and tragic, with a special kind of dignity. The racist language in all three works is meant to characterize the various speakers, and does not reflect the writer himself. This language is true to the idiom of the southern world of the forties.

Physical battling takes place in all three stories: between the narrator and the aunts and maid in "My Side of the Matter"; between the black girl and two white bullies in "Children on Their Birthdays"; and between a large number of people in *The Grass Harp*. However, the fighting is nastier in "My Side of the Matter," where, for example, the narrator slaps his wife around and one of the aunts uses a hog knife on him, and because of this nastiness is not particularly amusing.

The verbal jabs of the story are humorous, though sometimes inconsistent. The occasional slippage between the voice of the whiney young man who speaks in a regional accent and uses somewhat vulgar language and that of the sophisticated writer reminds us the author was also very young and still learning his craft. Sexual accusations intended to be funny fall flat in "My Side of the Matter." One of the aunts says of the narrator, "Why, this isn't any sort of man at all." Her statement is reinforced by her sister, who adds, "Why, he isn't even of the male sex!"[40] Later she queries, "How can a girl have a baby with a girl?" ("My Side," 16). In a revealing psychological turn, the subject, precarious masculinity, which is the humorous focus of these accusations, becomes the central and serious question in one of the writer's last stories, "Dazzle." After "My Side of the Matter," Capote went on to use sexual humor much more effectively a decade later in *Breakfast at Tiffany's*. By the seventies the sexual humor had become both salacious and malicious, as it appeared first in a nonfiction essay called "Blind Items," and then in all the pieces of his last, unfinished work, *Answered Prayers*.

That Capote could be inventive in his use of incongruities is shown in the description of one of the Southern maiden aunts, who having delivered a "terrific . . . punch" to the narrator, celebrates her victory standing out in the yard loudly singing "The Battle Hymn of the Republic," for all to hear. The author's lifelong reputation as the strikingly humorous teller of tales is borne out in such glimpses even in the first pieces he published.

"A Diamond Guitar"

The question of love is treated very differently in "A Diamond Guitar," first printed in 1950. Here, where the issue is homosexual love, Capote finds no room for humor, sexual or otherwise. The story does not fit neatly into the limited categories generally applied to Capote's work. The setting of the story, a prison, leads the reader to expect another of Capote's dark stories, but "A Diamond Guitar" is actually a quiet and reflective piece. It is written in a realistic mode rather than a fantastic manner, and is the first of his stories to reveal his interest in crime, criminals, and prisons.

Set entirely in a Southern jail, 20 miles from the closest town, the narrative concerns loneliness, love, and betrayal. The major character, Mr. Schaeffer, a model prisoner, is serving a life sentence. Although Schaeffer has spent a third of his 50 years in prison, he does not rail against what the omniscient author states is an unjust fate. Like all the other men in the prison, he has learned to survive by withdrawing into a kind of twilight torpor, without hope or desire. Prison is a world without women, sex, or love—although some of the prisoners do find sexual partners within the male group.

A young Cuban, sentenced to two years in the prison, changes Mr. Schaeffer's world dramatically, and also alters the lives of the other prisoners. With his arrival, "it was as if lamps had been lighted through all the gloomy dead rooms."[41] Tico Feo, a golden-haired, blue-eyed boy, brings lightness, laughter, and music to the endlessly repetitive, dull, quiet, cold existence of the men. His youth, beauty, and gaiety entertain them; however, his presence also has a negative side, for he awakens memories of life outside the prison walls, of freedom and the company of women.

Tico Feo has the greatest effect on Mr. Schaeffer. He falls in love with the boy, and it seems as if he is loved in return, although they never become sexual partners. What draws them together is puzzling. Like the characters in the stories of Carson McCullers, the lover and the beloved here have nothing in common.[42] They are separated by age, experience, temperament, and character. The love they share is both inexplicable and unsuitable. The beloved depends totally on the lover for help, support, and protection, and gives little or nothing in return except the opportunity for the experience of love itself.

But it does not matter to Schaeffer that Tico Feo is selfish, greedy, and lazy, nor that he lies about most things. His golden beauty and his ability to create magical moments with his "diamond"—that is, his glass-studded guitar—suggest Orpheus and his lyre. Those who listen to him play are enchanted. The moment Schaeffer meets Tico Feo everything in nature seems to flower for him. Only then does he awaken again to life and recognize the devastating loneliness he has endured. Life comes rushing back to him, with all its joy and sensuous images. Recognition of what he has missed and the sudden happiness he feels bring tears to the eyes of this prisoner who has forgotten what it is to live in the outside world. The tears are not only a reminder of lost hope and opportunities but also a representation of the breaking down of the barrier that has separated him from others. That barrier, of course, has also protected him.

While Schaeffer is satisfied to experience love, Tico Feo uses love as a way to survive, to get more food, more cigarettes, and ultimately help in escaping from the prison. Although he persuades Schaeffer to flee with him, he uses Schaeffer, knowing full well the older man will not be able to accompany him, and he abandons him when he is injured. Despite the shock of recognition, Schaeffer, like all the betrayed and lonely lovers in McCullers's stories, forgives his beloved. Continually grieving and longing for Tico Feo, he is forced once more into the solitude that was his former lot; loneliness is absolute, for he never hears word of Tico Feo again.

Schaeffer is a good man, kind, and generous. Unlike most of the prisoners, he can read and write and add, and he gives help to anyone who asks. Even the guards like him. After Tico Feo's escape, the prison captain lies about Schaeffer's role in order to protect him. Still, all of

Schaeffer's decency does not insulate him from the suffering that comes with unrequited love. His desolation is revealed through the depiction of him at night as he brushes his fingers against the strings of the guitar Tico Feo has left behind.

Capote is particularly effective in creating the impressions of separation and seclusion in the prison environment. Not only does he describe the isolation of the prisoners from society, but also the isolation of the prisoners from each other. Segregation separates whites, blacks, and Chinese. The sleeping quarters divide men hierarchically, with the important men near the single stove, lesser men positioned further away. The cold winters are both imagistic and metaphoric: they heighten the sense of the prisoners' distance from the rest of the world and also suggest the emotional chill these men must endure: to survive they must allow their emotions to atrophy. Furthermore, there is a sense of circularity in the images of coldness. Winters are cold before the ice in the heart is cracked by love. However, when love is gone, the winters grow successively colder and longer, and constant rain makes the single road to or from the prison more and more difficult to traverse. Thus the imagery of isolation not only comes full circle, but is intensified.

The "jewels" in Tico Feo's guitar are glass, but when he first comes to the prison they sparkle like diamonds, the most precious gem. After his escape, the glass begins to yellow and fade, as if the stones were old love letters, or the old newspaper clippings about Tico Feo Schaeffer keeps in an envelope, clippings that will also yellow and crumble with time. There is a strong air of melancholy attached to all these images, a tone of poetic sadness that characterizes many of Capote's best stories.

"House of Flowers"

"House of Flowers" is another story of love, but one concerned with a happy, heterosexual relationship. First written as a short story and later made into a play, it bears only a few resemblances to the writer's other fiction. This is a joyful piece from first to last, without any of the melancholy touches that sometimes frame even the light and humorous stories. Nowhere is the author's presence felt; he is neither narrator nor participant. The country in which "House of Flowers" takes place is Haiti, an exception to the fact that almost all Capote's fiction of the first two decades is set in the places in which he grew up: rural Alabama, New Orleans, and New York. Although the late fiction spreads over a wider geographical range than both the first novel, *Other Voices, Other Rooms*, and the early short stories, there is always an American base. *Handcarved Coffins*, written in the seventies, and said to take place in a small western state, has the feeling of the Midwest of *In Cold Blood*. The stories in *Answered Prayers* may include the European continent, but New York City remains central.

Not only is the setting of "House of Flowers" totally new for a Capote fiction, so too are most of the characters. A young prostitute, her friends in the brothel, her husband, and his grandmother comprise the cast. Only the grandmother bears any resemblance to people in other works, and her familiarity is in type rather than anything else. She is a witch figure, but nothing like the women in other stories who have unusual talents. The witchlike figures of other books know secrets and seem to be able to perform magic, at least in the eyes of the young boy (Capote or his persona) who is reporting. But in "House of Flowers," the grandmother, Old Bonaparte, truly believes herself to be a witch, as do all the people in the little mountain community in which she lives. Furthermore, the witchlike figures of the American stories are, for the most part, childlike, gentle, do-gooders, whereas the old grandmother here is a fierce, vindictive, and jealous woman who terrorizes everyone: "A charred, lumpy creature, bowlegged as a dwarf and bald as a buzzard, Old Bonaparte was much respected for miles around as a maker of spells. There were many who were afraid to have her shadow fall upon them."[43]

The idea of sorcery, spells, and voodoo is not confined to the grandmother: it is an integral part of the life and beliefs of the simple Haitians Capote depicts. When the 17-year-old whore, Ottilie, worries about her inability to fall in love, she turns to a Houngan, a voodoo priest, for assistance. His advice leads directly to a major change in her life. She finds love with Royal, the handsome young grandson of Old Bonaparte, and leaves Port au Prince, the capital city, to live with Royal and his grandmother in the hill country. Far away from the music, the electric lights, the glitter of silk and gold, Ottilie becomes embroiled in a battle for survival with the old witch who wants her dead.

That Ottilie wins in spite of the reputed force of voodoo is an ironic twist. In secret she takes every menacing animal or animal part (a cat's head, a lizard, a snake, a buzzard's breast) that the old woman uses in her magic spells to destroy her rival, and cooks these in the meals she serves the grandmother. So much does the old woman believe in the validity of her own magic that she dies instantly when she discovers that the spells have been turned on her. However, even after the death of Old Bonaparte, Ottilie continues to believe in the power of her ghost, and it is only through punishment by her husband that she can be rid of the menacing spirit of the grandmother.

Capote did not invent the story entirely out of whole cloth. A few years prior to the publication of "House of Flowers" he had written a travel piece about Haiti; it was republished in the nonfiction collection, *Local Color.* Many of the details of the essay appear in the short story. The description of brothels in "Haiti" is very close to the one in the fiction. Material success for both the nonfictional and the fictional whores in Haiti is measured by the possession of gold teeth. A number of the girls Capote met came from the Dominican Republic to work in the bordello, as do Ottilie's two closest friends. The Houngan whose ceremony Capote goes to witness and the Houngan Ottilie seeks out both lived in the hills above the town.[44] Rahrah weekends and Carnival with their drums, singers, and bands create atmosphere and exoticism in both works. An actual funeral, with mourners who are total strangers putting on a ritualistic display of grief, is the forerunner of the fictional funeral in which people from the village and the hills come to put on the ceremonial show of mourning for Old Bonaparte, in spite of the fear and hate she had inspired as a spellmaker.

Although "House of Flowers" is a story based on the reality of Haitian life, it is also a fantasy about love. It resembles in some ways the early legendary tales about the life of the painter Gauguin in his reputedly happy primitive existence on a remote island, where he lived a passionate life with beautiful maidens in flower-covered huts. The sentimental view of kind whores and generous benefactors also seems related to two of John Steinbeck's novels from the same period, *Cannery Row* and *Sweet Thursday.*

Capote's use of romance and myth is so attractive that the reader forgets the seamy and harsh actuality of life in Haiti. Even illiteracy is made to seem delightful in the endless season of summer and flowers. The story's title comes from the description of the house to which Royal Bonaparte brings his bride to live. It is as lovely as something from a fairy tale, and the mean old woman who lives there reminds us of the wicked old witch in "Hansel and Gretel," with her constant pinching and planning to take the life of the young girl. References to superstitions and folk tales abound. A name out of mythology, though entertainly inappropriate, is given to Royal's beautiful iridescent cock: Juno, queen of heaven, wife of Jupiter, and more important to this story, goddess of marriage. This bird brings the sweethearts together, when Royal takes him into Port au Prince with the idea of putting him in a cockfight. That he does not do so is an indication of his kind and gentle nature, and it is that nature, in addition to his beauty, that captivates Ottilie. Love wins out over an existence of ease, primitivism over electric lights and silk dresses, satin shoes, and gold bracelets.

It is little wonder that the humor, the sweetness, the lure of romantic faraway places led a producer to propose to Capote that he convert the story into a play for Broadway. But Capote was never very successful as a playwright, even though *House of Flowers* ran on Broadway for a fairly respectable period of five months.

"Among the Paths to Eden"

Love in Capote's fiction is not always caught up in melancholy or sentiment. One of his most successful stories, "Among the Paths to Eden," performs a delicate balancing feat between humor and serious-ness. Surprisingly, it is not well known, nor have anthologists discov-ered it. Perhaps the major reason is that the piece is atypical, lacking the familiar tone, theme, and characters of Capote's other work. The story is set in New York, as are many of his other pieces. However, this is a different New York, the home of ordinary middle-class people, far removed from the bizarre world of the gothic stories and also the jet-set surroundings of the rich, the famous, and the infamous. Although many of Capote's characters seem to belong in *The Diaries of Andy Warhol*, the people in "Among the Paths to Eden" do not.

A happily widowed, middle-aged man, Ivor Belli, meets a husband-seeking woman, Mary O'Meagan, and ends up planning matrimony, but not to Mary. This is only one irony in a story filled with ironies. Delighted with his lot, now that his sharp-tongued, suspicious wife has been dead for some time, Belli feels pleased with himself, with fate, and with the opportunity to live exactly as he wishes. He is free to enjoy the company of women, something his late wife constantly accused him of, probably with some accuracy. Everyone seems to think Belli should wed again, so he has become wary of entanglements and quickly and uneasily recognizes Mary's motives when she engages him in con-versation. But Mary serves as the major catalyst in his decision to remarry, and another irony is added; the woman he resolves to propose to is his elegant secretary, who, unlike other women, has never pursued him. Still, she has let it be known somehow that she is approachable.

Although Belli's wife was jealous of his secretary, "nothing unto-ward, very untoward" ever happened. Avoidance of any unpleasant-ness is characteristic of Belli. Capote humorously delineates his character with an apt line: after the death of his wife, Belli "absent-mindedly," began to call his secretary by her first name. And he who has had no conscious marital intentions, indeed who declares to Mary he will never marry again, can hardly wait for the wedding and honeymoon with his secretary once he has changed his mind.

Belli and Mary meet in the cemetery where Mrs. Belli is buried. Ever the practical man (ironically, Capote has made him a tax accountant), he goes for his first visit to his wife's grave in March, when he wants to be out of doors and get some sunshine and exercise. He is also going to the grave in hopes that his visit will placate one of his daughters, who suspects he is leading too happy a life. Mary, also attempting to be practical, is following the advice of an old friend. After reading obituaries in search of eligible widowers, she seeks them out at the cemetery, not far from her home. In an amusing reversal of an old statement, Mary seeks life in the midst of death.

The two meet at noon, a strongly symbolic time. Belli is 55, and Mary is somewhere under 40. Because it is the lunch hour, Mary offers Belli peanuts which the two of them eat while sitting on the grave of Mrs. Belli. Not only is the incongruity of that act humorous, but so too is the callousness of their behavior. That they are eating peanuts, a snack associated with parties, movies, and television, also adds to the irony. Still sitting on the grave of Mrs. Belli, after Mary confesses she likes to imitate a long dead blues singer, she sings a sad ballad. Mr. Belli's praise of her singing emboldens her to suggest he might want to come to her home for dinner some time, but he has no intention of doing so. Quickly rising, he says, with unconscious humor, "Sitting on cold stone too long, you can catch something."[45]

The likelihood of Mary's success in catching anyone seems doubtful, although she tries desperately and uses her wiles. A plain-looking woman with a crippled leg, she has little to offer except the ability to cook.[46] In another ironic twist, it is the discussion of cooking that brings back to Belli the first kind thoughts he has of his wife. He remembers her virtues: her ability to prepare elegant meals, the celebration of holidays, her loving and successful mothering of their children. Pleasant memories help dispel unpleasant ones, and thoughts such as these soften him enough to give marriage another try.

Something else is also functioning, however: the underlying and unconscious force that drives Belli. Although he has awareness of mortality—after all, his wife has recently died—he has not yet addressed his own mortality. He has been through "a hard winter," and while he is thinking in terms of the weather, the period that followed his wife's death included a winter of his emotions. At the unconscious level, the hard winter is a symbol of the inevitable, the "black-sailed unfamiliar."[47] Now the possibility of spring is in the air, a time of beginnings not endings. When he starts out for the cemetery the wind is "pleasant," but not for long. As he bends to "jam" flowers into a stone urn at his wife's grave he feels chilled by the wind. Again, the weather images the mortality/immortality theme. The sun holds no "real warmth." It, like everything else except his wife's grave, is deceptive.

Belli has brought early spring flowers, jonquils, to the grave, wishing he could water them to "delay their doom." But even if that were to occur, they, and he, cannot put off their doom for more than a brief time. There is further irony in his bringing jonquils to the cemetery, for the flowers his wife most loved and that he never gave her were orchids, the expensive, hothouse flower associated with special occasions. When his recollections of his wife are sweetened through the meeting he has with Mary, Belli regrets he never gave his wife orchids. After deciding he will marry his secretary, and looking forward to taking her out on a first date, he also thinks about buying her an orchid. His thoughts are symbolically related to the new life he seeks, to the honeymoon he wants to take soon, surely no later than April or May. Suddenly, he is a man in a hurry, for it is already March.

When Mary flatters him about not looking 51 (he has lied about his age), he claims he does not feel his age. Again, Capote relates this to the image of the wind: "the wind had subsided, the sun grown more authentic" ("Eden," 132). In spite of the cold wind that blew only a few minutes before, Belli has a renewed sense of immortality. Eager for the future that will be his, he wants to contemplate love. In the "spring-shiny parade weather" he is full of hope; even the graves all around him do not detract from his pleasure. That parades pass, flowers fade, spring eventually becomes winter does not give him pause in his quickened step as he leaves the cemetery.

Capote concludes his story with a final ironic scene. Coming through the gates as Belli exits is another cheery widower, full of life, whistling as he enters, although around his sleeve is the black band that denotes a recent loss. Mortality, the author suggests, is what we think belongs to others. Eden may exist in a heavenly world for the silent dead, but Eden, the longed-for paradise, is what the living expect to find here on earth.

The Caravan Moves On: Last Stories

"Dazzle"

"Dazzle," which appeared first in *Vogue* in 1979 and then in the collection *Music for Chameleons* in 1980, has multiple connections to the new kind of fiction Capote was writing by this time. Although the story is more focused than the pieces in the unfinished *Answered Prayers*, the works are similar in their revelations of details from the author's life. "Dazzle" also has links to his final story,[48] *One Christmas*, for both these pieces share subject matter and setting related to Capote's early childhood experiences in New Orleans. Like all the intimate and rather bitter pieces written in the last decade of his life, here the writer offers another version of himself and the people who were part of his often unhappy boyhood.

In the 1987 compilation *A Capote Reader*, the editor divided Capote's writings into genres and placed "Dazzle" with the essays. The logic behind the decision is puzzling, but perhaps the editor was misled because Capote himself called "Dazzle" nonfiction. Capote's categorization raises a number of questions, given his view that all truth is altered when it becomes a story. What, then, is "truth" in "Dazzle"? Is there any great difference, insofar as the labels "fiction" and "nonfiction" are concerned, between works in which the author does not appear or appears only as a minor character (*Breakfast at Tiffany's* for example), and works in which he takes the major role? Why should we think that, "Dazzle" is less fictional than *A Christmas Memory*, since both are remembrances of childhood?

The answer may lie in Capote's decision to end "Dazzle" by returning to the present and, without mask or other distancing device, introducing an episode that focuses on the relationship between himself and his lifelong nemesis, his father, Arch Persons. The major part of "Dazzle" is set in the past: Capote relates a mortifying childhood event that reflects his youthful confusion about his sexual identity. But at the end of this part of the story, he abruptly shifts to the present and introduces his father, who played no part at all in the incident recalled. We leap ahead 44 years. The grandmother, who had a major role in the disturbing incident, has died, and her grandson, Truman, did not attend the funeral. The drunken Truman Capote has an angry telephone conversation with the father he reviles, yet still fears. Is this the nonfictional aspect of the story? Perhaps. Though the feelings between father and son seem real enough, the dialogue does not sound realistic or truthful. The father's angry and sentimental statement that Capote's grandmother died with Truman's picture in her hand reads too much like nineteenth-century melodrama.

Apparently Capote in his late stores was trying to write autobiography as a means of explaining and justifying his life. Yet the resulting pieces contain too much fiction to be categorized as "real" autobiography. In "Dazzle" too many of the details sound like bits and pieces from Capote's early fiction: The mysterious Mrs. Ferguson, unmarried with "a raft of children," suggests Sister Ida of *The Grass Harp*. Mrs. Ferguson's praise of the boy's girlish beauty reminds us of Sam Radclif's comments in *Other Voices, Other Rooms*, and the little boy's journey to the Ferguson home also reminds us of that novel. Mrs. Ferguson's son, Skeeter, happens to have green eyes, always a significant symbol in Capote's stories. A belief in magic, witchlike characters, charms, and spells are all characteristic of the writer's fiction, and all appear in "Dazzle."

The story itself tells of a theft the boy commits while staying with relatives in New Orleans. To achieve a hoped-for transformation from male to female, he seeks the magical help of a local sorceress, Mrs. Ferguson. Mrs. Ferguson demands that he steal his grandmother's yellow, rock-crystal stone and give it to her as payment for her magic. The boy succeeds in taking the jewel without ever being discovered, but Mrs. Ferguson's sorcery fails. Not only is the boy's desire for a female identity disappointed, but the guilt he feels as the result of stealing from and betraying his grandmother stays with him throughout his life in memory. His grandmother's death revives the entire experience for him. However, his inability in middle age to handle his sense of shame, and the hostile confrontation with his father, seem completely separate from the other parts of the story. The mood and tone shift too abruptly as the narrator moves from past to present, and even the last words of the story, invoking the power and appearance of Mrs. Ferguson, do not succeed in bringing back to the reader the boy's sense of the frightening knowledge of that witchlike figure.

Should readers care whether "Dazzle" is fiction or nonfiction?

Perhaps. Certainly we must exercise caution in accepting all the author tells us about his own reality. Georges Gusdorf, author of a study on autobiography, has said that there are two types of autobiography: one is a form of confession; the other is "the artist's entire work, which takes up the same material in complete freedom and [is] under the protection of a hidden identity."[49] Unquestionably, some of Capote's works are forms of confession, and all of his works offer a composite, psychological autobiography by means of characters that serve as masks for Capote himself. Gusdorf also states: "Autobiography appears the more or less anguished uneasiness of an aging man who wonders if his life has not been lived in vain, frittered away haphazardly, ending now in simple failure. In order to be reassured, he undertakes his own apologia" (39). This analysis appears to fit as explanation for the last cycle of Capote's stories. Retracing segments of the past, he appears to be saying that this is true, that was not true. However, intended or not, the parts are all pieces of the whole, fragmented though they may be.

Answered Prayers

"Dazzle" was printed when Capote was struggling to recover from the aftershock of social and professional rejection brought about by the publication of fragments from a projected new novel. However, neither "Dazzle" nor publication of a well-regarded collection a year later could restore him to his previous position. Although much of Capote's writing had excited strong reactions from readers over the years, only his late stories provoked outrage. Supposedly conceived as part of his long-promised new novel, *Answered Prayers*, these pieces were first published in *Esquire* in the 1970s. The earliest story, "Mojave" (1975), was republished in the collection *Music for Chameleons* (1980). After Capote's death in 1984, his editor put together the remaining three stories as the work that was retitled *Answered Prayers: The Unfinished Novel* (1987).

To whet the appetite of the public, *Esquire* began "Mojave" on the cover of its June issue. It was Capote's first story in many years, and it elicited both negative and positive responses. Some who praised this so-called beginning of *Answered Prayers* were to change their minds when other stories followed. Capote, however, reportedly was delighted he had overcome the writing problems that had set in after the high point in his career in the late sixties.[50]

"Mojave" uses the techniques of the frame, that is, a story within a story, and of doubling. What is unusual in this approach is that the second story is made the double of the first. Both are about women who betray the men who love them, although one betrays in secret, and the other does it flagrantly and cruelly. One woman is young, the other old; one is rich, elegant, upperclass, and idle; the other is poor and lower class, a former burlesque queen and stripper. Both give their lovers gifts, paid for with their husband's money. Through the doubling of the two women, a theme is developed that surfaces throughout all the stories in *Answered Prayers*: beneath the skin all women are the same, "the Colonel's Lady an' Judy O'Grady." Capote's animus toward women is epitomized in a sneering remark about women and snakes: "The last thing that dies is their tail," says the old man, a central character in the inner story of "Mojave."[51] That Capote shares the old man's attitude becomes clear when Capote repeats the same statement in the later piece "Unspoiled Monsters," here without benefit of an intermediary, apparently having forgotten he had already used this abusive remark in "Mojave."

The doubled women are matched with doubled husbands. Actually, the doubling is made even more emphatic with the men because both share the same first name: George. On the surface the first George, George Whitelaw, appears to be the opposite of the second, George Schmidt, whom the former meets when he is just out of Yale, hitchhiking across the country. George Schmidt is old, fat, and blind, a man who has been a masseur for 50 years. (Capote seems to favor this occupation as a plot device that enables the masseur character to learn intimate details about the lives of the rich and famous people he serves; in this story of the device seems acceptable enough. However, when Capote repeats this device with his major figure, the narrator of "Unspoiled Monsters" and "Kate McCloud" in *Answered Prayers*, it becomes inappropriate, given the narrator's other talents and his social milieu.)

Twenty years after this meeting in the Mojave Desert, George Whitelaw tells his wife, Sarah, the story of his encounter with Schmidt. The blind Schmidt had been abandoned by his wife, Ivory, perhaps to die in the intense heat. In the course of a ride out of the desert with a truck driver, Schmidt tells Whitelaw about his meeting, courtship, and marriage to Ivory Hunter, who betrays him almost immediately with a younger man. Ivory Hunter lives up to her much too obviously symbolic name by taking all of her husband's possessions and driving off with her lover after leaving George alone amidst the "sand . . . mesquite and . . . boiling blue sky."

Sarah Whitelaw is far more subtle than Ivory Hunter when she betrays her husband. Refusing to share George's bed because she has had two unwanted children and fears having another, Sarah slyly takes a lover. Ivory never refuses to have sex with her husband—quite the opposite—and her relationship with her lover is scarcely concealed. Ivory's motivation for her treachery is sexual passion, but Sarah's motive is unclear. Sarah choses as her lover her former psychoanalyst, a man described in most unattractive terms: he is short, fat, and wears dentures, and he is a vulgar and greedy man who grunts and grimaces and expects gifts and money from her. Sarah derives no sexual pleasure or other satisfaction from this relationship. The pointlessness of Sarah's affair seem to suggest that betrayal for no motive other than betrayal itself is women's nature.

Capote provides no realistic cause for Sarah's deceitfulness, drawing her as a superficial, selfish, even prudish woman who chooses to ignore her husband's obvious suffering. She takes on the role of his pimp in order to keep him, as well as to keep him satisfied. Capote apparently recognized that Sarah is the least successfully drawn character in "Mojave," and therefore in an attempt attempt at providing a psychological motive for her actions, he says that Sarah married George because of his resemblance to her father. But this damage control does not work. The bits and pieces of her character and personality are an uncoordinated mixture: she is an anxious poseur with her husband; cruel and insulting to her lover; confiding, sympathetic, but also cynical to her hairdresser, whose pain at his betrayal by his lover she dismisses by telling him there is always someone else.

Her cynicism is leavened with fear the night her husband tells her his tale about George Schmidt and Ivory Hunter. As Sarah listens to her George he seems to become the other George, coarse and street-smart, blind, but possessed of a clear inner vision. Tired and feeling old, for the first time in their marriage George artfully hints to Sarah that he knows about her affair. When George turns to his wife for solace, she gives him the same comfort she had earlier given her hairdresser: there is always another lover down the road. Yet what her husband has given her is a far greater and deeper kind of love than the love that George Schmidt had given Ivory, for it includes forgiveness both for her refusal to share her bed with him and for her betrayal of his trust.

George tells Sarah that everyone, at some time, leaves the "other out there under the sky" and never understands why. This is one of Capote's themes in the story. Another theme, more hidden and dark, in the last part of the story, briefly reveals the Capote touch of earlier days. As Sarah draws the heavy silk draperies against the snow-misted night, the images leave us with the subliminal recognition of the swift passage of time, of the coming of night and the long winter of death that no draperies can block out.

"La Côte Basque," the second story published in *Esquire*, was a disaster for Capote. Although general readers took pleasure in the entrée the story provided into the secret world of stars, artists, and high-society glitteratti, those who belonged to that world were outraged by Capote's revelations. Capote's jet-set friends and acquaintances felt that he had betrayed them.

From the moment "La Côte Basque" appeared in 1975, Capote lost almost every society friend he had. The stories in *Answered Prayers* were all based on true incidents from or gossip concerning the lives of people in Capote's rich and famous circle. Once these people read "La Côte Basque" and recognized what he was doing—how he was turning the sordid details of their lives into stories for the public to read—they closed ranks and turned on him. Overnight, his friends became enemies; the reviews savaged him; and his career was destroyed. Soon he was reduced to appearing on talk shows, where often obviously drunk or under the influence of drugs, he pathetically tried to defend himself and to attack the people who had rejected him.[52]

Whether the unfinished "novel" would ever have been printed had there not been so much publicity about it following Capote's sudden death is a matter of speculation. For a number of years Capote and a few loyal supporters insisted the work was almost complete. But no manuscript has been found. For a time rumors that some people had seen, or read, or heard Capote read other parts of the book circulated. Speculation about a more complete manuscript version of *Answered Prayers* continues, but whether Capote actually wrote more than we have is doubtful considering his imaginative decline in the years before his death.

In book form, *Answered Prayers: The Unfinished Novel* is much the same as the stories *Esquire* published. There are only two significant differences. Where the sequence in the magazine was "Mojave" (June 1975), "La Côte Basque" (November 1975), "Unspoiled Monsters" (May 1976), and "Kate McCloud" (December 1976), the book places "Unspoiled Monsters" as part 1, "Kate McCloud" as part 2, and "La

Côte Basque" as part 3. The second change is the removal of any references to the story "Mojave." In the magazine version of "Unspoiled Monsters" the major character speaks about beginning to write "Mojave," and in the first lines of the *Esquire* "Kate McCloud" he notes having spent a week writing "Mojave." Clearly, Capote made almost no changes in the work, although for years he and his publisher announced he was revising it.[53]

Where "Unspoiled Monsters" and "Kate McCloud" have some slight connection to one another, "La Côte Basque" has nothing in common with either except that it, like the other two, is supposedly told by a narrator named P. B. Jones. One wonders about the publisher's choice of the term "novel" to describe the work, although it is the word the author himself used. If Capote had some large overall plan for the structure of his book, the plan is not revealed by the fragments that he managed to complete.

The first two stories make some attempt at plot, but plots so steamy and fitful as to appear ludicrous to the reader. Although Capote and a few other people spoke of the planned work as Proustian,[54] the plots and characters in "Unspoiled Monsters" and "Kate McCloud" might have been borrowed from a combination of popular romance and pornographic film and fiction. The third story, while recounting gossip, as do the other two, has no plot at all.[55]

P. B. Jones, identified by various people (including Capote's editor), as a "dark doppelgänger" of the writer, is a strange peripatetic figure, who, for no clear reason, flits between New York and the Continent. At some point he remains an expatriate for 12 years. He is a failed writer, a prostitute, and a masseur. While the reader quickly discovers that Capote often intends Jones to be himself, the secret self Jones seems to embody is like the painting of Dorian Gray. Almost nothing of the charming, witty, poetic writer remains. Instead, there stands in his place, a vulgar, vicious purveyor of gossip, a one-time man about town, who now is little more than the teller of dirty jokes.[56] In many respects Jones is an older, more worldly, and more world-weary Walter Ranney from the early dark story, "Shut a Final Door."

In "Unspoiled Monsters" the narrator tells us more about himself than anyone else in the story. The story consists of a number of vignettes about people whose names are household words. Many appear with names unchanged; others are given pseudonyms, but most of the pseudonymous characters can be easily identified. In "Kate McCloud" the focus shifts from the narrator and his angst to a soap-opera plot that is larger than the cardboard characters. And in "La Côte Basque" the narrator serves as little more than an ear for the malicious gossip of his luncheon companion.

In all this work, Capote used some of the techniques of earlier years: circularity, remembrance of things past, time shifts, cinematic devices, humor, and the poetic configuration of images and symbols. Yet the things that worked so well for him before rarely succeed here. "Unspoiled Monsters" and "La Côte Basque" have circularity of structure: each begins in the present, goes back to events in the past, and ends back in the present. "Unspoiled Monsters" and "Kate McCloud" include remembrances of the past, nostalgia for beginnings, and time shifts of multiple kinds; cinematic devices are strongest in these two stories as well, with collage and stills and scene shifts. All three pieces are very visual, but without the symbolic implications of previous fiction. An important component of each work is humor; much of this humor is farcical and sexually oriented; the gossip, which is meant to be funny, is almost entirely of a sexual nature.[57]

The person seeking to learn more about Capote—his likes, dislikes, attitudes, visions of himself in middle age—will find "Unspoiled Monsters" interesting. A mask is removed, but are we to believe what appears? In part, yes. Here is Capote taking vengeance on the academic world, mocking the scholars who either ignored him or considered his work insignificant. Jibing at them, suggesting they spend their time in tiny, petty pursuits, he calls attention to his use of alliteration, to his recognition that he is indeed borrowing the name of a graceless character out of a Flannery O'Connor story. He sneers at the process of obtaining grants, at writers-in-residence programs, at those writers whose work is read only by intellectuals. Having scorned the latter, he procedes to tell the kind of story he seems to have suggested they would never write.

Hostility permeates segments of the story, although it is meant to be humorous and honest about the way the world turns. In striking out at critics and reviewers, he suggests that much that is published under an author's name is not the work of that author, himself as Jones, for example.[58] He claims that many writers get into print because they trade sexual favors for assistance from editors, publishers, or other famous writers.[59]

Self-hatred is very strong in this first story. Jones describes himself as a failure, something Capote undoubtedly felt at this point in his career. But the author shifts gears at times, briefly separating himself from

Jones. Unlike Capote, Jones has had only one book published, and that was a flop. But Jones's failed book was called *Answered Prayers*. Capote appears to be saying he knows in advance that the public will reject his novel. Further, Jones is planning to rewrite *Answered Prayers*, an act Capote himself planned but did not accomplish during his sad last years. Doubling is used in the description of an attention-getting book-jacket photograph, although the picture of Capote used for his first book, *Other Voices, Other Rooms* was taken by Harold Halma, and Jones's portrait for *Answered Prayers* was done by Beaton, the photographer who became a very close friend of Capote after the publication of that first novel.

The subject of Jones's book, he tells an acquaintance, is "Truth as illusion," surely an important theme in all Capote's work. Briefly, Jones becomes the reflective writer, the thoughtful Capote, mulling over questions he has addressed before in other works. What is truth? What is fiction? How does the artist use them? Writers turn everything into stories. Do stories become lies when altered by the transforming imagination?

This conversation about writing, truth, life, and fiction occurs during a discussion Jones has with his friend about ways to make a living. The friend convinces Jones he can make easy money by selling his services as a prostitute. At first the shift in the conversation from writing to prostitution appears to be little more than another instance of the meandering structure of the story. Yet the juxtaposition of these two subjects presents a Jones/Capote view of the writer, part of the darkness, the hatred within: the writer as prostitute, prostitute of the self, or prostitute for the self, two very different views, yet each a cruel vision, albeit concealed by humor.[60]

Capote's Jones mask is held up to hide his own face, shifted to reveal a piece of his face, or dropped entirely at various times in this and the other two stories. At times Jones seems to disappear, or perhaps he and Capote become one and the dark side is hidden from view. Some of the melding takes place in episodes that remind us of the early poetic writer. When he is still a young, hopeful novelist, Jones, like Capote, met the French author Colette. When Jones described this meeting we hear not Jones, but the familiar voice of Capote talking; specifically, we hear the Capote of "The White Rose," when he remembers Colette and his introduction to her symbolism of paperweights.

In "Unspoiled Monsters," Capote places the Colette episode immediately before his discussion of prostitution of the self. He uses it to allow Colette to talk about art, about the penalties the artist must pay, the sacrifices he must make. Although life is flawed, it is warm compared to the coldness of art. The artist's life does not matter.[61] What matters is the purity of art—a true enough point, but one Capote was making defensively at this stage in his career.

Scattered throughout the story are a few other poetically wrought depictions of people and places. Still, the general tone is that of a writer suffering malaise. The cities described in Capote's collection of travel pieces, *Local Color* (1950), cities that once were magical, become now, through Jones's eyes, unattractive, unappealing places.

The touch of the painter-poet, Capote himself without the Jones/ Hyde element (even though Jones remains the narrator), is seen twice more, in the endings of "Kate McCloud," and "La Côte Basque." A dream concludes "Kate McCloud," a dream described as resembling a late-nineteenth-century painting, though one might also imagine it as a haunting scene created by a cinematic artist. Images of color, of delicate, graceful motion, and the shimmer of the sea remind us all too briefly of ways the writer once captivated us. So too does the final paragraph of "La Côte Basque" hold us momentarily with its description of the waning afternoon, the words "exhaustion" and "failing" creating the air of melancholy often found at the close of Capote's best stories.

The least satisfactory of the three stories, "Kate McCloud" is disjointed, and, far worse, uninteresting. The major character is a composite, fantasized figure drawn from several women Capote knew or had heard about. The story, told by Jones (here as masseur, with no sign of the novelist), moves back and forth between past and present, shifting abruptly at times, recounting the inevitable dirty jokes, gossip, and episodes that have absolutely no relationship to the story of Kate.

In contrast to "Kate McCloud," "La Côte Basque" is a well-structured piece, although the headnote, a salacious joke, at first seems unrelated to what follows. The jest, or prologue, is told by two ordinary people in an ordinary bar in the west. Yet the short story turns out to have many resemblances to it. Both are bawdy and are told by two people over drinks. No matter that the two luncheon companions are themselves widely known, that the restaurant, a real one, is elegant and expensive, or that the drink is Roederer's Cristal, one of the most costly champagnes. Everywhere life is a joke, we are being told, and a dirty one at that.

The story takes place in the course of a single afternoon. Here the function is extremely simple as compared to the two previous pieces: its entire concern is gossip, the telling of unpleasant truths about the private lives of people. There are two narrators, Jones, again the tale-bearing, wittily cruel persona, who moves among the monied celebrities of international society, and his hostess, Lady Coolbirth (Capote's playful naming of a friend whom a number of readers were easily able to identify). Jones's narrative function is limited, for it is really Lady Coolbirth who provides most of the gossip, taking great relish in demolishing the reputations of people in the restaurant and other people she and Jones (and Capote) know—and the reader may know of.

"La Côte Basque" adds nothing to what we have learned about Jones. The story is set in the present, and there is no clue about Jones's status either as writer or gigolo. That he is still "in" as part of the jet-set is suggested by the intimate knowledge he reveals concerning fellow members. In retrospect, however, the reader recognizes with some regret that it is this story which brought Capote's fall from grace, the finish to his charmed life, and those last imagistic words of the story, "exhaustion" and "failing," seem all too apt a description of the end of his meteoric career.

Reprise

Capote's career, while brilliant and unique in many ways, bears an uncanny resemblance to that of other American authors. Two that immediately come to mind are Hemingway and Fitzgerald, who gained fame after the World War I. Although Capote belonged to the generation that followed theirs, like them he gained instant recognition as a young writer in a postwar period. The success of all three was heady, yet their drive towards self-destruction was unstoppable. All three were successful with their first works and found a ready public. Each new work brought increased interest from newspapers, magazines, and filmmakers. But all three—for whatever reason or combination of reasons—seem in retrospect death-driven.

Attention, even adulation at times, love, friendships, money, elegant living—none of these rewards was enough to ward off the "mean reds," words Capote spoke through his fictional heroine Holly Golightly to describe a special kind of depression. All three novelists drank too much, lost the discipline that quality writing requires, developed illnesses they could not control, and eventually suffered a loss of will and talent. In their last years, Hemingway and Capote parodied themselves in their lives and in their fiction. Hemingway killed himself with a bullet, Fitzgerald with liquor, and Capote with alcohol and drugs.

Capote was little more than a boy when he began to write fiction. His first story, "The Walls Are Cold," was published when he was only 19. He charmed both beginning and established writers when he spent several summers at Bread Loaf and Yaddo. In his early 20s, working on his novel, *Other Voices, Other Rooms*, he was naive, eager to please, beautiful to look at. Everyone sought him out. He had a personal appeal that was to last for many years. At first he was taken up by several highly regarded academicians, and soon thereafter by editors who recognized in him a different strain of writer. His work was nothing like the social fiction of the previous decade, nor the war novels of the forties. It was subjective, imagistic, and symbolistic; some of his writing offered a new type of fantasy, spun from a combination of autobiography, regionalism (a sense of a particular place), and a longing for a lost or nonexistent world. The fiction he wrote in the forties was often dark. His first novel and five of the stories in his first collection led to his being labeled "gothic." However, Capote also was a humorous writer, and that side is easily pointed to in the earliest work.

Although the reviews of the first novel and short story collection were mixed, Capote found an audience, and he kept it for the remainder of his life. He attracted more and more readers as he broadened his writing interests and polished his skills. By the fifties his nonfiction prose, travel pieces, essays on people and places, was capturing more readers. His skills as a satirist were at their height in *The Muses Are Heard*, a work whose humor is as effective today as when it was first published. The comedy, the ear for dialogue, the ability to capture a particular time and place are also characteristic of Capote's fiction of that decade, especially one of his most admired stories, *Breakfast at Tiffany's*. The fifties also saw the publication of *The Grass Harp*, as both novella and play, the production of the theatrical version of his short story "A House of Flowers," and the publication of his mixed-media collaboration with photographer Richard Avedon, *Observations*.

Capote reached the pinnacle of his career in the sixties with the work that brought him fame, fortune, and finally, the interest of more than a handful of critics. Never modest, he announced that he had created a new form of writing with *In Cold Blood*. Whatever side people took, they read the book, and read about the author himself in newspapers, magazines, and literary journals. His every doing and pronouncement seemed to be noted by the press, TV, or the world of letters.

But following a string of successes that included *In Cold Blood*, *A Christmas Memory*, and *The Thanksgiving Visitor*, Capote began to falter. Although his collection *The Dogs Bark* was well received when it was published in 1973, the writer was already in personal and professional difficulty. Not only was his best work behind him, but both his fiction and occasional pieces revealed a writer who had lost his sure instinct, his critical sense, and his control of his material. The stories he wrote for *Esquire* in the seventies would probably not have been published if they had been written by anyone else. However, in 1980, still another collection of Capote's work appeared and seemed to redeem somewhat his tarnished reputation. *Music from Chameleons*, consisting of works from several genres, and including intimate revelations about the writer, is Capote's declaration that he is still serious, important, and a writer to be reckoned with. But, he was to complete only one more story, *One Christmas*, a minor piece that went out of print almost as soon as it was published. Capote never finished the "novel" he proclaimed would surpass *In Cold Blood*, the new work that was going to establish him forever as the American Proust. *Answered Prayers* was published in the rough form it had when the stories appeared a decade earlier in *Esquire*. In spite of the uproar they caused, those weak stories will be forgotten in time, but people will continue to discover the pleasure of the best of Capote.

Notes to Part 1

1. For a thorough discussion of the new gothic, see Irving Malin's *New American Gothic* (Carbondale: Southern Illinois University Press, 1962).

2. *The Selected Writings of Truman Capote* puts the publication date of "A Tree of Night" as 1943. However, Gerald Clarke states in his *Truman Capote: A Biography* (New York: Simon and Schuster, 1988) that the story was published in *Harper's Bazaar* in October 1945, after the publication of "Miriam" in June 1945; hereafter Clarke's biography will be cited in text.

3. "A Tree of Night and Other Stories," in *A Capote Reader* (New York: Random House, 1987), 22; hereafter cited in text as "Tree."

4. It is not coincidental, given Capote's predilection for autobiography, that the author's age was probably the same as Kay's when he wrote "A Tree of Night" and that her home is New Orleans, Capote's birthplace.

5. Eyes are always important in Capote's work and other new gothic fiction.

6. See Clarke's *Truman Capote*, page 9, for a discussion of Capote's childhood and his father's use of gimmickry.

7. The lyre of Orpheus here becomes the green guitar carried by Kay and is an example of Capote's alteration and reversal of the myths from which he borrowed. In Capote's story the guitar has no association with art, but is connected with death.

8. Capote had earlier used a slave bell to sound a warning to the boy Joel in *Other Voices, Other Rooms*.

9. See Clarke on Capote's entry into the world of magazine publishing.

10. Capote made this or a similar remark to many people. I quote from William Nance, *The Worlds of Truman Capote* (New York: Stein and Day, 1973), 22.

11. "Miriam," in *A Capote Reader*, 48; hereafter cited in text. Psychological studies describe the formation of the narcissistic personality in childhood. Narcissistic adults are driven by childhood longings.

12. Mrs. Miller cooks a favorite meal of Capote's: tomato soup and scrambled eggs. He was not much of a cook: various interviewers have said that he kept only champagne in his refrigerator.

13. "The Headless Hawk," in *A Capote Reader*, 48; hereafter cited in text as "Hawk." Because the hawk is headless and blind, Freudians might see it as a castration symbol indicative of Vincent's inability to maintain any sexual relationship. For D. J. it then suggests androgyny.

14. "Master Misery," in *A Capote Reader*, 80; hereafter cited in text as "Misery."

15. *Oxford English Dictionary*, compact edition, 1987, S.V. "reave."

16. Is it merely coincidental that Ranney and Capote have the same number of letters?

17. "Shut a Final Door," in *A Capote Reader*, 65; hereafter cited in text as "Door."

18. Walter's rationalization has a prophetic note; in the last years of his life, Capote also appeared driven to self-destruction.

19. Note the resemblance to line 54 in Shelley's "Ode to The West Wind."

20. We do not know whether Walter was born in New Orleans; his trip to that city suggests, because of the doubling, a regression, a symbolic return to the womb.

21. The color green is frequently associated with death in Capote's stories.

22. Helen S. Garson, *Truman Capote* (New York: Ungar, 1980), 186.

23. "Children on Their Birthdays," in *A Capote Reader*, 93; hereafter cited in text as "Children."

24. There is an autobiographical element here, in that the author's family life was somewhat like Miss Bobbit's: her mother is mute, and her father is absent, and Capote grew up without mother or father.

25. Capote associates the color green with death, and usually combines green with gothic images of horror, terror, or violence. Capote also associates the color yellow with death, but links this color with nostalgia or sadness.

26. *The Grass Harp* in *A Capote Reader*, 155; hereafter cited in text.

27. The southern parallel, at least as described in Faulkner's novels, is Memphis.

28. Although Manny Fox, in "Children on Their Birthdays," is not called a Jew, this identity is suggested. Dr. Ritz is often referred to as the "little Jew," usually by Catherine, who is an outspoken woman. She says things others are too polite or kind to voice.

29. See Michener's "Foreword" in Lawrence Grobel's *Conversations with Capote* (New York: New American Library, 1985).

30. Capote also makes an oblique reference to another autobiographical detail, when he speaks of being fired for "an amusing misdemeanor." He is probably referring to the Robert Frost episode at *the New Yorker*. See Helen S. Garson's *Truman Capote* and Gerald Clarke's *Capote: A Biography*.

31. *Breakfast at Tiffany's*, in *A Capote Reader*, 241–242; hereafter cited in text as *Breakfast*.

32. The names Lily Jane in "Children on Their Birthdays" and Lulamae in *Breakfast at Tiffany's* appear to have a relationship to the author's mother, whose name was Lillie Mae before she changed it to Nina.

33. "A Jug of Silver," in *A Capote Reader*, 32.

34. The technique reverses what he does in "Children on Their Birthdays," where fall and winter are almost ignored.

35. *A Christmas Memory*, in *Selected Writings of Truman Capote* (New York: Modern Library, 1963), 151; hereafter cited in text as *Memory*.

36. *The Thanksgiving Visitor* (New York: Random House, 1967), 14–15.

37. There is even a significant error on the dedication page, where the name "Dunphy" is misspelled.

38. Capote, in interviews and reminiscences, often spoke of his father's failings. Clarke devotes much attention to this topic.

39. *One Christmas* (New York: Random House, 1982), 28.

40. "My Side of the Matter," in *A Capote Reader*, 15; hereafter cited in text as "My Side."

41. "A Diamond Guitar," in *A Capote Reader*, 109; hereafter cited in text as "Guitar."

42. See Clarke on the Capote/McCullers friendship.

43. "House of Flowers," in *A Capote Reader*, 121.

44. "Houngan" in "House of Flowers" is spelled "boungan" in "Haiti," in *A Capote Reader*.

45. "Among the Paths to Eden," in *A Capote Reader*, 134; hereafter cited in text as "Eden."

46. See the difference between what William Nance says about Mary (*The Worlds of Truman Capote*) and what Capote writes of her in his essay about Jane Bowles (1966).

47. This phrase is from Philip Larkin's poem, "Next, Please."

48. The story "I Remember Grandpa" was published posthumously under Capote's name, but few people believe he was the author.

49. Georges Gusdorf, "Conditions and Limits of Autobiography," in *Autobiography: Essays Theoretical and Critical*, ed. James Olney (Princeton: Princeton University Press, 1980), 46.

50. For further discussion of this topic, see both Clarke's biography and *The Diaries of Andy Warhol*, ed. Pat Hackett (New York: Warner Books, 1989).

51. "Mojave," in *A Capote Reader*, 146. In spite of these hostile jokes, Capote did have a number of women friends he loved and admired. The anger toward women revealed in these stories shows Capote's disintegration and inability to accept rejection.

52. For accounts of specific episodes, see Andy Warhol's *Diaries*.

53. Capote even made the statement in his "Preface" to *Music for Chameleons*.

54. That Capote thought of himself as the American Proust may be seen in "Blind Items," a forerunner of the short stories that followed.

55. Not all readers, reviewers, critics, and other writers found the stories inferior. Clarke thinks "La Côte Basque" is "a tour de force" revealing "superb craftsmanship, storytelling at its most skillfull." Joseph Fox states, in the introduction to *Answered Prayers: The Unfinished Novel*, that he found "Unspoiled Monsters" flawless.

56. See John Richardson's "A Côte Capote," a review of *Answered Prayers*, *New York Review of Books*, 17 December 1987.

57. Sexual humor is not new in Capote. It is an element in *Breakfast at Tiffany's*, but only an element. Sexual humor engulfs *Answered Prayers*.

58. See Warhol's *Diaries* on this point.

59. This is an example of the self-hating element new to his work. Capote had always seemed confident about his talent up to this point.

60. Revelation and concealment seem to be part of Capote's temperament. An instance of this is seen in the account Warhol gives of a visit he made with Capote to the writer's psychiatrist to do a taping for *Interview*: *Diaries*, 7 July 1978, p. 150.

61. A Keatsian view, as seen in the "cold pastoral" of "Ode On A Grecian Urn."

Part 2

THE WRITER

Inventing a Self and a World

Truman Capote both as an individual and as a writer was an enigma. Did anyone really know him? In spite of his frequent and seemingly intimate pronouncements, he was a man who "travels alone, except that there's always someone with him."[1] Although John Malcolm Brinnin made this comment about Capote in the late 1940s, it was psychologically accurate throughout Capote's life. Many Capote watchers believe he did not want to reveal what lay beneath the facade of the clever quip, the showman personality, the eye-catching clothing—the trailing scarves, the oversized hats, the Holly Golightlyesque dark glasses. Capote created almost as many fictions about himself as he did in his writing. He invented multiple personae partly out of his sense of fun and and delight in mischief making and partly from a need to guard the vulnerable, wounded part of his psyche, the child inside him that had never recovered from the trauma of his bitter early years. He told various interviewers that he protected himself from pain by keeping people at a distance, a statement that seems to contradict the impression readers take away after entering the world of his writings. His lack of truth about himself was noted as early as 1972 by the writer who was to become Capote's only approved biographer, Gerald Clarke. The problem of getting "a fix" on Capote, Clarke said, was that he is a man who tells everything and nothing, using confession to turn interviewers away from knowledge.[2]

Facts and Fictions

Numerous pieces written by himself or about him by others are filled with references to his childhood. Although the events and characters in his stories and novels more often than not have a link to actual experiences in Capote's life, it is almost impossible for anyone to state flatly, "This happened to Capote," or "He witnessed these events," or "He knew the person who is this character," or "This is what Capote believed." For almost every declaration there is an opposite one. Capote was not much concerned with what most of us think of as truth.

In an interview with David Frost, Capote claimed that he made up most of the details of his life.[3] He embellished, altered, played with "facts." He had "a reputation for rearranging facts to suit his fancy or his need," a rearrangement he called "a form of art" (Clarke 1972, 201). On a talk show in the eighties Capote discussed "the non-falsehood lie"—Capote liked such oxymorons. Earlier, in the sixties, he had coined the term "nonfiction novel." "The non-falsehood lie" is "true," he claimed, "because it amuses me more that way."[4]

Contradictions abound, not only in interviews given over the years, but sometimes within a single piece. An example of Capote's method of embroidering actual occurrences may be seen in the various stories he told about his early employment at the *New Yorker*. Whereas he was actually hired as a clerk or copyboy, he manipulated the facts imaginatively and told an interviewer that Ross, the legendary editor of the *New Yorker*, sent for him in the forties, after reading his work, and hired him as a staff writer. Capote also changed the truth about why he left the *New Yorker*: although he was fired, he told people he quit because his kind of writing was not the kind the magazine printed.[5] He once told Donald Windham that he remembered "things the way they should have been" (Windham, 39). However, self-aggrandizement was characteristic of him. Perhaps he felt justified in fabricating early recognition by Ross and the *New Yorker* because he eventually did become a prized contributor to that magazine, and had the satisfaction of hearing William Shawn, the publisher, call his profile of Marlon Brando "a masterpiece."[6]

Many of Capote's "revelations" depended on his own sense of success, whether measured personally, professionally, or socially. He frequently denounced a piece Anne Taylor Fleming had written about him in the July 1978 *New York Times Magazine*. Speaking to Donald Windham, he accused Fleming of fabricating his admission that he wanted to be a beautiful woman. Yet a year after Fleming's article appeared, Capote's "Dazzle," an autobiographical story that hinges on the male protagonist's desire to be a female, was published in *Esquire*. When Charles Ruas described it as a story about "a crisis of sexual identity," Capote responded, "It was a true story; it was exactly what happened."[7]

Because he always had his eye on the media and his hand on the public pulse, he had no hesitation in dishing up what he knew would keep both the media and its audience interested in him. Furthermore, as Thomas Inge points out, Capote's response to interviewers depended on his evaluation of "their gullibility. An uninformed or stupid question would bring out an amused hostility which resulted in outlandish statements, but someone adept at reading his moods could elicit serious and honest answers." Inge also notes that Capote, because he was "an expert interviewer" himself, knew "how to manipulate the questions to his own advantage."[8]

At first self-publicizing was a challenge he met by means of provocative photographs and interviews; then, when he became famous, it was something of a game; finally, in the last unhappy decade of his life, it was his defense against the world. He had owned a large piece of that world and in the end he lost it.

As knowledgeable critics frequently said after he became a celebrity, the rearrangement or invention of details about himself, other people, and his work never bothered Capote because he saw such acts as the artist's prerogative. Indeed, if a reader turns to an early Capote essay, he or she will discover that the writer always held such views. In "New York" (1946) he indicates that truths become lies under the influence of the writer's pen. As a young author living in the city, he would store up experiences to report to the old family cook in Alabama. She would say, "Tell stories about that place, true stories now, none of them lies." Defensively, he confesses, "But mostly they were lies I told; it wasn't my fault, I couldn't remember, because it was as though I'd been to one of those supernatural castles visited by characters in legends: once away, you do not remember, all that is left is the ghostly echo of haunting wonder."[9] Everything a writer experiences, sees, and hears is filtered and then undergoes radical changes as it is processed and refined in the imagination before it is recast and presented in fictional form. As Capote noted, "life is life and art is art. You can't take actual life and make it into art."[10] In his "Self-Portrait" Capote asks himself whether he was truthful and responds: "As a writer—yes, I think so. Privately—well, that is a matter of opinion; some of my friends think that when relating an event or piece of news, I am inclined to alter or overelaborate. Myself, I just call it making something 'come alive.' In other words, a form of art. Art and truth are not necessarily compatible bedfellows."[11]

Beginnings

Within a certain framework, one is able to recognize the child who was destined to become a literary wunderkind in the forties. Whether he says he had a sense of what he would become as an adult or states more positively that he knew he would be a writer does not detract from the fact that he began to write very early; perhaps it was at 8, perhaps at 10 or 11; but writing absorbed him from his youth. If in his late essays he exaggerates his boyhood dedication to his art, he is only stretching a truth. Although he knew no one who wrote, and "few people who read," while still a child he began writing all kinds of stories and started to keep a journal: "Descriptions of a neighbor. Long verbatim accounts of overheard conversations. Local gossip. A kind of reporting, a style of 'seeing' and 'hearing' that would seriously influence me, though I was unaware of it then, for all my 'formal' writing, the stuff that I polished and carefully typed, was more or less fictional."[12] He was in his teens when a discerning teacher recognized his talent, and as he notes in his "Preface" to *Music for Chameleons*, he was already sending stories to the magazines by age 17. He may have erred about the age at which he recognized his vocation as an imaginative writer, and he may have overstated his artistic precocity, but the fact remains that he was very young when his first story was published.

In interviews, in confessional essays, and in fictionalized autobiography, Capote suggests that although or because he was a lonely and fearful child, he had a rich fantasy life. John Malcolm Brinnin—a close friend of Capote's for years, even though Capote later denied their intimacy—has written of Capote's ways of escaping from the unpleasantness of everyday life. When he was a boy and supposed to be in school, he would play truant and spend much of his time in Central Park, near the Plaza Hotel. He would sit in the park dreaming of "paperweight cities and towns where everything happened the way I wanted it to" (Brinnin 1981, 36).

Family and Home

Capote told Gloria Steinem that he had shared his fantasy life in part with his elderly spinster cousin, Miss Sook Faulk, the one person he had loved and trusted.[13] Still, his views concerning fantasy are marked by inconsistency. In the first decade of his career he observed to an interviewer that he disliked having critics call his work "fantasy." He indicated that he respects the form, which is "one of the most difficult things to do," but he then goes on to say "I just don't write it. . . . I'm trying to do something that's psychologically and emotionally true. If it is true, it just isn't fantasy."[14] However, by the late sixties, Capote acknowledged that fantasy was important in his early work, and that it came from his need to turn away "from the realities of my own troubled life, which wasn't easy. My underlying motivation was a quest for some kind of serenity, some particular kind of affection that I needed and wanted and have finally found."[15]

Capote was also ambivalent about being labeled a "southern writer." He often bristled at the southern designation, for he did not want to think of himself as a regionalist. In an interview in 1964, almost two decades after the publication of *Other Voices, Other Rooms*, he denied that it was a "southern" story. Only *A Christmas Memory*, he insisted, depended on a southern setting, and after that he had never written again about the South.[16] Apparently it did not occur to him that his rejection of a southern identity was odd, a refusal to put himself in the category of such distinguished writers as Faulkner and Flannery O'Connor, who are southern yet are not classified as "regional." Nevertheless, Capote in one of his last published conversations told the interviewer "everything important happened to me there," that is, in the South.[17]

Miss Sook Faulk, his cousin, not only shared his fanatasy life when he was a child, but also served as the model for some of his best-loved characters, most notably as his unnamed friend in *A Christmas Memory*, apparently Capote's personal favorite. But even on this topic he was contradictory, naming different works at different times as his favorite. In 1985 he said, "The way I ended that story [*Handcarved Coffins*] was my all time favorite piece of writing" (Ruas, 55).

Miss Faulk was Capote's companion and playmate for a number of the activities woven into the fabric of the early stories, such things as nut gathering and kite flying. His life as a child was spent with her and his mother's other middle-aged cousins in the small Alabama town of Monroeville. Those years provided him with the material for his southern stories. The southern world is seen in Capote's delineation of the changing seasons, particularly the heavy, lush, long-lasting summers; the little shops and the town characters; the religious atmosphere. Although even as a child he did not believe in religion, he had to go to church: "In the South, on Sundays, I went to church three times—morning, midday, and early evening. . . . I know what it is to have had to do all of these things without believing in any of it for a minute. . . . I was five, six years old and had to go to the Baptist church continuously in Alabama and I just didn't believe any of it. I wrote a short story about this very same subject, which my publisher published as *One Christmas*" (Grobel, 224–25).

Miss Sook embodied his vision of family and home throughout his life; when she died, he claimed many times in conversation and in his fiction, he lost both forever. Home was a place where he never went, the boy Buddy (Capote's own nickname as a child) tells the reader at the conclusion of *A Christmas Memory*. Capote's favorite character, Holly Golightly, in a statement that reflects Capote's own feelings, says to the young narrator, "Home is where you feel at home. I'm still looking" (*Breakfast*, 277). Like Holly, Capote wanted "permanence and stability" (Clarke 1988, 313–15), but in actuality Capote, like Holly, became something of a wanderer, a man who lived in many places in the world. Even though in his 20s he found a lifetime companion, Capote always considered himself as a family-less and homeless wanderer.[18]

Capote was reluctant for a number of years to admit to his use of autobiography in his work, particularly in the fiction that first made him famous, *Other Voices, Other Rooms*, but a quarter of a century after its publication he looked back at that novel and said he recognized the boy that had been himself in his search for a father: "the fact that the old man [in the story] is crippled and mute was my way of transferring my own inability to communicate with my father; I was not only the boy in the story but also the old man" (Norden, 53). By the time he was writing his last stories Capote no longer put a screen between himself and that never-to-be-satisfied longing for parental love, and in his final pieces he and his father both appear without any disguises.

The Changing Writer

In looking back over his career, Capote spoke of his writing as belonging to cycles, the first of which came to an end with the publication of that first novel. During the 10-year period between the publication of *Other Voices, Other Rooms* and *Breakfast at Tiffany's*, he "experimented with almost every aspect of writing, attempting to conquer a variety of techniques, to achieve a technical virtuosity as strong and flexible as a fisherman's net. Of course, I failed in several of the areas I invaded, but it is true that one learns more from a failure than one does from a success. I know I did, and later I was able to apply what I had learned to great advantage."[19]

His second cycle, he claimed, was concluded in 1958 with the publication of *Breakfast at Tiffany's*. To someone looking at the totality of Capote's work that "second cycle" clearly is his most productive. In this period he was creating what would be the most varied forms of his career: not only the novella and short stories, but also essays, portraits, plays, film scripts, and journalism. Although *The Muses Are Heard*, the author's memorably ironic work of nonfiction written during this time, did not sell well in spite of its many good reviews, it led to his interest in developing another prose work based on an actual occurrence. That became the "nonfiction novel," his best-known book, *In Cold Blood*, and the end of his third cycle of writing. Prophetically, Capote said that his fourth cycle would be his last ("Preface," 720). What he did not foresee, or at least would not admit to, was that the last cycle was also the one that stripped from him all the rewards he had worked so hard to win throughout his writing life.

Hostility toward Academia

Capote always liked to write in longhand on yellow, lined pads of paper. His other work habits—where he wrote, what time of day he wrote, how long he spent writing—varied over the years. However, many of his ideas about writers, writing, and literary critics did not change. Throughout his life he often voiced his disdain for literary critics, even though he admitted that critics were necessary for writers and public alike, for they interpret the former for the latter, and he himself read the reviews and critiques of his works. He also disliked the academic branch of the literary establishment. He had a low opinion of writing courses as a means of teaching people to write, asserting that writing cannot be taught. He scorned academics, who were like the "gray people" and the "drab quarterlies,"[20] in spite of the fact that two of his early lovers were professors at Harvard and Smith.[21] Brinnin speaks of Capote's scorn for Yalies who worked on doctorates. Capote's view is reflected in "Shut a Final Door," where the protagonist tells the reader that undergraduates from Yale and Princeton "made green birds fly in his stomach." Whether these feelings came from a sense of jealousy, or of not belonging, or of competition, is unclear, but Capote seems to have stated his own view in "A Tree of Night" by means of a sinister female character who says that college is not the place where one learns anything.

Style

Capote insisted that style could not be learned because it is the reflection of the self, of the writer's personality: "Style is what you are"

89

(Clarke 1988, 273). Almost invariably he called himself a craftsman, more concerned with style than content. Even when he spoke to a group of Soviet writers during the *Porgy and Bess* trip that became the subject of *The Muses Are Heard*, he stressed the fact that style was his main writing interest. To the Russians Capote was "a great literary figure" (Clarke 1988, 293). Nevertheless, many American critics have faulted him as being shallow, finding his range narrow and his content thin. They have also minimized the importance of his style, and labeled his work as "stylistically interesting but minor."[22] Such judgments did not seem to ruffle Capote much, at least not while he occupied the pinnacle of popular success. When the world clearly seemed to lie before him, he admitted he took pleasure not in what a work is "about, but the inner music words make" (Steinem 1967, 88).

In the eighties he told an interviewer, "I always stick to a strictly classic writing style, where everything is timeless. Nothing is going to date it—not the quality of the writing, not the subject" (Grobel, 134). Perhaps this statement was intended as a defense against those who were attacking his late work. Years earlier, as he entered middle age, he had admitted to a growing "need for admiration [that] had become insatiable" (Clarke 1988, 400). He wanted fame, and as his lifetime companion, Jack Dunphy, said to a reporter who interviewed him after Capote's death, "[The desire for fame] dictates to you. It makes you start to lie, deceive everyone but most of all yourself. . . . and the less that last book worked, the more he had to talk of it." Another old friend, Leo Lerman, blames Capote's insatiable appetite for fame on "the wound" of "his impoverished childhood," which was comparable to a Dickens story.[23]

Problems and Conflicts

As his ability to judge his own work began to falter, his fear of failure became so strong that kudos even from people whom he mocked and caricatured seemed sweet to him. Praise from Tennessee Williams for "Mojave," though, did not prevent Capote shortly thereafter from painting a scatological portrait of Williams in *Answered Prayers*. In the same vein of giving with one hand and taking away with the other, Capote told an interviewer that Williams has "total sensibility" but "absolutely no intelligence."[24] One finds that statement difficult to reconcile with Capote's decision to dedicate *Music for Chameleons* to Williams. Perhaps it had to do with his own feeling of rejection by the public and his identification with other writers who had similar experiences. He told Charles Ruas that it happened "to everybody" in the United States, to "writers . . . painters . . . composers. They'll build somebody up and then totally destroy him" (Ruas, 39). He saw himself as a victim, much like his fictional characters.[25] Donald Windham, who had been both an intimate of Williams and a friend of Capote, states in the foreword to his book *Lost Friendships: A Memoir of Truman Capote, Tennessee Williams, and Others* that both writers considered themselves "underappreciated . . . badly treated by public and critics" (12).

Capote frequently compared writers to racehorses. The metaphor suggests the artist's sensitivity, vulnerability, and need for special care. Brinnin said of the young Capote that he feared "what he's got most of: animal intelligence" (1981, 68). This attraction/repulsion is but another instance of Capote's duality.

A snake figures prominently in Capote's first novel, where it threatens the precarious masculinity of the young protagonist. Snakes figure as instruments of death in the late novella *Handcarved Coffins*. In two of his essays, "Self-Portrait" (1972) and "Nocturnal Turnings" (1979), Capote speaks of a cottonmouth water moccasin. The earlier essay describes Capote at age eight, bathing in a creek, seeing a snake, but not being afraid. The later essay changes and expands the incident: now he describes his feeling of terror, fear-induced paralysis, and the pain of being bitten and treated for snakebite. The memory of Capote's encounter with the deadly snake haunted him throughout his life. "And there, *just* there, swiveling, tangoing on the sun-dappled surface, the exquisitely limber and lethal cottonmouth moccasin. But I'm not afraid; am I?"[26] The snake represents fear as well as depression. Apparently the snake is symbolic of all the disasters that can befall a person. As Capote explained, when interviewed at a low point in his life and career, writing is the "antidote for snakebite."[27]

Capote knew, as most artists do, that there was danger from within as well as from without. Nevertheless, when that danger was obvious to others, he failed to recognize it. He held on to faith in his talent.

Defenses

Capote was full of contradictions. In the sixties, the decade before his fall from grace with friends and most critics, Capote was at the height of his powers and believed that "no one of his generation . . . had such a clear ear for the music and rhythm of the English language," that there was "no one else who wrote with such style and grace" (Clarke 1988, 331). In a television documentary, compiled after his death, we can see Capote, near the end of his life, speaking of himself as a poet in his early work.[28] Yet, two decades earlier, Capote had denied any claim to being judged as a prose-poet. Apparently stung by his friend Brinnin's misgivings about the inspiration for some of Capote's writing interests in the sixties, Capote angrily retorts, "I've never pretended to be that prose poet you and the others tried to make me." Brinnin was critical of Capote's social life and wealthy friends. He told Capote he was "recording," not "creating" as he had in the forties and fifties (1981, 91).

Nevertheless, for most of his writing life Capote continued to refer to himself as a stylist above all and insisted that technique concerned him more than any other aspect of writing. But by the time he wrote his "Preface" to *Music for Chameleons*, the author again seems to have changed his lifelong thoughts about style. Here he muses that he focused too much on technique in the past and that with the writing of the stories for *Answered Prayers* he wanted to change his mode. He asks: "How can a writer successfully combine within a single form—say the short story—all he knows about every other form of writing? . . . A writer ought to have all his colors, all his abilities available on the same palette for mingling (and, in suitable instances, simultaneous application)" (721). Unfortunately that realization seems to have come too late. In spite of the inclusion in the book of some fine journalistic pieces and interesting stories (many of them written originally for Andy Warhol's *Interview* magazine), by that point it was clear, because of the publication of the *Answered Prayers* stories in *Esquire*, that Capote had lost his sure touch and unerring judgment about his own work, in terms of style and subject matter alike. By 1980 the writer who in 1968 was labeled by an interviewer as "the Toscanini of the colon,"[29] thought he was tightening, stripping away, minimalizing, when in fact he was wandering, losing the thread of narration, mixing up ideas and writing in more styles than the frail subject matter could bear.

Hostile Contemporaries

One thing he never lost, though, was his love of titles. From his earliest interviews to the last one he spoke of the pleasure choosing titles gave him. Thus it is surprising to read Donald Windham's declaration in *Lost*

Friendships that he gave Capote the title for *Breakfast at Tiffany's*. Obviously, since Windham made this claim after Capote's death, Capote himself could not dispute it. Further, Windham asserts that Capote was lying about getting the book title for *The Dogs Bark* from André Gide. Windham declares that Capote never had such a discussion with Gide and that the title was actually taken from Quentin Bell's biography of Virginia Woolf. In view of Capote's well-known enthusiasm for choosing titles, Windham's statements seem at least open to question.

Windham's hostility toward Capote extends to the inclusion in *Lost Friendships* of statements he attributes to Carson McCullers, who is also dead and therefore unable to support or challenge Windham's story. McCullers claimed, writes Windham, that Capote had used "her subject matter" for his story "A Tree of Night," and that one of the passages in *The Grass Harp* had a strong resemblance to her story "A Tree, a Rock, a Cloud." Windham adds to the bill of Capote's literary piracy the charge that "the assembled properties" of Capote's "A Diamond Guitar" were taken from Windham's own novel, *The Dog Star*. It is a common practice for scholarly critics to engage in the time-honored art of finding resemblances between the works of writers. Many Capote stories have been analyzed in relationship to the work of other writers, but only Windham has declared Capote a plagiarist.

Techniques

Although several of his last stories seem to contradict Capote's frequent assertion that he always knew when he started a story the way in which it would end and that generally he wrote the ending before going on to write the rest of the story, there seems no reason to doubt that this practice was part of his technique during the years when he was totally in control of his material. Indeed, not knowing how he was going to end *In Cold Blood*, since the determination of the fate of the murderers remained in the courts for several years after the novelist had begun the book, made him anxious and depressed. However, it is a matter of record that Capote's depression also resulted from his too close involvement and identification with one of the criminals. Many critics have pointed out that Capote's battle with drugs and alcohol really began after the two men were executed. In other words, his inability to preserve objective distance as writer helped destroy him. Although he had told interviewers that writers must maintain distance from their material, such detachment did not work for him as an individual.[30]

One characteristic of Capote's writing technique was the keeping of journals. He would mine these journal entries to create his sketches, vignettes, and other nonfiction prose. Sometimes the journal entries were so detailed that he could transfer them almost in their entirety as a finished piece, as he said he did with his portrait of Marilyn Monroe ("A Beautiful Child," in *Music for Chameleons*). However, as the writing of *In Cold Blood* demonstrated, Capote also had a remarkable memory. While doing research for *In Cold Blood*, he did not take notes during interviews or discussions, but would write them up at the end of each day. For this work he also utilized another technique for the first and only time: to support his memory and observations he brought along as cohort and assistant his friend, the writer Harper Lee. They would separately record what they had heard, then talk about their findings. If necessary, they would see people again. The notes were filed and cross-indexed, becoming the factual part of *In Cold Blood*. In gratitude for Lee's help, Capote dedicated the work to her (and to his friend Jack Dunphy).

Contradictions and Attacks

Curiously, according to Donald Windham, Capote never communicated with Lee again after the book was finished (269). That he would dedicate *In Cold Blood* to Lee and then never talk to her again manifests his contradictory, even enigmatic personality. Capote and Lee had been friends from childhood, and Lee was the origin of the girl Idabel in *Other Voices, Other Rooms*. Windham claims Capote changed after the writing of *In Cold Blood*, that he lost his sensitivity to other people, that it no longer troubled him to "score at their expense." He could be "vicious" about people he had been "best friends with," said Andy Warhol, commenting on some of the public and indiscriminate remarks Capote made about various members of his social circle in the seventies. "When Truman turns, he really turns."[31] Nevertheless, Clarke and other writers tell of Capote's friendship with some people he had known since boyhood.

Warhol made some wild speculations about the origin of Capote's work, turning on him in his *Diaries* in a much more damaging way than Capote had ever employed even at the most unhappy, insecure time in his life. Warhol theorized that Capote was incapable of writing.

Warhol's August 1978 entry says, "maybe Truman never did write any of his own stuff . . . maybe he always had some butch guy there to do it. To do rewrites" (164). A few months later, in November, Warhol notes that Capote was in a surprisingly happy mood, and concludes that "he went out to Long Island and saw Jack Dunphy and . . . Jack Dunphy finally agreed to write *Answered Prayers*" (182).

Except for Windham's claims about titles and McCullers's supposed complaints about the use of her subject matter, Warhol appears to be the only person who questions the authorship of Capote's work. Authorship, however, came under scrutiny in a quite different situation that occurred after Capote's death. An aunt of his, Marie Rudisill, had published a work, *I Remember Grandpa*, which she claimed had been written by Capote before the publication of *Other Voice, Other Rooms*. Capote's biographer, his editors and publishers, and Capote scholars refused to take the claim seriously, but some reviewers treated *Grandpa* as if it actually had been the writer's own early work. During her nephew's lifetime Mrs. Rudisill wrote a book about his childhood, a work that he, Harper Lee, and members of Mrs. Rudisill's family repudiated. Even if there had not been such a rejection of Mrs. Rudisill's biography, the so-called find of that childhood work bears no resemblance even to Capote's earliest style.

Capote's Duality

In the television documentary, Mrs. Rudisill stated that people could always tell what mood her nephew was in by what he was writing. There is no telling whether Capote would have accepted or rejected that observation, but he did object to the designations scholars gave to his stories. Although critics from the time his work first was published have applied adjectives such as "dark" or "bright," "shadowy" or "sunny" to various works, the writer's position was that his style did not change; only the sounds of the language he used varied: "There is . . . a melodic adjustment of language to suit shifting material" (Norden, 56). But the work reflects the writer, as Conrad Knickerbocker noted in a review of *In Cold Blood*: "There are two Truman Capotes. One is the artful charmer, prone to the gossamer and the exquisite, of *The Grass Harp* and Holly Golightly. The other, darker and stronger, is the discover of death" (Clarke 1988, 363). Capote is the man of "Janus faces," said another, the man who is "killer and saint" (Medwick, 263).

Capote told numerous interviewers that he had a tragic vision of life. In reaction to this core belief, he assumed the external role of a frivolous person to help him cope with his internal, pessimistic image of himself as someone "standing in a darkened hallway" (Grobel, 110). Though some of his characters find joy everywhere they go, he did not. The world for him was not a magic place.[32] The only magic in his life took the form of superstitions: telephone numbers, yellow roses, three burnt cigarettes in an ashtray, a 13th day, a hat on a bed, nuns, and Fridays.[33] And, even though someone like Miss Bobbit may represent "the dreamer in him, the delicate spirit wandering in search of ideal happiness" (Nance, 71), he also has many terrible dark doubles, whose drive toward death and self-destruction is manifested from the earliest Capote stories.

Even the other authors he read show his duality. Faulkner disturbed him. When he was very young he described his feelings to Brinnin about reading Faulkner: "I feel threatened by something in the back of my head, something maybe too close to home" (1986, 55). He was drawn to the work of Dickens and Henry James—the gothic and psychological elements in their works clearly influenced him—and to mystery writers such as Raymond Chandler. He was attracted to such disparate observers of society and manners as Jane Austen and F. Scott Fitzgerald. There were three women writers whose work he admired unreservedly throughout his life: Willa Cather, whom he met as a schoolboy; Flannery O'Connor; and Isak Dinesen (Baroness Karen Blixen), about whom he wrote a prose "Portrait" for the photographer Richard Avedon's book, *Observation*. Two years before her death in 1962, Dinesen returned Capote's compliment by contributing a laudatory "Preface" to the Danish version of *Breakfast at Tiffany's*, known as *Holly* in Danish.

Love of Gossip

Although for unknown reasons he claimed in the latter part of his life that he had lost interest in James's work, Capote's film script of *The Turn of the Screw*, retitled *The Innocents*, is one of the two outstanding scripts he wrote. (He wrote four in the course of his career.) He told people he preferred *The Innocents* to his script for *Beat the Devil*, but both have become film classics. The writers he elevated to center stage were Flaubert and Proust. He wanted to become the American Proust. However, his desire to write prose "as pure as a distilled glass of water"[34] was not fulfilled in his later works, when he was reduced to offering gossip disguised as fiction.

Capote enjoyed gossip very much (he was a great reader of the tabloids and scandal sheets). He had something of a reputation as a raconteur. A friend interviewed after Capote's death spoke of the attraction he held for people "because he was so amusing."[35] Even though he often proclaimed that writing was his life, he also confessed to various people that he really liked to talk more than anything else. Because he was a good listener as well as a good talker, men and women, particularly women, confided in him. Unfortunately, he found some of the stories they told him too good to keep to himself; his inability to keep confidences led to his downfall, in spite of his declaration that he was doing for his age what Proust had done for his. He defended his practice by saying, "All literature—from biographies to essays to novels to short stories—is gossip" (Grobel, 92).

The Best Work

He was attracted to dark material from the beginning of his career as a writer. According to Clarke, themes such as "loneliness, the death of innocence, and the danger that lurks in every shadow" permeate all Capote's works (1988, 357). He was able to use what he learned from his short fiction and the novels and journalism to write that darkest of works, *In Cold Blood*. Still, he tells Grobel, the short story is formidable: "For the person who's a short-story artist it's the most difficult because it requires the greatest control and precision. Lots of writers write short stories, but they don't *write* short stories, so they don't know what they're doing" (93). His views of the importance of the short story changed little over the decades. Years earlier he said much the same thing and attributed "whatever control and technique I may have entirely to my training in this medium" (Hill, 132). Working within the confines of the short story, one learns discipline, the importance of rhythm, of paragraphing, of punctuation.

Journalism also prepared him for his best work. Good writers have seldom used that art form, but he learned it. As he said, "Journalism . . . always moves on a horizontal plane, telling a story, while fiction—good fiction—moves vertically, taking you deeper and deeper into character and events." Only someone who knows how "to write good fiction" is able to synthesize the two to produce the nonfiction novel (Clarke 1988, 357). "Playwriting," on the other hand, "has very little to do with literary talent. The theatre is so extraordinarily visual, and in order to write for it I had to forget the novel" (Breit, 236). Although here Capote was trying to defend his failure as a playwright, the fact is his writing was extremely visual.

From the beginning Capote was an extremely imagistic writer and became even more so as he developed an interest in film techniques. His works include many passages that might be aptly described as prose equivalents of wide-angle shots; he employed a kind of cross-cutting in scenes to move from character to character; he was also a master of the prose version of the camera close-up.

Neglect of Critics

Distracted by Capote's flamboyance, too few critics have pointed to the strengths of the psychological aspects of Capote's work. Although such significant literary critics as Levine and Hassan[36] wrote careful studies of Capote's early works, the works from Capote's middle and late periods have rarely been subjected to psychological analysis. Perhaps this critical neglect is attributable to Capote's outspoken hostility to the establishment, to his peers, and to entire groups of writers whom he faulted for having power to harm the careers of those outside their circle. Over the years he became more outspoken and hostile to artists he labeled "the Jewish Mafia," claiming they controlled the literary scene, the press, the theater, and the movie industry. He told friends and interviewers that many non-Jewish writers had been frozen out by influential Jewish reviewers and Jewish-owned intellectual publications. Bitter that he had not won either the acclaim or the prizes he believed he deserved, he lashed out at other writers as well.

Last Years

He would not, could not accept what happened to him after the publication of his stories in *Esquire* in the seventies. When the word "decline" was used to describe him in a 1978 newspaper article, he protested to Warhol, asking "What decline? I'm the most written about writer in the world." Warhol writes scoffingly in his diary: "I guess he's confusing written-about with writing" (*Diaries*, 149). At a large party Capote held in April 1978, few important people came, a devastating blow to the writer who in the sixties had given the "Party of the Decade," the party to which everyone sought to be invited.

That Capote was suicidal in his last years is not surprising. Close friends feared a possible suicide for some time before his death on 23 August 1984, a month short of his 60th birthday. Capote did not take his life, although it is possible his death could have been prevented, according to Clarke. When Capote became ill at the home of Joanne Carson, he would not allow her to get medical help. Clarke speculates that a combination of drugs and alcohol brought on "cardiac-rhythm disorder," which probably could have been treated. Instead, Capote "chose death" (Clark 1988, 546).

Capote might have been writing his own epitaph when he said, "I've written eight or nine short stories . . . as good as any in the English language" (Documentary). While there are people who might quibble with the number, most would agree with the point. That he failed at the end does not diminish the contribution he made to literature or the influence he had on other writers. When he was just starting out he spoke of art as "an act of faith and therefore an act of love" (Breit, 237). At the top of his career he described art as "the consolation for being human" (Steinem, 91). Although the history of American literature should have taught him that being a successful writer, a rich celebrity, carried with it an enormous freight, he did not learn that lesson. For a time, like Fitzgerald, whom he had admired, and Hemingway, whom he did not like, he had gone to Olympus; but as Gerald Clarke puts it, he "had been expelled" (1988, 470). In his expulsion he learned it is "the world [that] hath the day, and must break thee / not thou the world."[37]

He tried to hold on, to explain again and again that a writer can only use what he has, what he sees, what he knows. He attempted to cover his failures, while at the same time he was deceiving everyone, insisting he was continuing to write. But, according to Jack Dunphy, "He couldn't. . . . It was over" (Documentary). In Capote's own words, he had "used up the world" (Clark 1988, 541).

The sadness that his friends feel about Capote's last bitter years might be summed up in this statement made by a newspaper writer: "It was as if the wizard man who had given him so much, also made sure he possessed that one perfect other thing to assure his undoing: unappeasable hungers for recognition, for celebrity, for the inconsequentialities of glitter"—in things, parties, or "friends" with "famous names" who "in the end . . . broke his heart" (Hendrickson, B1).

Notes to Part 2

1. John Malcolm Brinnin, *Sextet: T. S. Eliot and Truman Capote and Others* (New York: Delacorte Press/Seymour Lawrence, 1981), 41; hereafter cited in text.

2. Gerald Clark, "Checking in with Truman Capote," *Esquire*, November 1972. Quote from reprint in *Truman Capote: Conversations*, ed. M. Thomas Inge (Jackson: University Press of Mississippi, 1987), 209; hereafter cited in text as Clarke 1972.

3. "When Does a Writer Become a Star? Truman Capote," in *The Americans* (New York: Stein and Day, 1970). Throughout the interview Capote is playful about truth.

4. Donald Windham, *Lost Friendships: A Memoir of Truman Capote, Tennessee Williams, and Others* (New York: Morrow, 1987), 158; hereafter cited in text. Windham is reporting Capote's remarks on Dick Cavett's show of 21 August 1980.

5. Richard Zoerink, "Truman Capote Talks about His Crowd," *Playgirl*, September 1975. Quote from reprint in *Truman Capote: Conversations*.

6. Gerald Clarke, *Truman Capote: A Biography* (New York: Simon and Schuster, 1988), 303; hereafter cited in text.

7. Charles Ruas, *Conversations with American Writers* (New York: Knopf, 1985), 47–48; hereafter cited in text.

8. Inge, "Introduction," *Truman Capote: Conversations*, x.

9. "New York" is part of a collection of travel pieces published in 1950 as *Local Color*. Quote from reprint in *A Capote Reader* (New York: Random House, 1987), 296.

10. Denis Brian, "Truman Capote," in *Murderers and Other Friendly People: The Public and Private World of Interviewers* (New York: McGraw Hill, 1972). Quote from reprint in *Truman Capote: Conversations*, 223.

11. "Self-Portrait." Quote from reprint in *A Capote Reader*, 633. Original date of publication was 1972.

12. "Truman Capote," *Vogue*, December 1979, p. 260.

13. Gloria Steinem, " 'Go Right Ahead and Ask Me Anything' (And So She Did): An Interview with Truman Capote," *McCall's*, November 1967. Quote from reprint in *Truman Capote: Conversations*, 93; hereafter cited in text, with page references to reprint.

14. Harvey Breit, "Truman Capote," in *The Writer Observed* (Cleveland: World, 1956), 236; hereafter cited in text.

15. Eric Norden, "Playboy Interview: Truman Capote," *Playboy*, March 1968, p. 53; hereafter cited in text.

16. Roy Newquist, "Truman Capote," in *Counterpoint* (Chicago: Rand McNally, 1964). Citation from reprint in *Truman Capote: Conversations*, 43; hereafter cited in text, with page references to reprint.

17. Lawrence Grobel, *Conversations with Capote* (New York: New American Library, 1985), 52; hereafter cited in text.

18. Mary Cantwell, "Truman Capote on Christmas, Places, Memories," *Mademoiselle*, December 1971, p. 176.

19. "Preface" to *Music for Chameleons*. Quote from reprint in *A Capote Reader*, 718; hereafter cited in text, with page references to reprint. Original date of publication was 1980.

20. John Malcolm Brinnin, *Truman Capote: Dear Heart, Old Buddy* (New York: Delacorte Press/Seymour Lawrence, 1986), 105; hereafter cited in text. Much of the material in this book is an expansion of Brinnin's *Sextet*. Capote also expressed these sentiments to Eric Norden in "Playboy Interview," 52.

21. For further discussion of these relationships, see Clarke's biography and both Brinnin books.

22. Gloria Steinem, "A Visit With Truman Capote," *Glamour* 55 (April 1966). Quote from reprint in *Truman Capote: Conversations*, 73.

23. Paul Hendrickson, "Capote: The Long Fade," *Washington Post*, 12 February 1988, pp. B 8–9; hereafter cited in text. Both quotations are from this article.

24. Josh Greenfield, "Truman Capote, the Movie Star?," *New York Times*, 29 December 1975. Quote from reprint in *Truman Capote: Conversations*, 326.

25. William L. Nance, *The Worlds of Truman Capote* (New York: Stein and Day, 1973), 211; hereafter cited in text.

26. "Nocturnal Turnings," in *A Capote Reader*, 641. Original date of publication was 1979. Capote altered this story frequently. In "Self-Portrait" he speaks of being bitten on the knee. In Grobel's *Conversations with Capote*, he says he was bitten on the toe.

27. Cathleen Medwick, "Truman Capote: An Interview," *Vogue*, December 1979, p. 312; hereafter cited in text.

28. "Unanswered Prayers: The Life and Times of Truman Capote: A Documentary." *American Masters*. Public Broadcasting, September 1987.

29. C. Robert Jennings, "Truman Capote Talks, Talks, Talks," *New York*, 13 May 1968. Quote from reprint in *Truman Capote: Conversations*, 165.

30. Haskel Frankel, "The Author," *Saturday Review*, 22 January 1966, pp. 36–37.

31. Pat Hackett, ed., *The Andy Warhol Diaries* (New York: Warner Books, 1989), 222; hereafter cited in text as *Diaries*.

32. Selma Robinson, "The Legend of 'Little T,'" *PM Picture News*, 14 March 1948. Information from reprint in *Truman Capote: Conversations*, 10.

33. Pati Hill, "The Art of Fiction 17: Truman Capote," in *Paris Review*, no. 16 (Spring–Summer 1957). Information from reprint in *Truman Capote's 'In Cold Blood': A Critical Handbook*, ed. Irving Malin (Belmont, Calif.: Wadsworth, 1968), 141; hereafter cited in text, with page references to reprint. See also Steinem, 98.

34. Patricia Burstein, "Tiny Yes, but a Terror? Do Not Be Fooled by Truman Capote in Repose," *People Weekly*, 10 May 1976. Quote from reprint in *Truman Capote: Conversations*, 333.

35. C. Z. Guest, speaking in the documentary, "Unanswered Prayers: The Life and Times of Truman Capote."

36. See Paul Levine's "Truman Capote: The Revelation of the Broken Image" in part III of this book. See also Ihab Hassan's "Truman Capote: The Vanishing Image of Narcissus," in *Radical Innocence: Studies in the Contemporary Novel* (Princeton, N.J.: Princeton University Press, 1961), 230–58.

37. Matthew Arnold, *Empedocles on Etna*, Act. II, LL. 17–19. In *Poetry of the Victorian Period*, eds. Jerome H. Buckley and George B. Woods, 3rd ed. (Chicago: Scott, Foresman & Co., 1965), 451.

Part 3

THE CRITICS

Introduction

Capote's career spanned almost four decades. From the beginning he and his work caught the interest of book reviewers and the public. Later, a few literary critics also began to pay attention to his fiction. Most reference books on modern American literature include essays about Capote's short stories and novels, as do those studies concerned with Southern writers. Nevertheless, the majority of pieces about Capote have been in the form of reviews in newspapers and magazines.

His greatest literary success, *In Cold Blood*, spurred the largest number of reviews; at the same time, some scholars became interested in his other work. Irving Malin's collection of critical essays *Truman Capote's 'In Cold Blood': A Critical Handbook*, explores more than the nonfiction novel. One such essay, reproduced here, is an example of that wider sweep: Melvin Friedman's study of Capote's aesthetics looks at the entire body of Capote's fiction up to 1968. Friedman describes Capote as a writer of his time, linking him to southern and French contemporaries. Another essay in Malin's collection, Robert Morris's "Capote's Imagery," links the images, characters, and setting of *In Cold Blood* with their antecedents in the writer's earlier fiction.

Over the years the bulk of Capote criticism has focused more on the personal and biographical than on the theoretical. Reviewers have generally been more attentive to Capote's life and idiosyncrasies, perhaps because he often behaved more like a performer than a serious writer. The great commercial success of the only complete Capote biography, Gerald Clarke's *Truman Capote* (1988), must be attributed to widespread interest in the public figure and television personality. The biography tells everything about Capote's life: his family, friends, lovers, triumphs, and failures, but it does not analyze or evaluate the work. For analysis of the work up to 1970, the readers should turn to William Nance's *The Worlds of Truman Capote*. John Malcolm Brinnin's two biographical books, *Sextet: T. S. Eliot and Truman Capote and Others* (1981) and *Truman Capote: Dear Heart, Old Buddy* (1986), written from the perspective of a Capote intimate, tell of the promise in the young writer and the disappointing changes that came with maturity. A combination of biographical information and criticism is found in both Helen Garson's *Truman Capote* (1980) and Kenneth Reed's *Truman Capote* (1981).

Capote's work does not lend itself readily to multiple forms of criticism. As Robert Stanton points out in the introduction to his annotated bibliography, *Truman Capote: A Primary and Secondary Bibliography* (1980), many critics have defined Capote's intellectual range as limited. Critics through the early sixties often faulted him for his failure to follow in the tradition of earlier novelists. Some seem to have applied the Arnoldian "touchstone" format, that is, a shared concern with the Victorian poet-critic over the preservation of taste and literary standards; these critics choose great pieces of literature to serve as "touchstones" in judging contemporary works. In *After the Lost Generation: A Critical Study of the Writers of Two Wars* (1951), John Aldridge sounds a note that is repeated by a number of critics during and after Capote's life: Capote, along with some of his contemporaries, is narrow in range and unconcerned with social issues. Instead of writing about war, the problems of returning veterans, and troubles in America's cities, Capote looked back at his childhood and produced fiction that focuses on his own private world. The Capote section of Aldridge's book is an expansion of the critic's hostile view of Capote expressed in "The Metaphorical World of Truman Capote" (1951). In this controversial essay, Aldridge describes the young writer as a failed symbolist. Carlos Baker, reviewing Capote's early stories in "Nursery Tales from Jitter Manor" (1949), scorns him as a fiction writer, yet praises him as poet. More generous than Aldridge or Hicks, Malcolm Cowley sees Capote as an important writer. Nevertheless, in "American Novels since the War" (1953), Cowley associates Capote with other writers of his time who lack an interest in and knowledge of history.

Capote's turn inward and away from the problems of contemporary society is often noted by critics whether they are analyzing his style or comparing him to other writers. His use of symbolism has met with mixed reactions. He is mentioned briefly by Ursula Brumm, in "Symbolism and the Modern Novel" (1958); she observes that Capote turns history into symbols. Thomas Curley calls him a rarity, a fine minor writer, and praises his technical ability in "The Quarrel with Time in Modern Fiction" (1960). Ihab Hassan, commenting on style, in "The Character of Post-War Fiction in America" (1962), speaks of Capote's devotion to language and, taking a totally different stance from the majority of critics, labels Capote a major novelist. In another essay, "The Victim: Images of Evil in Recent Fiction" (1959), Hassan explores the symbolic meanings of loneliness and isolation in Capote's stories, a subject that several other critics have also discussed. The Capote chapter in Hassan's book *Radical Innocence* (1961) contains a lengthy analysis of the dual aspects of Capote's fiction, the dark and the light motifs.

Albert Moravia likes Capote's impressionistic techniques but contends that his forms of fiction are not new and unique. In "Truman Capote and the New Baroque" (1960) Moravia argues that a reaction against realism had begun before Capote's first work was published. Moravia's view meshes well with a discussion by William Van O'Connor in *The Grotesque: An American Genre* (1962). O'Connor asserts that the South has produced more literature of the grotesque than any other region in America, and explains why this is so. Irving Malin allies himself on the side of critics who like Capote's gothic mode. In "From Gothic to Camp" (1964), a review of Capote's *Selected Writings*, Malin focuses on the theme of fear that makes the fiction superior to the journalism.

In *The Literature of Memory* (1977) Richard Gray alleges that style became a trap for Capote. He decries Capote's lack of moral engagement. In 1966, in *Time to Murder and Create: The Contemporary Novel in Crisis*, Aldridge repeats his earlier judgment of Capote, but he further claims that Capote burlesques the subject matter and modes of Faulkner.

Comparing Capote to other southern novelists as well as to other gothic writers is a common practice. In "Variations on a Dream: Katherine Anne Porter and Truman Capote" (1969), William Nance contrasts the ways the two writers use their material. A more recent essay, Blair Allmendinger's "The Room Was Locked, with the Key on the Inside" (1987), analyzes the influence of Eudora Welty's fiction on Capote. The essay, reprinted here, is a rarity in its feminist theoretical approach. Walter Allen, like Aldridge and Gray, measures Capote against Faulkner: the ingredients are the same, the style is poetic, but the work is empty, he avers in *The Modern Novel in Britain and the United States* (1965). Allen also compares the fiction of Carson McCullers and Christopher Isherwood with Capote's and ranks Capote's as the lesser work because he has created a toy world. Other critics note resemblances between Capote's Holly Golightly and Isherwood's Sally Bowles, but not all pronounce Capote hollow. Paul Levine's review of *Breakfast at Tiffany's* (1959) mentions Isherwood but reminds readers of the specifically American qualities of Holly; he also lauds the perfection of form in Capote's novella. Alfred Kazin, in *Contemporaries* (1961), speaks of Capote's comic flair in the novella, as well as his pity for the underdog. Kazin rejects the tag of superficiality that some critics have applied to Capote's fiction. In "The Prophetic Vogue of the Anti-Heroine" (1962), Nona Balakian, while describing Holly as an "asexual clown," nevertheless sees Capote's view as humanitarian in his vision of love.

Several critics have spoken of the debt Capote owes to Poe. Ray West, in *The Short Story in America* (1952), connects Capote to both Edgar Allan Poe and Paul Bowles. West maintains that Capote goes beyond any other writer in his experimentation and use of symbolism. Chester Eisinger's *Fiction of the Forties* (1963) discusses the similarities of the dark stories of Capote and Poe: resemblances exist not only in situations but also in the focus on the divided or opposing self. The matter of the divided self or the double is the subject of Michael Larsen's essay "Capote's 'Miriam' and the Literature of the Double" (1980), reprinted here. In *Violence in Recent Southern Fiction* (1965) Louise Gossett's view is similar to Eisinger's and others': Capote is interested in psychological disorder but has no concern for the moral issues behind it.

Psychoanalytic criticism continues to provide readers with insights into Capote's most difficult stories. Much of this criticism has been influenced by Paul Levine's timeless essay, reprinted here, "Truman Capote: The Revelation of the Broken Image" (1958). Levine provides a detailed discussion of the early fiction. A more recent piece of psychoanalytic criticism, Robert Davis's "*Other Voices, Other Rooms* and the Ocularity of American Fiction" (1980), links Freudian and Lacanian theory to Capote's frequent use of eyes, a central metaphor in his fiction.

Some mythological theory has been applied to Capote studies. Peter Hays's book *The Limping Hero: Grotesques in Literature* (1971) looks at archetypal lame figures and relates several Capote characters of myth. Hays's discussion of mythical elements in "Among the Paths to Eden" is excerpted here. Nancy Blake's "*Other Voices, Other Rooms*: Southern Gothic or Medieval Quest?" (1950) associates myth and Arthurian legend with Capote's first novel. David Kirby writes of fear and fairy tales in "The Princess and the Frog: The Modern American Short Story as Fairy Tale" (1973); although redemption is a characteristic of fairy tales, that does not happen in "Miriam."

Aside from reviews, very little has been written about Capote's late work. The exception is *Handcarved Coffins*, which has provoked some interest among critics. Robert Siegle's "Capote's *Handcarved Coffins* and the Nonfiction Novel," reprinted here, scrutinizes the story in an examination of the ambiguities of truth and cultural fictions.

All of the selections that follow, except one, are reprints of material that appeared elsewhere. The new essay, Baroness Karen Blixen's (Isak Dinesen) "Introduction" to *Holly*, the Danish version of Capote's *Breakfast at Tiffany's*, has never before appeared in English. I am very grateful to the Rungstedlund Foundation for allowing me to include in this book Jan Nordby Gretlund's translation of Blixen's piece. Blixen and Capote were friends, and the American writer was one of the Danish writer's greatest admirers. Without meaning to, he offended her, but she wrote the essay because she admired his work.

In spite of his decline in the decade before his death, Capote's name continues to have an aura about it. At the end of the eighties and into the nineties, people flocked to see the one-man show "Tru" on Broadway and elsewhere. The play, by Jay Presson Allen, captures some of the many moods and styles of the original. In my summary of the four decades of criticism and in the essays collected here I have attempted to provide the reader with an awareness of the differing responses of other writers to those moods and styles.

Blake Allmendinger

Grobel: "Has any American writer had an influence on you as a writer?"
Capote: "No American writer has."

— *Conversations with Capote*

I

"The apartment was in the wildest disorder—the furniture broken and thrown about in all directions. There was only one bedstead; and from this the bed had been removed, and thrown into the middle of the floor. On a chair lay a razor, besmeared with blood. On the hearth were two or three long and thick tresses of gray human hair, also dabbled with blood, and seeming to have been pulled out by the roots."[1] So Poe describes the scene of the crime, in "The Murders in the Rue Morgue." He startles the reader with a graphic depiction of the bedroom, but he stumps the reader with a detail that has since become a staple of detective fiction. Auguste Dupin learns, on forcing the door, that no person was seen. The windows, both of the back and front room, were down and firmly fastened from within. . . . The door leading from the front room into the passage was locked, with the key on the inside.[2] Dupin wrestles with the right of access to a locked room. In a similar fashion, critics struggle with the seductive image and mythic biography of Truman Capote. In conversations, interviews, and the preface to his last book, *Music for Chameleons*, Capote denies the influence of other writers on his work. Describing his own development, he conjures up the image of a locked room—of a writer who withdraws from the influence of society, to create. Critics have been less successful than Poe's detective in solving the puzzle of the room, locked from within. In the last thirty years, they have accepted the proclamations of a man whose conversation was often more convincing

Reprinted from "The Room Was Locked, with the Key on the Inside: Female Influence in Truman Capote's 'My Side of the Matter,'" *Studies in Short Fiction* 24 (Summer 1987): 279–88. Reprinted with permission of *Studies in Short Fiction* at Newberry College.

than his prose; whose own texts contradict the denials of literary influence. Books and articles have linked Capote to the work of his contemporaries in only a vague, suggestive sense, but a piece from his early period draws specifically upon Eudora Welty. "My Side of the Matter" is a clear reconstruction of her short story, "Why I Live at the P.O.," and a case study in the anxiety of female influence. In his response to Welty, Capote alters the gender of his characters to depict a battle between the sexes and centers the plot on a male protagonist, accused of stealing from a woman.

II

In the preface to *Music for Chameleons*, Capote says: "I started writing when I was eight—out of the blue, uninspired by any example.[3] Capote means to impress the reader with the emergence of his art, as a magician seeks to startle the audience, pulling a rabbit out of his hat. Here and elsewhere, Capote loads the denial of literary influence with a rhetorical force that seeks to amaze the audience and suggest that writing is an uninspired feat. In *Conversations with Capote*, the author belittles Ezra Pound by telling Lawrence Grobel that the poet sought help from T. S. Eliot. He adds: "I've never had anybody that I could show things to and ask their opinion."[4] He insists that Norman Mailer and other contemporaries have drawn from his work to produce the non-fiction novel and have won awards for their unacknowledged debt to his own novel, *In Cold Blood*. But he denies that he, in turn, has drawn from Henry Adams or Hemingway, as Malcolm Cowley suggests.[5] He reiterates this statement throughout a series of interviews with Grobel and insists upon it with an air of protestation: "I don't think of myself in terms of relationships with other writers at all and I don't feel in competition with other writers. Because I don't write about the same things as any other writer that I know of does. Or have the same interests. Or as a personality that's in any kind of conflict with any other writer. I have absolutely no envy of any other writer.[6] Capote suggests that literary influence is not a tradition, which bonds together writers in a helpful sense, but a psychological abnormality which brands the writer as psychotic with a "personality" disorder, in "conflict" or "competition" with tradition. Capote relates self-sufficiency to self-esteem and isolates himself from the canon.

In doing so, he builds an image around his own identity as an autonomous writer. He tells Grobel that he hid in his bedroom and started to write when he was eight years old. "I mean, really seriously, so seriously that I dared never mention it to anybody. I spent hours every day writing and never showed it to a teacher."[7] Capote allows the reader to imagine that he has fought off the curious and withdrawn from the world to write in his room. In the preface to *Music for Chameleons*, he says that his family sought to discover the purpose of his confinement. "Yet I never discussed my writing with anyone; if someone asked what I was up to all those hours, I told them I was doing my school homework."[8] Grobel accepts the scenario or finds the image of the locked room sufficiently interesting to include in a preface to his interview. He tells the reader that Capote was inspired to write *Other Voices, Other Rooms* during a winter walk in the forest. "When he finally reached home, he went straight to his room, locked the door, got into bed fully clothed, and . . . wrote: '*Other Voices, Other Rooms*—a novel by Truman Capote!' "[9]

III

The image of the locked room seems to have satisfied critics for the last thirty years. *In Cold Blood* has drawn attention because of the connection between the non-fiction novel and its precursors: *The Education of Henry Adams* and Theodore Dreiser's *An American Tragedy*. But "My Side of the Matter" has been overshadowed by other stories in *A Tree of Night*. Since winning the O. Henry Awards, both "Miriam" and "Shut a Final Door" have received scrutiny, but articles dealing with these stories discuss themes and predicaments that attract most readers of Southern American fiction: the Gothic, the grotesque, the obsession with the past, the use of local color and dialect. American critics have skirted the issue of influence since the publication of *A Tree of Night* and have focused on major stories in the collection.

"My Side of the Matter" borrows its plot from Welty's work, "Why I Live at the P.O." Both stories tell of a woman who returns home to her family, with child, and precipitates an argument that leads to the withdrawal of the narrator from other members of the household. Stella-Rondo returns with Shirley-T., a child she has "adopted."[10] Sister challenges the parenthood of Shirley-T., accuses Stella-Rondo of having borne the child herself, and provokes an argument which broadens in scope as it builds to climax. Systematically throughout the narrative, Papa-Daddy, Mama, Uncle Rondo and Shirley-T. turn against Sister and persuade her to leave the house. She moves to the post office: "And if Stella-Rondo should come to me this minute, on bended knees, and *attempt* to explain the incidents of her life with Mr. Whitaker, I'd simply put my fingers in both my ears and refuse to listen," (56). Marge returns to her aunts, three months pregnant, in "My Side of the Matter." Both Eunice and Olivia-Ann disparage her husband—the narrator—belittle his manhood, and question the fatherhood of the child. They antagonize Sylvester and succeed in turning his wife and their maid against him. After a skirmish, Marge's husband locks himself in the parlor, defies the other members of the family and, like Sister, determines to spite them: "Oh, yes, they've started singing a song of a very different color. But as for me—I give them a tune on the piano every now and then just to let them know I'm cheerful."[11]

Capote characterizes the people in his story by exploiting particular elements that occur in Welty's earlier work. Uncle Rondo becomes ridiculous when he appears "in the hall in one of Stella-Rondo's flesh-colored kimonos, all cut on the bias, like something Mr. Whitaker probably thought was gorgeous" (48). Capote uses the same garment to undercut the authority of Eunice and to mock her romantic self-image. "She troops around the house, rain or shine, in this real old-fashioned nighty, calls it a kimono, but it isn't anything in this world but a dirty flannel nighty" (197). Olivia-Ann has a pathetic, romantic attachment to Gary Cooper and has "one trunk and two suitcases full of his photos" (200). Her fantasy has its counterpart in the trivial feud between Sister and Stella-Rondo, who fight over Mr. Whitaker while sitting for "Pose Yourself" photos (46). Papa-Daddy intimidates the community of China Grove, as well as his family, by exploiting his alleged wealth and power. He uses his position to procure the office of postmistress for Sister and to marshal the town against her when she leaves. "There are always people who will quit buying stamps just to get on the right side of Papa-Daddy" (56). Welty exploits the comedy by characterizing Papa-Daddy as a man who denies the rumors of wealth, but capitalizes on them to wield power. Sister says: "He's real rich. Mama says he is, he says he isn't" (47). Capote puts Eunice in the same position. "Not that she hasn't got plenty of money! Naturally she says she hasn't but I know she has . . ." (197). Sylvester attributes the influence of Eunice to her status in Admiral's Mill: "Of course anything Eunice says is an order from headquarters as not a breathing soul in Admiral's Mill can stand up and say he doesn't owe her money . . ." (197). Capote caricatures the battle between David and Goliath by juxtaposing the status of Eunice with that of the narrator. While Eunice conceals her funds and denies her wealth, Sylvester exaggerates the importance of his job in Mobile, and consistently refers to his "perfectly swollen position clerking at the Cash'n'Carry" (196–197). Welty also pits the authority of Papa-Daddy against the subordinate Sister, who runs "the next to smallest P.O. in the entire state of Mississippi" (47).

Welty and Capote tell their stories in the first-person. In part, they do so to color the narrative with a silly urgency and impromptu exaggeration, both of which help to characterize the tall tale. Sister and Sylvester are obsessed with their own importance, the injustice of "life," and the righteous indignation which motivates their behavior. Their ramblings also enliven the events of the past, turning them into oral reconstructions of the immediate present. Run-on syntax, slang, idiomatic phrases, and italicized words animate experience and imitate the inflection of vocal speech patterns. Sister and Sylvester talk to their audience and recreate their scenes, using rhetoric to grab the attention or gain the sympathy of the reader. Sister uses one device which occurs nowhere else in the works of Welty: the recreation of speech tempos through the hyphenation of letters within a single word. She prepares the reader for the reaction of Papa-Daddy, who rebels against the notion that he should cut off his beard. Stella-Rondo says: " 'Papa-Daddy, Sister says she fails to understand why you don't cut off your beard.' So Papa-Daddy l-a-y-s down his knife and fork!" (47). The reader anticipates the response of Papa-Daddy, who slowly l-a-y-s down his utensils and prepares to put up his dukes. Capote appropriates the same device in a dialogue between Eunice and Marge. Marge describes the narrator as "the best-looking" man she knows, and the narrator says: "Eunice eyes me u-p and d-o-w-n and says, 'Tell him to turn around' " (198). Again, the elongation of the phrase "u-p and d-o-w-n" enables the reader to see Eunice, as she scans the body of the narrator with careful scrutiny, and prepares the reader for the sarcastic comment which follows the pause. " 'You sure must've picked the runt of the litter. Why, this isn't any sort of man at all' " (198).

Two other strategies have their counterparts in "My Side of the Matter": the comic one-liner, used to describe a character, and the rhetorical question, addressed to the reader. Sister systematically slays her antagonist-of-the-moment with comic barbs throughout the story. "Papa-Daddy is about a million years old and's got this long-long beard" (47). "You ought to see Mama, she weighs two hundred pounds and has real tiny feet" (50). She exaggerates the age and weight of her family and undercuts one aspect of their appearance by insisting on the incongruity of another. Welty turns the longevity of Papa-Daddy into a joke and makes the grandfather into a caricature of Methuselah, with a "long-long beard." Sister's description of Mama cannot bear scrutiny, any more than her mother's "real tiny feet" can possibly bear the weight of her "two hundred pounds." Capote's description of Eunice bears more than a faint resemblance to Welty's description of Mama. "Eunice is this big old fat thing with a behind that must weigh a tenth of a ton" (197). Elsewhere, Olivia-Ann is "real pale and skinny and has a mustache" (197). Marge has "no looks, no body, and no brains whatsoever" (196). The narrator resents the interference of Eunice, Marge, and Olivia-Ann by telling Eunice about Mrs. Harry Steller Smith, a canary that Olivia-Ann has released from its cage. Sylvester silences Olivia-Ann and turns aside to the reader. He says, triumphantly: "Remember Mrs. Harry Steller Smith?" (202). He begs the reader to side with him and uses the rhetorical question in the same way that Sister does, to win the sympathy of the reader. When Stella-Rondo says that her uncle looks like a fool in her kimono, Sister comes to his defense. "'Well, he looks as good as he can,' I says. 'As good as anybody in reason could'" (49). Stella-Rondo tells Uncle Rondo in a later scene that Sister has described him as "a fool in that pink kimono" (52). Sister responds, by asking the reader to pity her plight. "Do you remember who it was really said that?" (52).

IV

Capote might well have entitled his story "My Side of the Matter: Or, Do You Remember Who It Was Really Said That?" His imitation of Welty and his denial of literary influence put him in an interesting position. His comments to Grobel suggest that a writer who bonds himself to tradition loses his identity and becomes psychotic, but his refusal to identify the source of his own work seems equally perverse. Capote's alterations of the earlier story reveal more clearly than the similarities that he struggles to resolve this paradox. "My Side of the Matter" transforms the narrator into an alter ego of the author and turns the antagonists into a successive string of females, who challenge Sylvester. The plot now centers on the accusation of theft—by a man, from a woman. The struggles between Sylvester and the women in Admiral's Mill have their counterpart in the acceptance and refusal of Welty as the original source, and represent the anxiety of female influence, which Capote must overcome.

The reassignment of the sex roles in the second story turns the battle between Sylvester and the opposition into a gender issue. Sister faces off against a series of enemies who are equally distributed between the male and female sex—against Papa-Daddy and Uncle Rondo on the one hand, and Stella-Rondo and Mama on the other. Capote turns the conflict between the narrator and the other characters into a battle between the sexes. Sylvester now confronts Eunice, Olivia-Ann, Bluebell, and eventually Marge in a series of encounters that test his manhood. He asserts his authority by insisting that he has a position of patriarchal importance at the Cash'n'Carry, by defending his ability to impregnate his wife, and by demanding to sleep with her. The women attempt to separate Sylvester from the rest of the house because of his sexual status. Eunice says: "Birds setting in their roost—time we went to bed. You have your old room, Marge, and I've fixed a cot for this gentleman on the back porch" (200). The women are horrified by the possibility that Sylvester could assert the male prerogative, impregnate his wife, and work on her affections. They seek to castrate the protagonist, who finds an alternate means of asserting his sexual strength. Sylvester describes the influence of Eunice over Marge, and his attempt to counteract it: "She has turned that girl against me in the most villainous fashion that words could not describe. Why, she even reached the point when she was sassing me back, but I provided her with a couple of good slaps and put a stop to that. No wife of mine is ever going to be disrespectful to me, not on your life!" (201). When he learns that he can't control his wife as a sexual male, he turns to force and seeks to assert his power, as a member of the "stronger" sex. He exerts physical power over the other women in the house as well. As the battle progresses, he picks a parasol off of the hat tree and raps Bluebell "across the head with it until it cracked in two" (204). He describes himself as a victor in the sexual sense—as a "man." Only Sylvester has the strength to barricade himself behind the parlor door with "that big mahogany table that must weight a couple of tons" (205). And only Sylvester can appropriate sexual power—pick and choose between Marge and "a five-pound box of Sweet Love candy" (205) that becomes a mock-romantic substitute for the female companion.

Sylvester creates a history for himself and other characters by building a sexual hierarchy that subordinates women and defines people by establishing their patriarchal roots. He undermines female influence by attributing the importance of Eunice and Olivia-Ann to the appropriation of masculine power. "There is a big table in one corner of the parlor which supports two pictures of Miss E and O-A's mama and papa. Papa . . . was a captain in the Civil War" (202). The male tradition empowers the past and enables the narrator to live for the future. Sylvester says: "Oh, if it wasn't for that little unborn George I would've been making dust tracks on the road, way before now" (200). Unlike Marge, Eunice, and Olivia-Ann, Sylvester has no parents or past, according to the narrative. He is completely self-created and, as the narrative progresses, the reader learns that he is also able to create little men in his own image. Sylvester determines that the unborn child is a boy, believes that it will grow to be a man, and decides to protect it until the man can protect himself. He names the child and confers upon it the attribute of male power. "George Far Sylvester is a name we've planned for the baby. Has a strong sound, don't you think?" (199). The "strength" of the male child is due to his distance from the female group, as the middle name "Far" suggests. The reader establishes the identity of Sylvester himself through a naming process in the narrative which is self-referential and gender-reflexive, within the male tradition. The narrator uses the reflexive pronoun "I" to refer to himself and withhold his name from the reader as he withholds his presence and power from the women, at the end of the narrative. Through the naming of George Far Sylvester, the reader learns to identify the narrator himself as Sylvester—to link the father and son together, through the patriarchal surname.

Eunice and Olivia-Ann acknowledge their "inferiority" by imitating men or assuming the costume and behavior of the opposite sex to achieve power. Eunice chases Sylvester with her father's Civil War sword—a comic, phallic symbol and a relic from the male world of war and bloodshed. Olivia-Ann "squats around most of the time whittling on a stick with her fourteen-inch hog knife" (198). Both she and Eunice brandish their weapons, wave them in the face of the protagonist, and challenge his potency. They represent a threat to the male and give him a "half-inch cut" (204) that harms him less than it hurts his masculine pride. Sylvester counters the authority of women, throughout the story, by telling the reader that Eunice and Olivia-Ann fail as men and function as comic, pathetic imitations of the real thing. Eunice "chews tobacco and tries to pretend so ladylike, spitting on the sly" (197). Olivia-Ann has a "mustache" (197). Sylvester portrays the women as sex-starved maiden aunts who envy Marge because they can't get a man for themselves. In the absence of actual men, they imitate the opposite sex and persecute Sylvester because he represents the real thing.

They mock his pretensions to manhood, as he mocks theirs. Eunice glories in the role of bread-winner and belittles Sylvester: "Why don't the little heathen go out and get some honest work? . . . If he was any sort of man you could call a man he'd be trying to put a crust of bread in that girl's mouth instead of stuffing his own off my vittles" (201). Olivia-Ann pokes fun of his small size and bad back, and refers to him as a "runt" (198). Both women devalue the man by denigrating his capacity to procreate and defining his status as a sexual failure. Olivia-Ann echoes her sister when she says that "he isn't even of the male sex" (198). "How can a girl have a baby with a girl?" (199). References to impotence and castration proliferate throughout the text and testify to the capacity of women to disarm their male opponents. Sylvester compares the tyranny of Eunice, in the community of Admiral's Mill, to the alleged rape of a woman by an elderly man: ". . . if she said Charlie Carson (a blind, ninety-year old invalid who hasn't taken a step since 1896) threw her on her back and raped her everybody in this country would swear the same on a stack of Bibles" (197). The sisters assert their presence in the house, as they do in the community. Sylvester finds that "the fancy man tore out of this house one afternoon like old Adolf Hitler was on his tail and leaped into his Ford coupé, never to be heard from again" (201). Olivia-Ann locates the source of the feud, below the belt, and gives Sylvester a terrific "knee punch" (204) before running into the yard and shouting: "Mine eyes have seen the glory of the coming of the lord; He is trampling out the vintage where the grapes of wrath are stored" (204). She brings the opponent to his knees—literally—and tramples the "grapes of wrath," neutering the man whose genitals threaten the women.

The conflict begins with the accusation of Eunice, early in the story. Sylvester says: "I happened to find close to a thousand dollars hidden in a flower pot on the side porch. I didn't touch one cent, only Eunice says I stole a hundred-dollar bill which is a venomous lie from start to finish" (197). Later, the accusation precipitates the final fight in the story.

> "Where is it?" says she. "Where's my hundred dollars that he made away with while my trusting back was turned?"
> "*This* is the straw that broke the camel's back," says I, but I was too hot and tired to get up.

"That's not the only back that's going to be broke," says she, her
bug eyes about to pop clear out of their sockets. (203)

The theft by a man, from a woman, summarizes the conflict between
men and women and symbolizes the central theme of the story: female
influence and the denial of it. Eunice proclaims the dependence of
men upon her and threatens to break the back of a man whose body is
weaker than hers. Sylvester maintains his innocence, first by fighting
Eunice, then by pushing her out of the parlor. The final image is an
answer to the accusation. Sylvester locks himself in the room, using his
physical isolation to assert his actual innocence, and to demonstrate his
independence.

V

Capote leaves the crime—and the issue of influence—unresolved at
the end of the story. He allows the reader to suspect Sylvester and
certainly means to suggest that the locked door is evidence of an empty
assertion. The isolation of the protagonist cannot, in itself, absolve him
of the crime or his complicity of it. The denials cannot function, on
their own, as an adequate defense. Capote compares the confrontation
between Eunice and Sylvester to an earlier scene of accusation and
denial. Eunice meets Sylvester, when he first arrives, and tells Marge
that he looks like the "runt of the litter." Sylvester says: "I've never
been so taken back in my life! True, I'm slightly stocky, but then I
haven't got my full growth yet" (198). Sylvester responds to the
accusation with a weak defense. The reader dismisses the reasoning
process of the protagonist and carries a skeptical reaction to Sylvester
over into the final episode of accusation and denial. To this extent,
Capote allows the reader to doubt Sylvester, to interpret the outcome
of the story, and to care about it. But ultimately he undermines the
issue of female influence by leaving it open-ended. He suggests that
the plot is irrelevant and that the accusation of theft is simply one in a
chain of petty incidents in the narrative, championed by ridiculous
people. The interaction of characters and the complication of events
create a diversion which subverts interpretation and subordinates the
issue of female influence to the illustration of the spectacle itself.

"In an interview with *Playboy*, in March, 1968, Capote said: 'I've
never been psychoanalyzed; I've never even consulted a psychiatrist. I
now consider myself a mentally healthy person. I work out all my

problems in my work.' "[12] Capote seems to work out the problem of influence in "My Side of the Matter," using the battle between Sylvester and the women to illustrate his own anxiety. He imitates Welty and reveals this intent, by tipping his hat to tradition in the title of the story. "My Side of the Matter" might well read "My Response to Eudora Welty," for Sylvester's battle seems to reflect Capote's own involvement with his predecessor. But in his comments on his work—in conversations, writings, and interviews—Capote contradicts the blatant link between himself and earlier writers. The psychological search for his own identity, within the text, leads the reader to suspect that the struggle between two images of the author—the psychotic and the "mentally healthy person"—never resolves itself. Taken in context with the author's statements about tradition and the struggle to create a literary identity, "My Side of the Matter" ultimately remains a problematic work. Sylvester's retreat to the parlor parallels Sister's withdrawal to the post office and indicates the extent to which the author draws upon his literary model. But Sylvester's rebuttal, behind the locked door, mirrors the protestations of the author, who uses the image of the locked room to illustrate his own autonomy. Capote's story, therefore, represents an intriguing compromise: a testimonial to tradition and a denial of it.

Notes

1. Edgar Allan Poe, "The Murders in the Rue Morgue," from *The Complete Tales and Poems of Edgar Allen Poe* (New York: Vintage Books, 1975), p. 147.

2. Ibid., p. 150.

3. Truman Capote, *Music for Chameleons* (New York: Random House, 1975), p. xi.

4. Lawrence Grobel, *Conversations with Capote* (New York: New American Library, 1985), p. 97.

5. Ibid., p. 116.

6. Ibid., p. 149.

7. Ibid., p. 52.

8. Capote, *Music for Chameleons*, p. xii.

9. Grobel, *Conversations with Capote*, p. 82.

10. Eudora Welty, "Why I Live at the P.O.," from *The Collected Stories of Eudora Welty* (New York: Harcourt Brace Jovanovich, 1980), p. 46. Further references to this story are from the same edition and are included, parenthetically, within the text.

11. Truman Capote, "My Side of the Matter," from *The Grass Harp and A Tree of Night and Other Stories* (New York: Signet Books, 1980), p. 205. Further references are from this same edition and are included, parenthetically, within the text.

12. William L. Nance, *The Worlds of Truman Capote* (New York: Stein and Day, 1970), p. 53. I borrow this passage from an interview in *Playboy*, which Nance quotes.

Karen Blixen (Isak Dinesen)

The magic of Truman Capote's oeuvre is in its characteristic combination of airiness and gravity. We observe it the way we observe a squirrel's flight in a tree, at one and the same time it is utterly fantastic and fully within reason,—the flying figure may be described as both lightfooted and lumpish.

When he performed in American literature for the first time with the story "Miriam" (1945), Truman Capote was nineteen. During the next four years he published the novel *Other Voices, Other Rooms*, and a collection of short stories, *A Tree of Night*. With those two books he asserted himself with acclaim as a wonder child and an enfant terrible among the preachers of the gospel of his generation: horror. Not the horror of burial vaults and apparitions by Hoffmann or Monk Lewis, in which it is the fear of a direct and sudden visitation of unforseeable consequences that will make your hair stand on end. But the horrible such as it manifests itself in a waiting room with a draft, bad lighting, and cigarette butts on the floor, where the grotesqueness is in the fact that in here nobody is concerned about anything, and where fear is at once claustrophobic and a horror vacui.

It is not, however, on this ungenial instrument that the young writer will become a classic in American intellectual life—or perhaps already has become one—here he has keen competitors. Already in one or two of the short stories from *A Tree of Night* he struck a new note, and in his next book, *The Grass Harp*, he grandly renounced the vacuum. And then we listened.

It was a curious experience: as if on the roof of the Church of Notre-Dame one of the Gargoyles all at once from a case under the black wing of bat had produced Puck's flute itself and had coursed through a number of his tunes. They may well begin as a night music macabre, in which the hungry lion roars and the schreech-owl schreeches loud.

Reprinted from the "Introduction" to *Holly* (*Breakfast at Tiffany's*). trans. Jan Nordby Gretlund (Denmark: Gyldendal, 1960). Printed with permission of The Rungstedlund Foundation.

But soon they acknowledge the world of fairies and true magic. Was the transformation in earnest?—After all there is always a more wonderful gravity in the fable than in the nightmare.

The tunes are revived in Capote's latest book. The Devil's trill is also sounded in *Breakfast at Tiffany's*, and we still have time to shudder. Old Bonaparte is bad enough, of much the same dye as our own Kulso [in Danish literature], maybe like one of the witches in Macbeth's moors, and in the struggle between the old and the young woman in "House of Flowers" the witches' cauldron is at the boil. Yet there is no void in the book's airy space—there is a universal presence that may be sensed as a nearness. Seen from a literary point of view, as a character in a book, the twenty-five year older Sally Bowles is better behaved than Holly Golightly. But Holly strikes the better note.

Even a conviction can be found in this book. Among echoes from far away and from all sides we find a truth in the truly unaffected, inspired mind of man and in the perfectly unbreakable, inspired loyalty of two people of this disposition. We have seen that kind of devotion between Sister Middy and Brother Appleseed—whose name could be entered direct in a presentation of Titania's sylvan servants—we find it again here between Holly and Fred and between Royal and Ottilie. A theme from *The Grass Harp* recurs in the friendship between the little, or half-grown, boy and the much older, half-crazed woman, and in their redeeming roaming in the forest. Even the enemies who come between the lovers are named in this open world, frankly and without resentment, as "those who knew better." And even when the flute sounds its most painful note, its singularity is retained: "I promise you, good Master Mustardseed, your kindred hath made my eyes water ere now."

All the experiences and thoughts in this book are rendered in a pure, aware, kind of unforced style, which in literature corresponds to what in company is called good manners. This is the author whose style says: "My Style is my Castle," and yet keeps an open house.

Translator's Note

Karen Blixen structured her evaluation of Truman Capote on golightly airiness vs. ambiguous gravity. She saw *Breakfast at Tiffany's* as a product of a magic flute that for once had lured Capote from his habitual gloom of the Gothic grotesque. She described the battle for the writer's soul in universal terms of lightness vs. darkness and found her examples in

Shakespeare's *Midsummer Night's Dream* and *Macbeth*. (There are obvious echoes of both plays in Blixen's text.) The importance of this little essay is that Truman Capote is evaluated on the grand scale of literary achievement by a writer of international fame. Blixen saw clearly that with Capote it would be an either/or, and she asked prophetically: will the transformation last? When she wrote this essay, she had no way of knowing that his main achievement would be *In Cold Blood*, but Blixen seems to have sensed that the old darkness and gravity would defeat Capote's new magic airiness.—Jan Nordby Gretlund

Melvin J. Friedman

November 14, 1959, is likely to become as important a literary date as June 16, 1904. This is the day when Perry Smith and Dick Hickock murdered the Clutter family of Holcomb, Kansas, "in cold blood." Capote, in late 1965 (when *In Cold Blood* appeared in four issues of *The New Yorker*), as indelibly marked our literary calendars as Joyce did in 1922. Just as Joycians hold an annual reunion in Joyce country (visiting the many familiar landmarks including the Martello Tower and 7 Eccles Street) on this sacred day in June, so may Capotians eventually gather, with some misgivings, on November 14 in and around River Valley Farm, Holcomb, Kansas. Joyce intended Bloomsday to be an affirmative and epiphanic day; Capote characterized his day as having "blood on the walls."

These two days, as Joyce and Capote presented them, yield paradoxically different impressions: Joyce's seems quite the more real, Capote's the more fictional. Joyce invented his day so thoroughly and convincingly that our disbelief is almost completely suspended. Capote gave his day such elaborate literary trappings that it is difficult to believe he has scrupulously stayed within the bounds of strict reportage. It were almost as if Joyce had written the "nonfiction novel" instead of Capote.

It might be said about Truman Capote that everything he touches turns to literature. He is what the French have fondly referred to as an *écrivain de race*. He is sensitively attuned to what he calls "interior temperatures" (*Paris Review* interview) and "scenery of the mind" (*The Muses Are Heard*). He cannot be anything but "literary" even when he is merely reporting on the capricious tour of a *Porgy and Bess* troupe about to perform in Russia, interviewing Marlon Brando for *The New Yorker*, recording some moment of frozen time in the life of a resident of Brooklyn, New Orleans, Hollywood, or even Haiti. Capote has

Reprinted from "Towards an Aesthetic: Truman Capote's Other Voices," in *Truman Capote's 'In Cold Blood': A Critical Handbook*, ed. Irving Malin (Belmont, Calif.: Wadsworth, 1958), 163–76. Reprinted with permission of the author.

himself indicated in his *Paris Review* interview that there should be no intrinsic stylistic difference between fiction and reportage: ". . . one of the reasons I've wanted to do reportage was to prove that I could apply my style to the realities of journalism."[1] Thus his entire *oeuvre* seems to form a coherent, textural whole—from the early stories like "Miriam" through the recent *In Cold Blood*. Stanley Kauffmann recognized several years ago in his "An Author in Search of a Character" (*The New Republic*, February 23, 1963) that Capote's means of characterization remains the same from the fiction to the reportage: "The characters of Holly Golightly and of Mrs. Gershwin in *The Muses Are Heard* are depicted by, essentially, the same method" (p. 22). *In Cold Blood* reinforces Kauffmann's position—and even extends it.

The unity of Capote's work has had even another dimension. He has achieved a contemporary realization of Horace's celebrated dictum *ut pictura poesis*, with the aid of a kind of pictorial alter ego, Richard Avedon. Avedon's photographs and Capote's inspired captions produced a unique blend of poetry and picture—which would have waylaid the suspicions of even a Lessing or an Irving Babbitt—in their work-of-collaboration, *Observations* (1959). Capote, for example, underscored Avedon's Isak Dinesen: "Imposing creation come forward from one of her own Gothic tales"; and spoke of Avedon's rather bizarre Chaplin as "a horned Pan sprite." Avedon was called upon once again to offer a photographic backdrop for *In Cold Blood* and the result appeared in a seventeen-page spread in *Life* (January 7, 1966) to celebrate the publication of Capote's latest book. This time Capote's words were absent (they were replaced by a canned bit of *Life* "coverage in depth" and a rather corny bit of literary reporting by Jane Howard), but the photographs would do well as an interlinear commentary for a new edition of *In Cold blood*.

Photographs were used to illuminate Capote's text on still another occasion, in his series of "travelogues," *Local Color* (1950). This is more the standard fare and lacks the unique cooperation which produced the later *Observations*—perhaps because Avedon was not involved in this collaborative venture. Still it is evident even here that Capote's prose has a pictorial equivalent and that the lushness of his style is somehow toned down by the sobering quality of the photographs. Capote's love of the near-clichéd image, like "bridge of childhood" and "imagination's earliest landscapes," is redeemed by realistic pictures of existing scenes.[2]

Photography has gained respectability as an art form in the past few years, as has cinema. Capote has also lent his talents to film-making. The script he wrote for *Beat the Devil* is probably better than anything Faulkner or Fitzgerald did during their Hollywood periods. And one should not forget the screenplay he co-authored with William Archibald for *The Innocents* (based on James's *Turn of the Screw*)—with its intriguing angles of cinematic vision—which seems so closely allied to his early stories and to *Other Voices, Other Rooms*. Several reviewers of *In Cold Blood* believe that he learned something from these experiences as they point to the cinematic shape of the book. Dwight Macdonald, writing his monthly film critique in *Esquire* (April 1966), speaks of "the Griffith cross-cutting in the first chapter," "the 'establishing' long shots of the Kansas milieu" (p. 44). Stanley Kauffmann, long-time film critic, remarked that "Capote's structural method can be called cinematic: he uses intercutting of different story strands, intense closeups, flash-backs, traveling shots, background detail, all as if he were fleshing out a scenario" (*The New Republic*, January 22, 1966, p. 19). Capote admits much of this himself when he remarks in his *Paris Review* interview: "I think most of the younger writers have learned and borrowed from the visual, structural side of movie technique. I have" (p. 293).

Several of the more inspired reviewers of *In Cold Blood* realized something else about Capote—that he was now entering a more authentically American tradition of story-telling than any revealed in his earlier work. Malcolm Muggeridge came closest to explaining this: "From Huck to Dick and Perry is quite a span; from Twain to Capote, too, for that matter. If Huck was the beginning of the American Dream, Dick and Perry are perhaps its end" (*Esquire*, April 1966, p. 84). We can now begin using such literary catchphrases as "Adamic myth" to explain Capote, just as we've used them up to now to explain the "great tradition" in American fiction from Cooper to Hawthorne through William Styron.

This brings us face to face with the central ambiguity in Capote's career: his successes and failures rarely seem to have much to do with his intentions. He has always been interested in the untried and the unprecedented both in his life and his work. Thus he told a number of attentive interviewers, following the publication of *In Cold Blood*, that he had invented a new genre to be known henceforth as the "nonfic-tion novel." He admitted a certain priority in Lillian Ross' *Picture* ("a nonfiction novella") and in his own *The Muses Are Heard* ("which uses the techniques of the comic short novel") but stood firm on the essential lines of his discovery. This has had an adverse effect on several reviewers of the book who viewed rather mockingly the assertion that a new literary genre had been uncovered. A sober critic like F. W. Dupee (writing in the February 3, 1966 *New York Review of Books*) was able to see beyond Capote's claim and feel that "whatever its 'genre,' *In Cold Blood* is admirable" (p. 3). But the general feeling was that the author's own view of his accomplishments—as expressed by him too often and at too great length—was seriously out of line with what *In Cold Blood* delivered.[3] It would probably have served Capote's purposes better if he had not insisted so much on the uniqueness of his undertaking and allowed the merits of his book to speak for themselves. In a sense the "public Capote," which has come out repeatedly for originality in his work as well as in his behavior and in his dress, has proved unworthy of the more private Capote who has sustained an impressive body of work over a twenty-year period.

Which brings me to the point of this essay—to prove that Capote is a very traditional writer who has managed admirably in a fictional mode expected of his generation. Like his contemporaries in the South, he has profited a great deal from reading William Faulkner. F. W. Dupee has pointed out how similar the portrait of Perry Smith as a boy ("half-breed child living in a California orphanage") is to Joe Christmas in *Light in August*. We can add to this the photograph of the African wood carving of Holly Golightly's head which opens *Breakfast at Tiffany's* and its uncanny resemblance to the photograph of Caddy Compson which the librarian uncovers in the appendix which precedes Faulkner's *The Sound and the Fury*; in each case the photograph points to a period later than the events of the novel proper and is a revelation of a woman who had passed out of sight several years before. In a more basic way, the division of the characters into tree-dwellers (eccentrics) and ordinary townspeople in *The Grass Harp* is a Faulknerian device: Faulkner used it in *As I Lay Dying* when he distinguished between the eccentric Bundrens, bent upon the burial of Addie, and the townspeople who act as a kind of chorus of "respectability"; we find the same sharp division in "A Rose for Emily" and even, to a lesser extent, in *Light in August* and *Absalom, Absalom!* Irony invariably accompanies the situation, as the author clearly prefers the eccentrics to the *consensus gentium* in each instance. (If Capote had more willingly taken sides in *In Cold Blood* the position might have been the same.[4] Still one feels a sympathy for Perry Smith which one does not feel for Alvin Dewey, even though Dewey's voice of respectability is the last one heard— much like the final pronouncement of the Greek chorus.)

The echoes of Carson McCullers and Eudora Welty have been amply pointed out already.[5] And Capote has been grouped on several occasions with Frederick Buechner and William Goyen.[6] A few words might be said about the links with Flannery O'Connor and William Styron. A story like "Jug of Silver" is very close to the tone of false evangelism and prophecy which runs through the novels and stories of Miss O'Connor. There is a clear connection, for example, between Appleseed's claim, in the Capote story, that he was "born with a caul on my head" and Enoch Emery's belief, in Flannery O'Connor's *Wise Blood*, that he came into the world with "wise blood." Willie-Jay, in *In Cold Blood* (whose name Capote admits he has invented), resembles in many ways the "Bible Belt" preachers of Flannery O'Connor, both in name (think of Onnie Jay Holy in *Wise Blood*), and in evangelical manner. And Truman Capote is careful to identify the region about which he is writing: "A hundred miles west and one would be out of the 'Bible Belt,' that gospel-haunted strip of American territory in which a man must, if only for business reasons, take his religion with the straightest of faces, but in Finney County one is still within the Bible Belt borders."[7] Despite the differences in geographical locale—most of Capote's fiction occurs in the South or involves displaced Southerners living in New York City—the Kansas Capote writes about is not significantly different from Flannery O'Connor country. Another O'Connor reminder in *In Cold Blood* is when we are told (p. 212) that Perry Smith's sister Fern changed her name to Joy when she turned fourteen: several of Miss O'Connor's characters undergo name changes, including Joy with the Ph.D. ("Good Country People") who perversely changes her name to Hulga.

It should be made clear before we continue that the connections which involve *In Cold Blood* are largely fortuitous. Truman Capote was very insistent in his *New York Times* interview with George Plimpton on his "factual accuracy" and on his refusal to "give way to minor distortions." Despite the convincing claims of unreliability put forth by Phillip K. Tompkins in his "In Cold Fact" (*Esquire*, June 1966), we must still believe in the essential authenticity and integrity of Capote's account. Yet even a "reporter"—especially one of Capote's temperament—will usually compromise his "reportorial distance" in favor of elements borrowed from his own reading and culture. Hence Faulkner and Flannery O'Connor have found their way through the back door of *In Cold Blood*.

The connections between Styron and Capote are less exact than those we have been looking at. They have in common a sense of the inviolability of style, and their metaphors have a way of straining towards eloquence. One has a Gallic sense of *de trop* when faced with their more extended imagery. Thus a sentence of Styron like "In the morbid, comfortless light they were like classical Greek masks, made of chrome or tin, reflecting an almost theatrical disharmony"[8] could easily have been written by Capote. On the very first page of *In Cold Blood* he speaks of "a white cluster of grain elevators rising as gracefully as Greek temples." Styron's image, in reference to marines on a forced march, seems as inappropriate, at first glance, as Capote's view of the western Kansas countryside; but the suggestive power of the figures has a way of dilating the experience into myth.

We notice from various interviews with Styron and Capote that they have marked similarities in reading tastes and habits. Their sense of craft, for example, makes *Madame Bovary* an essential book. Thus Styron writes in his *Paris Review* interview: "*Madame Bovary* is one of the few novels that moves me in every way, not only in its style, but in its total communicability, like the effect of good poetry" (*Writers at Work*, p. 274). Capote is less poetical on the subject; he told Jeanine Delpech, ". . . je relis tous les ans *Madame Bovary*" (*Nouvelles Litéraires*, April 12, 1962, p. 10).

It should be no surprise that these *bovaryistes* are well received in France. Almost all of their work is available in French translation. Capote has had the benefit (like Styron with *Set This House on Fire*) of M. E. Coindreau's always sensitive renderings of his prose. Capote joins Faulkner, Flannery O'Connor, and other American novelists who have profited from Coindreau's inspired translations and commentary.

We can then begin to speak of a Franco-American Capote in a double sense. His reputation is at least as assured in France as it is in America, and he has himself been responsive to the French tradition in the novel from Flaubert on. In fact, it seems to me that any discussion of his work from *Other Voices, Other Rooms* through *In Cold Blood* would profit from a consideration of the French novel from Alain-Fournier's *Le Grand Meaulnes* (1913) through the *nouveau roman*. This tradition in French fiction should serve as an apt metaphor for Capote's entire career. The Italian novelist Alberto Moravia[9] and the French critic and translator Michel Mohrt[10] have already suggested a kinship between Alain-Fournier's novel and the early Capote. Fournier and Capote both partake of a Proustian magic-lantern-of-childhood atmosphere. (Jeanine Delpech quotes Capote as saying "je plonge voluptueusement dans Proust" and speaks of "le fantôme de Proust" hovering over him.)

Le Grand Meaulnes and *Other Voices* are examples of a genre which Fournier's close friend and brother-in-law, Jacques Rivière, has christened *roman d'aventure*. Both novels involve elaborate itineraries into the unknown. Augustin Meaulnes, Fournier's seventeen-year-old hero, has spent a miraculous evening at a palatial manor in the company of a certain Yvonne de Galais. He subsequently devotes all his attentions to recapturing this experience, but in spite of his uncovering of most of the mystery he never manages to recreate the "moment of being" he has irreparably lost. Meaulnes asks the question of the narrator, Seurel, "But how could a man, who had once leapt at one bound into Paradise, get used to living like everybody else?" He says a page later: "I was at the height of what stands for perfection and pure motive in anyone's heart, a height I shall never reach again."[11] There is only a thin line separating the world of Sainte-Agathe School, which offers the hero a here-and-now *point de repère*, and the world of Meaulnes' "Lost Land."

Joel Knox of *Other Voices, Other Rooms* is a somewhat younger and more effeminate Augustin Meaulnes. His "Lost Land" is Skully's Landing. He voyages there to find his father, but finds instead the wreck of a man whose only occupation is bouncing red tennis balls down the stairs. Like Meaulnes, Joel uncovers the mystery of his "Lost Land" but must settle for a reality in every way inferior to his dream. Joel has a caricatured Yvonne de Galais in the tomboy Idabel Thompkins— whom he finally loses to the dwarf Miss Wisteria. Consumed finally by "a sleepwalker's pattern of jigsaw incidents," Joel must settle for the transvestite Cousin Randolph and accept his world and "the zero of his nothingness" (a phrase from *Other Voices* which could easily have been written by Samuel Beckett or Roland Barthes). Joel's *roman d'aventure* ends on the same note of resigned despair as Augustin Meaulnes'.

Other Voices, Other Rooms must have seemed very old-fashioned when it appeared in 1948, especially in the manner of its telling. Many of the experiments with point of view and displacement of chronology had already been tried and Capote seems to have completely ignored them. He stays with the standard omniscient author of nineteenth-century fiction and tells a story which naively conforms to clock time. *Other Voices, Other Rooms* could easily have been published in 1913 (the year of *Le Grand Meaulnes*), but even then it would have been declared old-fashioned next to Proust's *Du côté de chez Swann* which appeared the same year.

Capote's next novel, *The Grass Harp* (1951), shows no advance in technique. There is, however, an important change in narrative: the story is told by one of the active participants, Collin Fenwick, another of Capote's adolescents. His is also a *roman d'aventure* which wavers uncomfortably between reality and the dreamworld. The temporary inhabitants of the tree house defy reality in much the same way that Joel Knox and Augustin Meaulnes did. The symbolism is not really so different: Collin and his companions look to the tree house as Joel did the Cloud Hotel and Meaulnes the lost manor house. The first-person telling, however, gives *The Grass Harp* an immediacy and colloquial nearness which *Other Voices* and *Le Grand Meaulnes* do not have.

Capote's third novel, *Breakfast at Tiffany's* (1958), is perhaps his most Jamesian work. The narrator, again a participant in the story although this time more a detached onlooker, has early counterparts in James's garrulous "posts of observation" and Fitzgerald's Nick Carraway. Once more we are faced with the old-fashioned story-teller in Capote, this time with some mild tampering with chronology—at least to the extent that we first hear of Holly Golightly, the main character, at a period later than the events of the narrative. *Breakfast at Tiffany's* has virtually nothing of the *roman d'aventure* of the two earlier novels but has much of the urban chic of a later tradition of French fiction which would include the Paris-centered novels of Gide (especially *Les Faux-Monnayeurs*), Roger Martin du Gard, Georges Duhamel, and perhaps Jean Cocteau. Françoise Sagan is probably at the end of this line and indeed Holly Golightly could easily be a Sagan heroine. The French have always been fond of the "up from the provinces" motif from *Le Rouge et le noir* on; and Capote has offered us, in *Breakfast at Tiffany's*, a female counterpart of Julien Sorel, Frédéric Moreau, and others, in the sense that Holly Golightly has confronted the urban scene with a vengeance and turned her back on her own provincial and backwoods origins. She has mastered the vocabulary of her new setting, with its many gallicisms. Yet there is something authentic about her language (which is the reverse of what René Etiemble has recently called *franglais*) and her modish behavior; this quality is captured in a remark of one of the other characters: "She isn't a phony because she's a *real* phony."

The short stories which Capote has been turning out since the early 1940's are thematically very close to the novels. The narrative devices are traditional. Most of them resemble in compactness and tightness of style the stories of Flannery O'Connor, Eudora Welty, and Katherine Anne Porter. The settings, as in the novels, are Southern or involve displaced persons living in New York City—all part of that diaspora which has experienced the bitter-sweet taste of exile. There is as much in the stories of what Irving Malin has aptly called "new American gothic" as in the novels. Chance meetings in a train ("A Tree of Night"), at a cemetery ("Among the Paths to Eden"), in a painting gallery ("The Headless Hawk"), in a neighborhood moviehouse ("Miriam") produce dire psychological consequences for the unsuspecting and innocent. The invasion of experience upon innocence (as in James's *Turn of the Screw*) is one of the central themes of the stories—with the ironical twist that children are often the experienced, adults the innocent.

These stories may have no precise equivalents in France, the way the novels clearly do. Capote's intermittent attempts at reportage, however, fit the French tradition I have been talking about. Most French novelists regard it as their solemn obligation to contribute to the day-to-day workings of the world by sounding a journalistic note. It is not surprising to pick up an issue of *Le Figaro* or *Le Monde* or any of the French weeklies and monthlies and find an editorial by an established writer. Sartre, for example, has his own journalistic and critical voice listened to regularly and attentively in the pages of *Les Temps Modernes*. Camus used the clandestine newspaper *Combat* for the same editorial purposes. There is no precise counterpart now in this country. In fact, most writers shy away from this kind of commitment. Capote is one of the rare American authors who believes in the value of reportage and remains convinced of its artistic possibilities.

The New Yorker has offered him the same literary haven as Sartre finds in *Les Temps Modernes*. He published his Marlon Brando "profile" ("The Duke in His Domain") and *The Muses Are Heard* in its pages. Michel Mohrt, who has elsewhere in *Le Nouveau Roman Américain* written perceptively about Capote, says about *The New Yorker:* "Ils se contentent d'en souligner les ridicules" (p. 255). Capote's portraits of Mrs. Ira Gershwin, Leonard Lyons, and the Ira Wolferts in *The Muses Are Heard* and the sustained "profile" of Brando ("just a young man sitting on a pile of candy") offer a systematic underplaying, in a very low key, of emotional frailty. Capote follows the formula for the "nonfiction novel," which he suggested to George Plimpton, that "the author should not appear in the work." Thus the Brando portrait, particularly, reminds one of the method of another of *The New Yorker*'s faithful, Lillian Ross; we are especially reminded of her famous Hemingway "profile" with its subtle ambiguities. Capote and Lillian

Ross have virtually invented in the pages of *The New Yorker* a new "school" of reportage built on a sensitive ear for the incongruous and depending on the correct measure of attentive eavesdropping.

The other kind of reporting Capote has done has acknowledged his "sense of place" (an expression Frederick J. Hoffman has accurately used in reference to recent Southern writing).[12] Most of his pieces in this genre, which read like tone poems, have been collected in *Local Color* (1950). They are brief sketches of places like Hollywood, Brooklyn, New Orleans, Haiti, and Tangier. The manner is not far from the Baudelaire of *Les Petits poèmes en prose*. Mark Schorer's expression "people in places" (in his introduction to the Modern Library *Selected Writings of Truman Capote*) explains how Capote's descriptions of landscapes are continually crowded by his "profiles" of anonymous people.

Capote has been mixing his reportage with his fiction through most of his career. Many of the reviewers noticed the two converging in *In Cold Blood*. Jack Kroll, writing in the January 24, 1966, *Newsweek*, saw something timely in the method: "In its refusal to analyze, to make judgments, *In Cold Blood* is supercontemporary. This is the attitude of the new international avant-garde—of the French 'anti-novelists' who with bland obsessiveness describe only the surface of reality" (p. 60). Indeed the *nouveau roman* has many techniques in common with *In Cold Blood*. Just as *Other Voices, Other Rooms* had an uncanny resemblance to *Le Grand Meaulnes* and *Breakfast at Tiffany's* had much in common with the French city novel written between the two world wars, so does Capote's book of 1966 seem more than passingly related to the post-war novels of Alain Robbe-Grillet, Nathalie Sarraute, Michel Butor, and Samuel Beckett.

The first point of comparison is the use of the mock-detective motif. Sartre has already defined this genre, in his famous preface to Nathalie Sarraute's *Portrait d'un inconnu*, as "an anti-novel that reads like a detective story." He further elaborated on this by saying; ". . . it is a parody on the novel of 'quest' into which the author has introduced a sort of impassioned amateur detective who becomes fascinated . . . by virtue of a sort of thought transference, without ever knowing very well either what he is after or what they are." Thus we find Robbe-Grillet's Wallas (*Les Gommes*) and Mathias (*Le Voyeur*) turning into implausible murderers. Nathalie Sarraute's "detectives" pursue clueless paths in her novels, and the accustomed detective motif always falls gracefully to pieces. The most revealing instance of all is probably Michel Butor's *L'Emploi du temps* in which the protagonist becomes obsessed with a murder novel he has just read about the English city which he has been inhabiting for a year. He manages to piece together an elaborate crime story, based ingeniously but inaccurately on details from the murder novel and incidents from his own experience. But his theories prove as ineffectual as those of Sarraute's heroes. Each of Beckett's novels is in one way or another "a parody on the novel of 'quest'" and his "detectives" always fail to solve crimes which have not been committed.

Even though *In Cold Blood* bears as its subtitle "A True Account of a Multiple Murder and Its Consequences," it is not automatically exempt from Sartre's fictional category. There are a variety of false leads and clueless paths exploited by Capote with particular relish. Thus he shows a peculiar interest in a certain Jonathan Daniel Adrian who turns out to have nothing to do with the Clutter murders; he dotes on Adrian more as a novelist than as a reporter of a crime would do. Capote goes out of his way to pursue a jagged course rather than the rectilinear one of a Georges Simenon or an Agatha Christie (both of whose serious detective novels have been linked to the mock-detective writings of the *nouveau roman*).

The method of uncovering the murderers in *In Cold Blood* also smacks of the mock-detective. Although Capote seems to have enormous respect for Alvin Dewey and his men, he is still not above suggesting that their methods were unavailing in capturing Smith and Hickock; he gives them credit for a variety of false leads and repeated, if honest, blunders. If Floyd Wells, an inmate of the Kansas State Penitentiary, had not revealed what he knew, the solving of the murder might have been delayed indefinitely. This is perfect *nouveau roman*: the detective is the last one to solve the crime and needs the help of a criminal in doing so.

The question of the imaginary Clutter safe with the imaginary money is vintage mock-detective. This touch is worthy of the "new novelists" who generally use the criminal investigation as a flimsy substitute for plot and action.

But probably nothing is quite so revealing as Capote's portrait of Perry Smith. He is clearly not the stock figure of crime fiction—Dick Hickock is closer to that. Several reviewers have even pointed out Perry's proximity to the *poète maudit*, almost as if Capote reinvented him to make him the implausible murderer that he is. Certain things about him, as Jack Kroll remarked in *Newsweek*, "fit uncannily into the pattern of Capote's previous fiction." Thus his collection of souvenirs and trinkets reminds us of Joel Knox's obsession "to keep and catalogue trifles." Perry's dream of "the yellow bird, huge and parrot-faced" is not unlike the bluejay Joel sees, after he arrives at the Landing, which seems almost to be "a curious fragment of his dream." Perry's urgency about correcting people's grammar also has an echo in Joel: ". . . he took odd pleasure in bringing to attention a slip of grammar on anyone's part."[13] Perry's devotion to his guitar reminds us of Tico Feo in Capote's short story "A Diamond Guitar."

All of these concerns of Perry Smith, beyond recalling earlier Capote works, succeed in making him an unlikely candidate for murder and eventual hanging, at least in the conventional detective-story sense. Although Capote is giving us a "true account" in *In Cold Blood*, he is still using his material in a very special way, in a way—as I suggested—to recall the devices of the *nouveau roman*. Just as Robbe-Grillet, Butor, Nathalie Sarraute, and Beckett are preoccupied with certain objects which keep recurring in their fiction, so does Capote keep reintroducing certain things. The Chinese elms which line the Clutters' driveway is such an example. The references to snow perhaps offer an even more poignant example. We are told, periodically, through the first three sections of *In Cold Blood* that the snow was late in coming that year to Kansas. The suggestion is that it was awaiting the capture of the criminals for, Capote tells us, it began to fall almost immediately following the arraignment of Smith and Hickock. The author dramatically saves this mention until the final words of Part 3: ". . . the miraculous autumn departed too; the year's first snow began to fall" (p. 280). Snow is everywhere in Capote's work, as most of his critics have already reminded us; a good example would be *Other Voices*, in which Zoo flees north to Washington, D.C., to find it; another is the lyrics to the song "I Never Has Seen Snow" which Capote wrote for the Broadway musical version of *House of Flowers* (based on one of his short stories).

The references to the Chinese elms and snow in *In Cold Blood* serve much the same purpose as the repeated references to the centipede (*La Jalousie*), the figure eight (*Le Voyeur*), the eraser (*Les Gommes*) in Robbe-Grillet. They serve as almost musical reminders and help to enrich the texture of the prose. Like Robbe-Grillet, Capote has worked in art forms other than literature. His cinematic experiences, for example, are quite like Robbe-Grillet's, although his work on *Beat the Devil* and *The Innocents* is scarcely comparable to Robbe-Grillet's vitally experimental *L'Année dernière à Marienbad* and *L'Immortelle*. Robbe-Grillet called his films *ciné-romans*, and indeed we are supposed to get a sense of the convergence of cinema and novel when we view them. *Marienbad* and *L'Immortelle* are clearly expansions on his career as a novelist and use many of the same devices. We shall recall now how Stanley Kauffmann and Dwight Macdonald found unmistakable cinematic signs in *In Cold Blood*. One has a strong sense of unreeling film as one reads the book; it seems in many ways the literary equivalent of montage just as so many of Robbe-Grillet's novels do.

Robbe-Grillet has spoken out, on several occasions, for the need of a new sense of space in fiction. He has dwelt on surface effects in his own novels and has come out strongly in an early essay for ". . . the complete rejection of the old myths of *profondeur*, or depth of meaning in objects." He has been intent on destroying the image of the novel as a "time-art" and reestablishing it spatially.[14] Capote does not go as far as Robbe-Grillet, but he does seem interested in exploiting the reality of surfaces and fragmenting time in *In Cold Blood*. Some of the breathlessness of the book is doubtless due to Capote's concern with juxtaposing the parts of his narrative to give the illusion of simultaneity. Thus we have the sense of many things going on at the same time, in a kind of continuing present. The Clutter murder hovers over the narrative just as vividly and immediately at the time of Hickock and Smith's execution in April 1965 as it did in November 1959. *In Cold Blood* seems to be without a past tense, as do most of the novels of Robbe-Grillet and Butor.

One of Capote's procedures for gaining this effect is in his skilled manipulation of point of view. He tries to present the events through as many eyes as possible. He sets up, as James said in his Preface to *The Wings of the Dove*, "successive centres" who manipulate the point of view. Capote allows us to see Hickock and Smith (again quoting from James's Preface) "through the successive windows of other people's interest." Thus the final point of view of *In Cold Blood* is that of Alvin Dewey, who wanders through the cemetery which houses the graves of the Clutters. Capote has turned over the final pages of his book to Dewey because he is probably in the best position to cast the final symbolical note. The scene described is not unlike that which ends Turgenev's *Fathers and Sons* (Capote lists Turgenev among his "enthusiasms that remain constant" in his *Paris Review* interview) when the old parents, in a most pastoral and elegiac sequence, visit the grave of their nihilist son, Bazarov. The alliterative final words of *In Cold*

Blood permanently freeze the experience: ". . . the whisper of wind voices in the wind-bent wheat." (There are reminders also of Joyce's "The Dead" in this final scene and especially in its alliterative ending.)

The view of Capote which I have expressed here—partly using as a metaphor the French convention in the novel from *Le Grand Meaulnes* through the *nouveau roman*—is of a writer who is very tradition-bound. His claim to having invented a new literary form, "the nonfiction novel," matters less than what he has accomplished in the last twenty years when he has consistently turned base metal into literature. He has brought the various art forms together harmoniously in his own work, using some of the devices of cinema, photography, and reportage to great advantage. His own writing gently holds up the mirror to what is being accomplished artistically around him. Capote likes to think of himself as being in advance of his contemporaries; it is probably more accurate to say that he is wonderfully in step with them.

Notes

1. *Writers at Work: The "Paris Review" Interviews*, ed. Malcolm Cowley (New York: Viking, 1959), p. 291. All references will be to this edition.

2. We might mention also the slick photograph-caption piece Capote collaborated in: "The Sylvia Odyssey—Photographs with (Handwritten) Comment, *Vogue*, January 15, 1966.

3. One of the interesting footnotes to the reception of *In Cold Blood* is the uncanny way literary history has a way of repeating itself. Walter Allen suggested the connection in his "London Letter" (*New York Times Book Review*, April 10, 1966): "It [*In Cold Blood*] reached us with the biggest fanfare of publicity that has accompanied any American book since *By Love Possessed*." *By Love Possessed* was faring remarkably well with the literary press in America until Dwight Macdonald took to dissecting Cozzens' style in the January 1958 *Commentary* and Irving Howe proceeded to close the lid on Cozzens' coffin in a now-famous review in the January 20, 1958 *New Republic*; Howe started out with his usual directness: "*By Love Possessed* is a mediocre and pretentious novel written by an experienced craftsman." Eight years later an inflatedly advertised *In Cold Blood* received a similar fate at the hands of *The New Republic*, whose reviewer, this time Stanley Kauffmann, took delight in deflating the Capote myth: "Are we so bankrupt, so avid for novelty that, merely because a famous writer produces an amplified magazine crime-feature, the result is automatically elevated to serious literature . . . ?" His proved not to be a lonely voice, as Macdonald's and Howe's were in 1958, and he was promptly joined by Sol Yurick (*The Nation*, February 7, 1966), Edward Weeks (*The*

Atlantic, March 1966), William Phillips (*Commentary*, May 1966), Dwight Macdonald (*Esquire*, April 1966). 3

4. Capote insisted in every interview on a Flaubertian detachment. Thus he told George Plimpton: ". . . for the nonfiction-novel form to be entirely successful, the author should not appear in the work" (*New York Times Book Review*, January 16, 1966, p. 38).

5. See especially Mark Schorer, "McCullers and Capote: Basic Patterns," in *The Creative Present: Notes on Contemporary American Fiction*, ed. Nona Balakian and Charles Simmons (Garden City, N.Y.: Doubleday, 1963); see also Frank Baldanza, "Plato in Dixie," *Georgia Review*, XII (Summer 1958). Paul Levine, in his excellent "Truman Capote: The Revelation of the Broken Image," *Virginia Quarterly Review*, XXXIV (Autumn 1958), points out the similarity between Eudora Welty's "Why I Live at the P.O." and Capote's "My Side of the Matter."

6. John W. Aldridge has a fine chapter, "Capote and Buechner: The Escape into Otherness," in his *After The Lost Generation* (New York: Noonday Press, 1958). Chester E. Eisinger likens Capote to Goyen in his *Fiction of the Forties* (Chicago: University of Chicago Press, 1963). Michel Mohrt places Capote and Goyen in a similar literary climate in his *Nouveau Roman Américain* (Paris: Gallimard, 1955). Finally, Ihab Hassan's *Radical Innocence* (Princeton University Press, 1961) is indispensable in this area.

7. *In Cold Blood* (New York: New American Library, 1967), p. 46. All references will be to this edition.

8. *The Long March* (New York: Random House, 1952), p. 29.

9. "Two American Writers," *Sewanee Review*, LXVIII (Summer 1960), pp. 480–481.

10. *Le Nouveau Roman Américain* (Paris: Gallimard, 1955), pp. 232–233. All references will be to this edition.

11. *The Wanderer*, tr. from the French *Le Grand Meaulnes* by Françoise Delisle (New York: New Directions, 1928), pp. 211, 212.

12. See his "The Sense of Place," in *South: Modern Southern Literature in Its Cultural Setting*, ed. Louis D. Rubin, Jr. and Robert D. Jacobs (Garden City, N.Y.: Doubleday, 1961).

13. *Other Voices, Other Rooms* (New York: New American Library, 1960), pp. 27, 26, 9.

14. The best book on Robbe-Grillet is Bruce Morrissette's *Les Romans de Robbe-Grillet* (Paris: Les Editions de Minuit, 1963). See also his very useful booklet, *Alain Robbe-Grillet* (1965), in the Columbia Essays on Modern Writers. I am personally indebted to Professor Morrissette for certain ideas in this essay connecting Truman Capote with Alain Robbe-Grillet.

Peter Hays

Truman Capote's short story "Among the Paths to Eden" treats the theme of death and spiritual rebirth suggested by the title and graveyard setting. The heroine, Mary O'Meaghan, is a spinster of nearly forty, whose life had been devoted to her father. But he is now dead and she, on the advice of a "practical" friend, is seeking a husband among the widowers she meets in a nearby cemetery, men who she hopes miss the comforts of a well-kept, well-cooked-for home. The man she confronts in this story is Ivor Belli, who has finally paid a grudging visit to his not terribly lamented wife's grave. It is a Saturday in March, "a hard winter had just passed," and the day is adorned with "handsome, spring-prophesying weather." As a token of the season, Mr. Belli brings jonquils to his wife's grave. Here . . . early spring flowers suggest rebirth, renewal; jonquils are especially appropriate since they are a variety of narcissus, named for the beautiful Greek youth who took his own life but was reborn as the flower.

Mary and Ivor talk, share her peanuts, and sit on the gravestone, though the very invitation to do so causes Mary to blush "as though he'd asked her to transform Mrs. Belli's bier into a love bed." One of her difficulties in finding a husband, besides her age and plain looks, is that she is crippled: her left leg will not bend. "An accident. You know. When I was a kid. I fell off a roller coaster at Coney. . . . Nobody knows why I'm alive." Like the Man Who Died, she has returned from death, entombed not for three days but for most of her life. And though she fails to interest Belli enough for him to wish to marry her, she does, like the Man Who Died, cause a renewal of life.

Her pleasant conversation, her reminiscences of times past, her very person make Belli feel younger and more alive: "'. . . I'm fifty-one' he said, subtracting four years. 'Can't say I feel it.' And he didn't;

Excerpted and reprinted from *The Limping Hero* (New York: New York University Press, 1971), 42–44, 88–89. Reprinted with permission of the author. Original page citations have been deleted.

perhaps it was because the wind had subsided, the warmth of the sun grown more authentic. Whatever the reason, his expectations had re-ignited, he was again immortal, a man planning ahead." He begins to think with more nostalgia of his past marriage, remembering the pleasant aspects of it, and wishes he had brought his wife, instead of jonquils, orchids like those she had saved after their daughters' dates and "stored in the icebox until they shriveled." With an increasing sense of vigor and rejuvenation—"clouds were fewer, the sun exceedingly visible" —he decides to take his secretary to dinner, to buy her an orchid, a flower named in Greek "testicle," appropriate to his resurging sense of masculinity. "And where, he wondered, do couples honeymoon in April? At latest May."

Lame Miss O'Meaghan has played the part of Pan: she has ushered in the spring, Ivor Belli's second. She brings no new life to herself, no renewed fertility, but Mr. Belli she brings to a "hopeful, zestful, life-forever mood."

. . . Truman Capote used maiming to suggest fertility in "Among the Paths to Eden"; he used it for the opposite purpose in his first novel, *Other Voices, Other Rooms* (1948). There Edward Sansom's physical paralysis symbolizes the state of all in Skully's landing: the wasted lives of Zoo and Jesus Fever; of homosexual, transvestite Randolph; of Randolph's sister [sic] Amy, who marries and spends her life caring for Sansom, the man her brother shot. The paralysis affects most severely Joel Knox, Sansom's son and the protagonist of this story of initiation. Joel's loss in wrestling to tomboy Idabel and his cut buttock foreshadow his emasculation as she takes his sword from him to protect him from the menacing snake, and his acceptance of sexual inversion as he prepares at the novel's end to enter the bedroom of his bewigged and begowned cousin. His maturity bears with it the realization that the decay of Skully's landing and the Cloud Hotel affects all their lives. The pain and disillusion that have blighted the lives of all the characters await him as well.

Michael J. Larsen

Truman Capote's short story "Miriam" appears regularly in anthologies as a contemporary example of fantastic literature. Critical notice of this story of the double or *Dopplegänger* has been rather scant; however, it is an accomplished piece of fiction that rewards careful study. Capote handles the device of the double with tact and authority, and we can appreciate his skill in portraying the encounter with a second self by comparing "Miriam" with other well-known stories of the double.

In the first place, the double in "Miriam" conveys an impression of objective reality that is rare for double stories. It is true that Miriam has no last name, is not seen by others, asserts suggestively (about the movies) that "I've never *been* before" (italics supplied), and seems to emerge at the end of the story from Mrs. Miller's reverie; however, the two meet in an ordinary public place, young Miriam has her own assortment of clothes and possessions, and she comes from the home of an old man who makes a brief appearance in the story. Thus, the double in "Miriam" is as much a character as a subjective phenomenon, which distinguishes the story from those where the *Doppelgänger* is obviously a figure of fantasy or hallucination (as, for example, Gogol's "The Nose" or Andersen's "The Shadow") or is clearly an allegorical figure embodying a psychological or moral aspect of the protagonist (as, for example, Stevenson's *Dr. Jekyll and Mr. Hyde*).

Capote, then, plays down the usual gothic and supernatural elements surrounding "the other" in the interests of verisimilitude. At first, we see Mrs. Miller, the kindly and ineffectual adult trying to help and understand an increasingly bold and self-assertive young girl. Only later do we sense that the older woman is experiencing a terrifying encounter with a repressed and stunted self. The ambiguous nature of the double figure adds to the uncanny quality of the narrative and to the thematic possibilities inherent in the relationship between Mrs. Miller and Miriam. In this respect, "Miriam" has an affinity with very

Reprinted from "Capote's 'Miriam' and the Literature of the Double," *International Fiction Review* 7, no.1 (1980): 53–54. Reprinted with permission of the author.

complex double stories, such as Hoffmann's *The Devil's Elixir* and Dostoevsky's *The Double*, which use the double motif to explore both extraordinary interpersonal relationships and psychological decomposition.

If the double figure is not a transparent authorial device whose significance is fixed and evident, the important question is the one asked by Mrs. Miller—"Why has she come?" At the beginning of the story Mrs. Miller's personality and character are so bland that she seems to have effaced herself from life altogether. In fact, she is described almost completely in negative terms: she lives "alone," is a "widow," her interests are "narrow," she has "no friends," has "rarely journeyed," was "never noticed," and so on.

Then she meets young Miriam, whose ethereal beauty and spontaneity bring a much-needed ray of light and gaiety into Mrs. Miller's drab world. The effect is almost magical. In the days following Miriam's first visit, Mrs. Miller feels exhilarated, goes on a shopping spree, dreams of leading a procession that has overtones of a fertility rite, and, in general, strays from the paths of thought and action that she has followed for years. In other words, initial contact with the rather exotic and mysterious Miriam taps a totally unexpected reserve of joy and imagination in the aging window.

Later in the story, Miriam's mysterious and uncanny attributes are given greater prominence so that we begin to see her not only as a strange young girl, but also as a double figure, the suppressed self that Mrs. Miller must confront and cope with. The transformation from elf-child to *Doppelgänger* brings about a dramatic change in the story's mood. Miriam becomes eerie, threatening, and wildly self-indulgent; consequently, Mrs. Miller's gaiety is replaced by paralyzing fear and torpor in her presence. Furthermore, images of flowers, bridal dresses, and sweets give way to cobwebs, skeletons, and funeral processions, while the seemingly endless images of white—white dresses, white flowers, white hair, and so on—begin "to appall," as Frost puts it in "Design."

Miriam's changing role and impact emphasize the disastrous consequences of life deferred too long. Once fully awakened, the long-dormant energies of Mrs. Miller quickly elude her attempts at conscious control and vehemently assert themselves as an autonomous and independent personality. The result is psychological disintegration, withdrawal from reality, and obsession with the demands and frustrations of the "other" or "hidden" self. Our final view of Mrs. Miller reveals an isolated and shattered woman passively succumbing to the double whose power over her is now complete.

Miriam, the frost flower that blooms in the autumn of Mrs. Miller's life, is, in other words, not only a child who refuses to be sent away, but also the hidden self that refuses to be suppressed any longer. Tragically, Mrs. Miller is unable to cope with this belated discovery of a vital and unsuspected self, especially since it forces her to recognize the utter vacancy of her past life. Thus, what seemed a step towards personal expression and vital contact with the outside world (that is, the meeting with a homeless, friendless young girl) turns out to be the prologue to psychological decomposition, obsession, and despair.

The double figure emerges into Mrs. Miller's life, then, shattering its placid surface and indicating depths of personality long suppressed and unacknowledged. This, of course, is the kind of experience we expect in a double story. Capote's contribution to the literature of the double can be seen in the way he deftly creates and maintains an aura of actuality about Miriam while he insinuates her function as a *Dopplegänger*. This ambiguity intensifies the mysterious atmosphere of the story, renders the double figure much more solid and threatening than is often the case when we are obviously dealing the hallucination or allegory, and allows for a surprising and moving reversal in the protagonist's life as the full truth about Mrs. Miller's "visitor" is gradually revealed. In other words, Capote injects new life into the double story and demonstrates dramatically the truth of Guerard's assertion that "We traffic with doubles at our peril."[1]

Note

1. Albert J. Guerard, "Concepts of the Double," in *Stories of the Double*, ed. Albert J. Guerard (New York and Philadelphia: J. B. Lippincott Company, 1967), 8.

Paul Levine

The inclusion of Truman Capote in any discussion that pretends to be at most scholarly and at least literary is usually frowned upon by the more stern-faced of our critics. The mention of his name conjures up images of a wispish, effete soul languishing on an ornate couch, emitting an ether of preciousness and very little else. The reaction to the amazing success of his early books, *Other Voices, Other Rooms* and *A Tree of Night,* has relegated Capote to the position of a clever, cute, coy, commercial, and definitely minor figure in contemporary literature, whose reputation has been built less on a facility of style than on an excellent advertising campaign. Even an earnest supporter would have to admit that Capote's stories tiptoe the tenuous line between the precious and the serious.

Yet the attacks on Capote seem more personal than literary. Critics like John Aldridge—whose essay appears in *After the Lost Generation,* a book that generally has little good to say about anyone (except Mr. Aldridge)—have blatantly confused the author's private life with his literary ability. The notion—as fantastic as any of Capote's stories—that Capote's style comes too easily is an excellent example. Not only is the banner of the tortured writer rather tattered by now but in Capote's case the charge of a "natural style" is false. His first stories—"These Walls Are Cold" and "The Shape of Things"—are written in the painfully realistic prose associated with those young writers in transition from the *Saturday Evening Post* to the *New Yorker.* Moreover, Capote is really no more precocious than a number of our outstanding writers. J. D. Salinger published his first story at twenty-one and Carson McCullers had written two novels before she was twenty-four. As with the legend surrounding Fitzgerald, critics have a difficult time discerning Capote from his work, a slight not only to the author but to the critic. Mr. Capote is no more an *enfant terrible* than Mr. Aldridge is.

Reprinted from "Truman Capote: The Revelation of the Broken Image," *Virginia Quarterly Review* 34 (Autumn 1958); 600–17. Reprinted with permission.

Perhaps the most frequent criticism leveled at Capote's work is that he is limited in scope and remote from life. While it is true that Capote writes fantastic and grotesque stories, it is not necessarily true that these stories, because of their genre, must be remote from life. In many ways, Capote has chosen the most universal medium in which to present his thematic material, because the genre of the fantasy, evolving from the day dream, the fairy tale, and the tall tale, is among the oldest and most elemental of fictional forms.

While we must acknowledge Capote's admission that "style is the mirror of an artist's sensibility—more so than the *content* of his work," we must also recognize that there is no dearth of content in his work. To understand that content fully we must first posit some very elemental points, because Capote is to a great extent an erudite writer about primal things. At the heart of his writing is the dichotomy in the world between good and evil, the daylight and the nocturnal, man and nature, and between the internal and external manifestation of things. As Harry Levin has pointed out in a different context:

> This takes us back to the very beginning of things, the primal darkness, the void that God shaped by creating light and dividing night from day. That division underlies the imagery of the Bible from Genesis to the Apocalypse, and from the word of life to the shadow of death. It is what differentiates the children of light from the children of darkness in the Dead Sea Scrolls.
>
> . . . But all religions, in accounting for the relation of the earth to the sun and for the diurnal and seasonal cycles, seem to posit some dichotomy, such as the Yin and the Yang of the Orient or the twin paths of the Bhagavad-Gita.

The dichotomy of good and evil exists in each Capote character just as the dichotomy of daylight and nighttime exists in the aggregate of his stories. We might almost say that Capote's stories inhabit two worlds—that of the realistic, colloquial, often humorous daytime and that of the dreamlike, detached, and inverted nocturnal world. This double identity must be viewed with a double vision because Capote stories can be interpreted either psychologically or as an expression of a spiritual or moral problem. In either case, whether the story be realistic or fantastic, the central focus is on the moment of initiation and the central character is either adolescent or innocent.

One way to distinguish the daylight from the nocturnal tales is to note the hero's position in relation to his private world and the public world. In the daylight stories the movement is out towards the world while in the darker tales the hero tends to move away from the world and in towards his inner Id or soul or imagination. In the daylight variety, there is a tension between the hero and his society which resolves itself often in a humorous and always in a creative or imaginative way. All these stories are told in the first person but none of them tries to move into the character's psyche or soul. The focus, instead, is on the surfaces, the interest and humor deriving from the situation and the action.

The realism in these daylight stories seems to evolve from Capote's early pieces, printed in *Decade Magazine*. But the warmth, humor, and ease of style lacking in these surface stories is picked up in "My Side of the Matter," which closely resembled Eudora Welty's "Why I Live at the P. O." in its colloquial use of language. This slim tale of a minor skirmish between a young, beleaguered hero and his querulous in-laws is slight in comparison to the later "Jug of Silver" and "Children on Their Birthdays." Both of these stories are markedly similar in that they are concerned with extraordinary, almost supernatural children. The hero of the first story, Appleseed, is blessed with a kind of extrasensory power for determining the amount of money in a jar filled with silver: a power acquired from being born with a caul over his head.

Similarly, the heroine of Capote's most perfect story in the daylight genre, "Children on Their Birthdays," is a precocious child with an uncanny power. Like Cousin Lymon in Carson McCullers' *Ballad of the Sad Cafe*, Miss Bobbit comes to a new town and disrupts its whole pattern of living with her awesome brand of animal magnetism. From her first appearance, grotesquely made up like an adult and sporting a parasol, Miss Bobbit impresses as a fantastic mixture of innocence and experience, morality and pragmatism. She sings like Sophie Tucker, dances like Gypsy Rose Lee, and possesses the business acumen of a Polly Adler. Miss Bobbit doesn't go to church because she finds the odor there offensive but she adds:

> I don't want you to think I'm a heathen, Mr. C; I've had enough
> experience to know that there is a God and that there is a Devil. But
> the way to tame the Devil is not to go down there to church and
> listen to what a sinful mean fool he is. No, love the Devil like you
> do Jesus: because he is a powerful man, and will do you a good turn
> if he knows you trust him. He has frequently done me good turns,

like at dancing school in Memphis. . . . I always called in the Devil to help me get the biggest part in our annual show. That is common sense; you see, I knew Jesus wouldn't have any truck with dancing. Now, as a matter of fact, I have called in the Devil just recently. He is the only one who can help me get out of this town. Not that I live here, not exactly. I think always about somewhere else, somewhere else where everything is dancing, like people dancing in the streets, and everything is pretty, like children on their birthdays. My precious papa said I live in the sky, but if he'd lived more in the sky he'd be rich like he wanted to be. The trouble with my papa was he did not love the Devil, he let the Devil love him. But I am very smart in that respect; I know the next best thing is very often the best.

It is necessary to distinguish here between the hero in the two worlds of day and night. Notice that the *mana*-laden child is the hero in the stories discussed so far, while this same figure becomes the shadowy antagonist in Capote's nocturnal stories. Instead, the protagonist becomes an impotent Prufrock, a character to whom things happen. Yet the relationship between the antagonist and the protagonist is ambiguous: one seems the alter ego of the other. The uncanny power in the daylight hero is a creative force—the manifestation of the imagination. In the nocturnal stories the hero is forced to come to grips with the destructive element—the power of blackness which resides in each of us. The confrontation of the psyche leads to the exposure of the constructive and destructive elements: the wish for death and the wish for life.

In Capote's nocturnal stories the movement out into the world becomes simultaneously the movement into the self. John Aldridge has compared Capote's novel *Other Voices, Other Rooms* unfavorably to Joseph Conrad's *Victory*. The comparison between the two writers is a just, almost obvious one when used in a different context. If we juxtapose Conrad's "Heart of Darkness" with any Capote twilight story, it becomes immediately apparent that the structures are the same. In Conrad's story, Marlowe moves into the heart of the dark continent at the same time he moves into the heart of his own subconscious or soul. In reality, the two movements are the same. The same idea occurs in Paul Bowles' *The Sheltering Sky*, in which two American moves into the primitive Arab world and the primal inner world simultaneously. Similarly, each Capote nocturnal hero must face a fiendish form of *mana*, an external force, and his inner guilt. The relationship in all cases is the same: there is an inescapable fascination with the outer and inner faces of evil. The moment of initiation, the shock of recognition, comes when the hero discovers that the two are the same: the *mana* which confronted him was an external manifestation of his inner identity. The dichotomy then is not only between the two worlds but between the two faces of each world: the constructive and the destructive.

The story of initiation is the search for identity. For instance, in "Master Misery," one of Capote's favorites by his own admission, his heroine, Sylvia, is caught between the outside world represented by her insensitive girlhood friend, Estelle, and the impersonal, mechanical Santa Clauses in store windows, and the personal world of her own dreams. In an attempt to escape the outside world. Sylvia sells her dreams to the anonymous Master Misery, only to discover that she had not escaped the outer world but only lost the inner.

Sylvia is befriended by Oreilly, a used-up clown with no more dreams to sell, who squints one eye and says: "I don't believe in Jesus Christ, but I do believe in people's souls; and I figure it this way, baby; dreams are the mind of the soul and the secret truth about us." When Oreilly leaves her with a smile to go "travelling in the blue" where *the best old pie is whiskeyberry pie*" and not "*loveberry pie*," Sylvia is left completely alone, having lost her dreams and her friend: "I do not know what I want, and perhaps I shall never know, but my only wish from every star will always be another star; and truly I am not afraid, she thought. Two boys came out of a bar and stared at her; in some park some long time ago she'd seen two boys and they might be the same. Truly I am not afraid, she thought, hearing their snowy footsteps following after her; and anyway, there was nothing left to steal."

In no other nocturnal story is the reader as conscious of the tension between the individual and society. Sylvia, in attempting to escape from society, discovers that the destructive element comes from within. Master Misery is himself a bogey man that "all mothers tell their kids about": a force outside the self and yet an extension of the self. Sylvia's surrender at the end of the story is not to society but to the dark side of her soul, the destructive element which dominates when the creative imagination is exhausted. In this lies the idea that the creative imagination of the dream world is the one *thing* by which the individual is identified; the surrender of identity and of the creative force is the acquiescence to the death wish.

The differences between the lighter and darker sides of Capote's writing come out more clearly in one of his most famous stories, "Miriam." In it, an old woman, Mrs. Miller, is haunted by a striking and uncanny child who is her namesake—Miriam. The story shows how Miriam moves in and takes over Mrs. Miller's home, person and life. The plot is similar to "Children on Their Birthdays" and "Jug of Silver": an uncanny child upsets the equilibrium of the drab routine of living. Miriam is in many ways similar to Miss Bobbit and we may almost think of her as that remarkable child's darker sister. But in "Miriam" there are some significant differences from the daylight stories, most important of which is the withdrawal from the outside world, a movement from the relationship of self to society to a confrontation of the self by the self in which Miriam becomes an uncanny device—a result of *mana* and projection. In fact, Miriam stands as the primal alter ego to Mrs. Miller: an extension of her destructive, unconscious instinct. The withdrawal from the outer world is accompanied by a complementary shift in style; the clarity and realism of "Children" is replaced by a filmy and surreal style in which Miriam's fingers "made cobweb movements over the plate, gathering the crumbs."

The hero's encounter with, and surrender to, *mana* is perhaps most richly stated in the inverted story, "The Headless Hawk," in which an extraordinary young girl, half child, half adult, innocent, experienced, demented, homicidal, naïve, and primitive, invades the sterile life of a young failure on the fringes of the art world. Vincent is "a poet who had never written poetry, a painter who had never painted, a lover who had never loved (absolutely)—someone, in short, without direction and quite headless. Oh, it wasn't that he hadn't tried—good beginnings, always, bad endings, always . . . a man in the sea, fifty miles from shore; a victim, born to be murdered, either by himself or another; an actor unemployed." Vincent falls under the spell of a demented young girl, D. J., whose painting of a headless hawk hovering over a headless body—a vivid symbol of his own disconnectedness—forces on Vincent "a note of inward recognition." Vincent takes the girl as his mistress because she recalls from his past his incurable fascination with carnival freaks, and because "it was true that about those he loved there was always a little something wrong, broken." D. J. thus becomes a mirror of his own disconnected self into which he can retreat. He shuns all his old friends because he does not know how to explain his relationship with the grotesque young girl.

However, Vincent's immersion in D. J. takes a sharp turn when he discovers her obsession with a Mr. Destronelli, a shadowy figure out of her past who she is sure will kill her. When Vincent discovers her dementia he knows he must betray her in favor of his old life, just as he had betrayed his other lovers, just as "he'd betrayed himself with talents unexploited, voyages never taken, promises unfulfilled . . . why in his lovers must he always find the broken image of himself?" He soon turns her out of the house and on the same day symbolically stabs the headless hawk in her painting as he is trying to catch a butterfly. But, of course, he has not escaped her. D. J. haunts him night and day, convinced that he is Destronelli. Vincent, returned to his old world which he now finds "sterile and spurious," discovers that he is held by "a nameless disorder . . . a paralysis of time and identity." Vincent's fascination with D. J. is the fatal confrontation with Mr. Destronelli—the executioner in each of us: he sees in D. J. the grotesque reflection of his own broken image.

The heart of the matter—the heart of darkness—is revealed significantly enough in a dream that Vincent has on the night of D. J.'s eighteenth birthday. He is at a huge party with "an old man with yellow-dyed hair, powdered cheeks, kewpie-doll lips: Vincent recognizes Vincent." The old man is on Vincent's back and Vincent feels out of place until he notices that he is not alone. "He notices then that many are also saddled with malevolent semblances of themselves, outward embodiments of inner decay." The host has a headless hawk attached to his wrist drawing blood with its talons. Suddenly the host announces in a soprano voice: "Attention. The dancing will commence." Vincent finds himself dancing with a succession of old lovers.

> Again, a new partner. It is D. J., and she too has a figure barnacled to her back, an enchanting auburn-haired child; like an emblem of innocence, the child cuddles to her chest a snowball kitten. "I am heavier than I look," says the child, and the terrible voice retorts, "But I am heaviest of all." The instant their hands meet he begins to feel the weight upon him diminish; the old Vincent is fading. His feet lift off the floor, he floats upward from her embrace. The victrola grinds away loud as ever, but he is rising high, and the white receding faces gleam below like mushrooms on a dark meadow.
>
> The host releases his hawk, sends it soaring. Vincent thinks, no matter, it is a blind thing, and the wicked are safe among the blind. But the hawk wheels above him, swoops down, claws foremost; at last he knows there is to be no freedom.

Part 3

The confrontation of the inner world becomes the confrontation of man's innate guilt. The dark side of the subconscious reflects not only the death instinct but the Christian sense of man's depravity. The burden that each carries becomes more than the darker alter ego: it is also the sense of original sin which each of us carries like a cross. Thus even the child is heavier than she looks; and thus Vincent cannot transcend his wickedness, even among the blind, even through love. Truly, there is to be no freedom from original sin.

The ingredients in all of Capote's nocturnal stories are present in their most striking expression, "A Tree of Night." Kay, a young college girl on her way back to her insulated environment from her uncle's funeral, is intimidated by two grotesque carnival performers: a deaf mute who plays Lazarus by being buried alive in tank towns and his one connection with the outside world, a woman made freakish by her huge head. Much against her will, Kay is coerced, almost mesmerized, into buying a worthless charm which she had previously refused to buy. Like Capote's other heroes, Kay finds herself acquiescing to an uncanny power: "As Kay watched, the man's face seemed to change form and recede before her like a moon-shaped rock sliding downward under a surface of water. A warm laziness relaxed her. She was dimly conscious of it when the woman took away her purse, and when she gently pulled the raincoat like a shroud above her head."

On the one level the story may be read as a tawdry and ironic parable of Lazarus—

> "I am Lazarus come from the dead,
> Come back to tell you all, I shall tell you all"—
> If one, settling a pillow by her head,
>   Should say: "That is not what I meant at all;
>   That is not it, at all."

—just as Carson McCullers' novel, *The Heart Is a Lonely Hunter*, can be read as an ironic parable of Christ. But perhaps the religious significance is being overemphasized:

(Confronted by the afflicted mute) Kay knew of what she was afraid: it was a memory, a childish memory of terrors that once, long ago, had hovered above her like haunted limbs on a tree of night. Aunts, cooks, strangers—each eager to spin a tale or teach a rhyme of spooks and death, omens, spirits, demons. And always there had been the unfailing threat of the wizard man: stay close to the house, child, else the wizard man'll snatch and eat you alive! He lived everywhere, the wizard man, and everywhere was danger. At night, in bed, hear him tapping at the window? Listen!

Fear seems the motivating emotion in these stories just as love is the motivating force in McCuller's novels. *"All our acts are acts of fear,"* remembered Walter Ranney, the hero of "Shut a Final Door," and perhaps he was right. For the wizard men and the Master Miseries are all personifications of some form of *mana*, formalized by superstition—that primitive and perhaps honest type of religious observance. At the same time, the Master Miseries and the Destronellis are not the products of our creative imagination but the very heart of darkness, the black, destructive, guilt-ridden side of our subconscious and soul. In each of these nocturnal stories, a seemingly normal but creatively bankrupt person encounters a destructive force at once outside himself and within his depths, which is so dreadful that he is utterly vanquished by fear and surrenders his very essence—his identity. The hero is drawn towards the source of power—the primal heart of darkness—and in doing so removes himself from the public world. Like Narcissus watching his reflection, Capote's hero becomes fascinated and mesmerized by his own evil alter ego. Like Jacob wrestling with the dark angel, the hero in these stories is wrestling not only with the outside world of reality but with his own personal world, losing the former while winning the latter. For the moment of defeat, of despair, of unconditional surrender, is also the moment of revelation.

What we have discovered about the two worlds of Truman Capote's short stories is equally true in his two novels. Conveniently, one novel describes each world: *The Grass Harp* seems the daylight metaphor of *Other Voices, Other Rooms*. And yet both novels exhibit a deepening of perception, a widening of scope, and an enrichening of the dense thematic material found in the stories. On the other hand, neither novel is entirely successful, whereas some of his stories—notably "Children on Their Birthdays" and "A Tree of Night"—are striking examples of their medium. Even Capote admits he is most at home in the short story.

Still, no piece of Capote's fiction has elicited as much comment, criticism, and bewilderment as the gothic and complex first novel, *Other Voices, Other Rooms*. Indeed, the dust jacket picture of the sensitive reclining face staring out from beneath boyish bangs was perhaps as great a cause for the excited confusion as anything in the book. But the difficult and fantastic remoteness of the book has been exaggerated by the mistaken identification of the hero with his exotic and precocious creator. Basically, *Other Voices* resembles Capote's twilight stories in that it concerns an adolescent's initiation into the private and inverted adult world, full of danger and evil. John Aldridge has called it essentially a search for the father and Carvel Collins has likened it to the quest for the Holy Grail: both are right. Yet Joel Knox's search for his father, which leads him from the realistic daylight of New Orleans to the fantastic twilight of Skully's Landing, can be considered as a search for identity. Joel moves from the outside world towards the personal, just as he moves from the bright afternoon heat of Noon City to the dream-like darkness of his new home—Skully's Landing.

John Aldridge has accused Capote of being metaphorical and remote, but his symbolic treatment of thematic material seems clear enough if examined in the same manner as we have examined his other stories. Like his other work, *Other Voices* can be read from either a psychological or a moral, perhaps Christian, viewpoint. Basically, Joel "was trying to locate his father, that was the long and short of it," for the discovery of his father's identity would cast some light on his own essence. But when Joel discovers the terrible truth that his father is a helpless, paralyzed invalid, he must look elsewhere for help in his search for identity. Joel stands as a stranger at Skully's Landing, poised between going further into the private world with his fascinating, witty, cynical, and homosexual cousin, Randolph, and moving out into the real world with the adolescent tomboy, Idabel. Joel's initiation can be seen as a straight-line development from the outside world of Noon City through the decadent limbo of Skully's Landing to the private, dreamlike ruins of the Cloud Hotel—and back again.

In order to tell his story, Capote has expanded the technique of metaphorical use of characterization seen in "Miriam" and "The Headless Hawk." Each character in *Other Voices* is a metaphor or alter ego of another. The tomboy, Idabel, has a twin sister, Florabel, because, as Florabel says, "the Lord always sends something bad with the good." Similarly, the dwarfish Miss Wisteria, "weeping because little boys must grow tall," is a grotesque reflection of Randolph's hopeless, homosexual quest for completion. Little Sunshine, the hermit who inhabits his own private world at the Cloud Hotel, mirrors the old Negro servant, Jesus Fever. And, finally, Joel himself is reflected in Jesus Fever's daughter, Zoo: both must reject their fathers in an effort to escape from the Landing.

Joel's first test comes when he is not allowed to meet his father. In his mind the illusions he had built around his father are confused with the reality of his father's absence. "He couldn't believe in the way things were turning out: the difference between this happening and what he'd expected was too great." With the confrontation of his father's impotence, Joel must look elsewhere for the key to his identity. Randolph offers him one possibility: the narcissistic immersion in the self: "They can romanticize us so, mirrors, and that is their secret: what a subtle torture it would be to destroy all the mirrors in the world: where then could we look for reassurance of our identities? I tell you, my dear, Narcissus was no egotist . . . he was merely another of us who, in our unshatterable isolation, recognized, on seeing his reflection, the one beautiful comrade, the only inseparable love. . . . Poor Narcissus, possibly the only human who was ever honest on this point." But even in the personal world Randolph cannot escape his own guilt, for "it is easy to escape daylight, but night is inevitable, and dreams are the giant cage." Like Vincent, in "The Headless Hawk," Randolph is "a victim born to be murdered, either by himself or another." He remains a broken figure hopelessly committed to, and castrated by, the destructive side of his personal vision.

Caught between a loyalty to his father and a need to escape his stultifying influence, Joel at first rejects his father for Idabel, with whom he plans to run away. But the final act of initiation—the revelation of his own guilt that smashes the tinted glasses of childhood—renders Joel powerless to escape. In leaving his father, Joel, like Zoo, is judged guilty by his father and must act as his own executioner. Both he and Zoo can never really leave the Landing; their dreams of escape from limbo are shattered. When Randolph takes Joel to the Cloud Hotel— the private world which Randolph never left—a revelation of identity comes to Joel in a flash of insight:

> (He looked into the fire, longing to see their faces as well, and the flames erupted an embryo: a veined, vacillating shape, its features formed slowly, and even when complete stayed veiled in dazzle; his eyes burned tar-hot as he brought them nearer: tell me, tell me, who are you? are you someone I know? are you dead? are you my friend? do you love me? But the painted disembodied head remained unborn beyond its mark, and gave no clue. Are you someone I am

Part 3

looking for? he asked, not knowing whom he meant, but certain that for him there must be such a person, just as there was for everybody else: Randolph with his almanac, Miss Wisteria and her search by flashlight, Little Sunshine remembering other voices, other rooms, all of them remembering, or never having known. And Joel drew back. If he recognized the figure in the fire, then what ever would he find to take its place? It was easier not to know, better holding heaven in your hand like a butterfly that is not there at all.)

Unable to live in either the private or the real world, Joel makes the compromise of the artist: finding his identity by walking the tenuous line between the illusory and the tangible, between the imaginative and the real:

> "I am me," Joel whooped. "I am Joel, we are the same people" . . .
> And Joel realized then the truth; he saw how helpless Randolph was: more paralyzed than Mr. Sansom, more childlike than Miss Wisteria, what else could he do, once outside and alone, but describe a circle, the zero of his nothingness? Joel slipped down from the tree; he had not made the top, but it did not matter, for he knew who he was, he knew that he was strong.

Yet Joel's search for his identity contains another and perhaps more significant level of meaning. At the very beginning of the book, while riding to Skully's Landing, Joel passes a sign—a sign for him and for the reader: "The Lord Jesus is Coming! Are you ready?" But the Christ figure we meet is one we are not prepared for: the paralytic father, Mr. Sansom, who drops red tennis balls like drops of blood, an ironic, afflicted Christ similar to the deaf-mute, Singer, in Carson McCullers' *The Heart Is a Lonely Hunter*. Joel's search for his father leads to the confrontation of his innate guilt—guilt symbolized in the desertion of his father and manifested in his sudden awareness of the disparity between illusion and reality and his perception of the impossibility of escape from the Landing. His situation is mirrored by Zoo, who leaves her father's grave to escape the Landing only to find that she has taken "the wrong road" to salvation. She is crucified by assaulters just as Joel, like Christ, is condemned and abandoned by his father and crucified by surrendering to Randolph. But in the act of the crucifixion are the seeds of redemption: Joel is crucified a boy and resurrected a man.

Every Capote character is scarred permanently just as Zoo bears the marks of a razor slashing on her neck. They are all marked men, marked perhaps by original sin. Even the artist—like Joel—is afflicted: "the feeble-minded, the neurotic, the criminal, perhaps, also, the artist, have unpredictability and perverted innocence in common." But Capote's nocturnal hero remains essentially the failure. And in Randolph he has created his most fascinating and grotesque failure, who speaks for Vincent and Sylvia, Mrs. Miller and Walter Ranney, when he says: "But we are alone, darling child, terribly, isolated each from the other; so fierce is the world's ridicule we cannot speak or show our tenderness; for us, death is stronger than life, it pulls like a wind through the dark, all our cries burlesqued in joyless laughter; and with the garbage of loneliness stuffed down us until our guts burst bleeding green, we go screaming round the world, dying in our rented rooms, nightmare hotels, eternal homes of the transient heart."

In *The Grass Harp*, Capote again moves to the daylight style. Essentially, it is the story of a group of innocents, alienated from society because of their innocence, who move into a tree house to escape the world and discover their true selves. The theme is again the search for *true* identity. For the tree dissolves all of society's restrictions and replaces them with a beatific feeling of freedom; it is a realm where wish becomes fulfillment. The tree becomes the refuge for the outcasts from society: the saintly Dolly, the most innocent of all, who, like J. D. Salinger's misfit hero, Seymour Glass, loves people so much she hides in corners for fear of scaring them with her love. With Dolly is her constant companion, Catherine, a zany mixture of Negro and Indian, harshness and loyalty, who brings to the tree house a sense of hard-headed reality, and Collin Fenwick, the adolescent narrator, who lives with Dolly and her brutish sister, Verena. These three have left home after a quarrel over Dolly's home-remedy dropsy cure: Verena wants to mass produce it and Dolly refuses to commercialize it. They are soon joined by a retired judge, Judge Cool, whose sons feel he has outgrown his usefulness. "I sometimes imagine," he says, "all those whom I've called guilty have passed the real guilt on to me: it's partly that that makes me want once before I die to be right on the right side." The fifth party is a "tense, trigger-tempered," directionless youth, Riley Henderson, who also happens to be Collin's idol.

Like Salinger's Holden Caulfield, these five stage a "quixotic" battle against hypocrisy, materialism, and anything that takes beauty away from the world. The small revolt from society forces them to move towards the inner world of the imagination. Judge Cool sums up the whole idea nicely:

"But ah, the energy we spend hiding from one another, afraid as we are of being identified: five fools in a tree. A great piece of luck provided we know how to use it: no longer any need to worry about the picture we present—free to find out who we truly are. If we know that, no one can dislodge us; it's the uncertainty concerning themselves that makes our friends conspire to deny the differences. By scrapes and bits I've in the past surrendered myself to strangers—men who disappeared down the gangplank, got off at the next station: put together, maybe they wouldn't've made the one person in the world—but there he is with a dozen different faces moving down a hundred separate streets. This is my chance to find that man—you are him, Miss Dolly, Riley, all of you."

But this leafy retreat seems hardly the place for soul-searching; Verena soon has the authorities there to demand that they return to their homes. A pitched battle occurs between the rebels and the authorities, which, with the help of the right of creative imagination and the might of an ingenious family of gypsies, is decided in favor of the rebels. However, they do leave the tree house when Verena returns broken by the swindler of her heart and money—the bogus doctor who was to bottle the dropsy cure. Dolly returns to Verena because she is needed and the magic of the "dissolving" chinaberry tree is gone.

In the story the end of innocence is two-fold. For Collin, it is an elegiac remembrance of things past, a vicarious initiation at Dolly's own loss of innocence, and his real initiation at Dolly's death. But for Collin the act of initiation brings the discovery of love and the redemption of the identity. It now becomes clear that for Capote love is the redeeming element in life. Echoing the judge's words in an earlier part of the book, Dolly tells Collin before her death: "Charlie said that love is a chain of love. I hope you listened and understood him. Because when you can love one thing . . . you can love another, and that is owning, that is something to live with. You can forgive everything."

Like Carson McCullers in her story, "A Tree, A Rock, A Cloud," Capote here shows "that life is a chain of love, as nature is a chain of life." Arching over the story of Dolly and Collin and the chinaberry tree is the grass harp, a symbol of the immutable moral order, an order of the good and the imaginative which always tells a story of the lives of the people, good and bad, with and without identity, who have lived and died there. And so the search for identity comes to rest in the shock of recognition—recognition of the primacy of the natural order, of the creative instinct—of love and imagination over the death wish. Both Joel and his daylight brother, Collin, have learned the same thing: the search inward for identity must eventually turn outward if it is to reflect anything but the broken image of the grotesque self:

> The world was a frightening place, yes, he knew: unlasting, what could be forever? or only what it seemed? rock corrodes, rivers freeze, fruit rots; stabbed, blood of black and white bleeds alike; trained parrots tell more truth than most, and who is lonelier: the hawk or the worm? every flowering heart shrivels dry and pitted as the herb from which it bloomed, and while the old man grows spinsterish, his wife assumes a mustache; moment to moment, changing, changing, like the cars on the ferris-wheel. Grass and love are always greener; but remember Little Three Eyes? show her love and apples ripen gold, love vanquishes the Snow Queen, its presence finds the name, be it Rumpelstiltskin or merely Joel Knox: that is constant.

Robert Siegle

The nonfiction novel makes us uneasy by its apparently oxymoronic nature—its mixing of reality and fiction, of journalist and novelist, of factuality and imagination. Uncomfortable with so indiscrete a mixture, many writers on the subject resolve specific works back into either the novel or nonfiction. William L. Nance, for example, speaks of the "flaws" and "limitations . . . inherent in the very concept of a nonfiction novel" and concludes that *In Cold Blood* "falls back into a category which may as well be labeled 'documentary novel.'"[1] In the most extended reflection on the type, Mas'ud Zavarzadeh shifts it in the opposite direction by calling it "the 'fiction' of the metaphysical void. In the absence of shared, preestablished norms, it maps the surrounding objectal world, without imposing a projected pattern of meaning on the neutral massiveness and amorphous identity of actual people and events. Its response to confused and contradictory interpretations of reality, which are all the product of an Aristotelian compulsion to explain and label experience at all levels, is to return to noninterpretive, direct contact with actuality."[2] Zavarzadeh's ideal of objectivity—"direct contact with reality"—may be stated so extremely in order to contrast the type with the two principal alternatives he sees in contemporary fiction, the "liberal-humanist novel" (Bellow, Malamud, Updike), and "transfiction" (Barth, Pynchon, Barthelme), but he nonetheless argues that the "fictual" realm of the nonfiction novel has both the factual authority of reality and the "aesthetic control" of the fictional.[3] One side of the debate approaches the work in terms of its novelistic artistry, the other side in terms of its ability "to circumvent the intervening imposed interpretations and to return to the elementals."[4]

This curious split response can be explained by thinking of the "nonfiction novel" not as an oxymoron, but as a tautology. That is, works of this type bring us not up to a barrier between two distinct

Reprinted from "Capote's *Handcarved Coffins* and the Nonfiction Novel," *Contemporary Literature* 25:4 (Winter 1984) (© 1984 by the Board of Regents of the University of Wisconsin System), 437–51. Reprinted with permission.

regions, nonfictional reality and fictional narrative, but into a vortex in which both kinds of accounts, together with the presumably metalinguistic commentary upon them, are drawn into the same discursive swirl. Each grounds itself by means of a figurative space, a literary triangle delegating specific zones to each, and allowing each to "cover" its limitations as discourse, as a way of knowing, by deferring elements of the "full picture" to the others—the way science defers matters of the heart to fiction, and fiction defers precise explanations of quantum mechanics to physics. Such a strategy of differentiation seeks to stabilize each kind of discourse by suiting its methods to its material. But part of the problem critics seem to have with the nonfiction novel is that nothing new or unique emerges from the "synthesis" of these supposedly distinct zones—not because it "falls back" into one or the other familiar kind, but because these kinds turn out to have been the same. Different methods all turn out to be varying conventions for framing, proportioning, and selecting from the same basic cultural myth of reality.[5] If such material is as much fiction as "reality," and if "method" is mainly convention—that is, fiction—then even the distinction of method and material turns out to be a version of the basic cultural logic from which all these illusory oppositions derive. They are, in other words, diacritical rather than independent variables.[6]

This redundancy in the nonfiction novel is the key to sorting out the anomalies readers find in it, and to look at Truman Capote's *Handcarved Coffins*—a brief and thus convenient piece for illustration—is to see how immediately useful this approach can be. In the preface to *Music for Chameleons*, the volume in which the story appears, Capote calls the book a "nonfiction short novel," and thus launches from outside the discourse of the narrative a presumably authoritative commentary upon it.[7] The rest of the document explains Capote's period of disorder after enraging critics with the publication of chapters from *Answered Prayers* in *Esquire*. Feeling himself "in a helluva lot of trouble," "suffering a creative crisis and a personal one at the same time," moving through a period of "creative chaos" that was "torment," Capote tells us he came to a new understanding "of the difference between what is true and what is *really* true" (p. xvi). The nonfiction novel, then, is the means of answering on both the personal and professional levels what amounts to the fundamental hermeneutical question, and *Handcarved Coffins* accordingly reproduces the hermeneutic investigator in the form of the sleuth and his scribe endeavoring to discover the truth and put it in writing.

This effort to establish the "*really* true" is the root of all cultural fictions. But as truth is a difficult goal at best, we had best return to Capote's preface to discover why and how he feels able to achieve it. There are curious aspects to the two basic ideas he advances at this point. Capote apparently considers the crisis in his writing as an unsatisfactory ratio between "the powers at my command" and "the total potential" of "all the energy and esthetic excitements that material contained" (p. xvii). If Nietzsche is right that "powers" are version of a will to mastery over the materials of one's experience, then this passage presents the dramatic confrontation of order with the "energy" and "excitements" of its counterpart, the chaos of the material before the writer brings out of it the "total potential" of its truth. The dream of "total potential" or plenitude is not reached, however; for some reason the resources of writing cannot triumph totally over the recalcitrance of its material. We may at this point at least speculate as to why: if fiction and nonfiction, or perhaps even method and material, are no different, then such a triumph is impossible. It is like the dream of sign and referent merging, text and world, desire and fulfillment.

Capote remains buoyant, however. He exudes the ecstasy of desire for such a crossing, and bubbles with metaphors that command our attention. The "apparently unsolvable problem" he poses is this:

> how can a writer successfully combine within a single form—say the short story—all he knows about every other form of writing? For this was why my work was often insufficiently illuminated; the voltage was there, but by restricting myself to the techniques of whatever form I was working in, I was not using everything I knew about writing—all I'd learned from film scripts, reportage, poetry, the short story, novellas, the novel. A writer ought to have all his colors, all his abilities available on the same palette for mingling (and, in suitable instances, simultaneous application). (p. xvii)

It is no wonder that the work he returns to is *Answered Prayers*, for this wish amounts to the theological conception of fulfilling the inner truth of the spirit. Capote seeks to make his practice of writing as comprehensive as possible, absorbing into this application all the forms he has known, as if sheer range of generic conventions and techniques would achieve his dream of plenitude. The "voltage was there," it seems, although one cannot tell whether the voltage derives from the material as an inner truth to be brought out, or from Capote's earnestness despite his self-restrictions in technique. Perhaps it is enough to see, however, that the voltage raging through the material left the work "insufficiently illuminated," darkened in its partial order. If, somehow, an additional intensity of the light of order could be brought to bear upon the material, it would shine brightly with its "total potential." The truth is there; it needs illumination.

But strangely enough, as the paragraph moves towards Capote's own enlightenment, the metaphoric configuration shifts, and what the writer needs is not more light, but all his "colors" on "the same palette." His techniques now are an impasto smeared upon the canvas, covering what is there in order to portray on one surface the illusion of what exists elsewhere. Here the truth is no longer within, an actual order to be illuminated, but a virtual order to be created, fictionalized, in a medium unmistakably alien to the material it pictures. The first of these images suggests a metaphysical ontology of truth, the second a rhetoric of figuration which obviously can at best only approximate, only disfigure, the subject. It clearly marks its difference from that subject, and indeed is what it is because of that difference. We are back, in other words, to the two views of writing with which we began—as a direct rendering of the actual entities whose inner truths we must reveal, or as virtual points in a fictional matrix. The novel itself suggests ways of thinking through the relation between the two as diacritical conventions of the basic interpretive activity of culture.

The extent to which narrative practice in the novel shows interpretive interests at work on the "nonfiction" material can be seen in a number of ways that echo the previously cited work of Nance, De Bellis, and Tompkins on *In Cold Blood*. Jake, a detective and a friend of Capote's, is one narrator worth comment. He selects the case for the character "TC" as "something that he thought might interest" a novelist (p. 68), and he draws on his own literary tastes (Dickens, Trollope, Melville, and Twain are mentioned) to present matters to TC. One sees a number of instances of this literary framing of the event. Jake literally reads from fiction to explain Quinn, he paces the timing of information for maximum effect, and he allows metaphor to introduce figurative displacement into a supposedly denotative case history in criminology (as when his chief is "jittery as a killer on Death Row," an interesting mixing of contraries). Perhaps he has no choice but to perceive events in terms of Dickens's search for hidden connections, people in terms of characters in nineteenth-century novels, referential "facts" in terms of metaphorical figures—nonfiction in terms of fiction.

As for the larger topic of TC's narrative practice, one's first observation is that he plays well the role of "narratee" for Jake. For example, when Jake tells him of the rattlesnake murders, TC plays the role of ideal reader, co-creating in his imagination the scene Jake outlines: "But the sound of the wind was only a murmur in my head underneath the racket of rattling rattlesnakes, hissing tongues. I saw the car dark under a hot sun, the swirling serpents, the human heads growing green, expanding with poison. I listened to the wind, letting it wipe the scene away" (p. 70). Besides being a prime example of Capote's skill at description, the passage shows TC's willingness to go beyond the factual to imagine how it has come to be. A fictional narrative line is projected back of the "facts" of corpses to explain them, a quite mythic origin posited that in its fictiveness reiterates the book's qualification of any naïve understanding of its method, or that of detection, interpretation, or nonfiction. It also, of course, shapes the responses of TC's own readers—of us, that is—as he does later when he marvels at the "mathematical element" in Clem Anderson's decapitation (p. 76), or when he underlines the suspense in Jake's tale of Addie ("You mean you're going to leave me hanging out here?" [p. 83]).

Lest we neglect our hermeneutic responsibilities, TC prods us from time to time by rendering facts as clues: "There were nine snakes. And nine members of the Blue River Committee. Nice quaint coincidence" (p. 97). By playing narratee so well, TC plots out within his novel the "real" readers' responses. In other words, those supposedly external to the narrative find themselves already anticipated there inside the text. One hears in the distance Roland Barthes collapsing the distinction between reader and text, but more conservatively, for the moment, we may note that TC exploits fully, as Capote's preface promises, the resources of fictional narratees in his nonfiction work.

TC exploits fictional narrators too, as it turns out. He paces his story as much like the omniscient novelist as Jake does; he finally remembers at one point of whom Quinn reminds him, but won't tell us until the time is ripe (p. 110). And he makes good use of Dickensian dreams; he speaks of "Addie: her hair, tangled in watery undergrowths, drifted, in my dream, across her wavering drowned face like a bridal veil" (p. 127), anything but an innocent metaphor. An even more intense example of the classic dream device occurs earlier in the narrative:

> Oddly, sleep struck me as though I'd been hit by a thief's blackjack. . . . I entered some sphere between sleep and wakefulness, my mind like a crystal lozenge, a suspended instrument that caught the reflections of spiraling images: a man's head among leaves, the windows of a car streaked with venom, the eyes of serpents sliding through heat-mist, fire flowing from the earth, scorched fists pounding at a cellar door, taut wire gleaming in the twilight, a torso on a roadway, a head among leaves, fire, fire, fire flowing like a river, river, river. Then a telephone rings. (p.84)

At first glance this seems only a marvellously evocative passage that collects for the reader the various murders that have taken place. But the least bit of attention to its figures finds more of interest as well. The puzzle of reality, represented in the novel as crime, seems to have become pervasive, as TC cannot even nap without theft and assault giving shape to his sleep. Moreover, the "spheres" that normally exhaust the alternatives are here split by another, nameless sphere in which he finds himself.

Perhaps more interesting than the cosmology is what takes place there. His mind becomes "a crystal lozenge" that "caught the reflections" of the images he lists. The very materiality of his mental theater is an interesting anachronism for our age, but its epistemological implications may be even more so. That is, the lozenge is "crystal" or clear, and the images are "reflections" of something external to that mind, since crystals reflect particularly those images "spiraling" around the crystal. But if Jake has indeed not described, but TC imagined, the details, as we saw a moment ago, then these cannot be external images at all. And if they are made by TC, then he is hardly the neutral, objective, crystal clear window upon them, but rather the opaque colorist or producer of them. The superrealist, the nonfiction journalist reporting on "the way it was," might indeed aspire to the method of the crystal lozenge, but it seems oddly out of place here. Ah—one remembers, this is a dream, Capote only dreams of himself as the objective, nonfiction reporter. If nonfiction is thus the dream element of the narrative, that is to say of the fictional element, does that make the fictional element *more* real, deriving as it does from the flow of actual fictional narratives in culture? The interchange of contraries

165

remains confusing, as in this passage when fire and water are equivalent. Fortunately for the analyst, "the telephone rings," giving us a line out of a literary device that absorbs pretensions to the nonliterary, nonverbal, and nonfictional into its own dream structure.

What he finds "outside" the dream-set is not necessarily reassuring, however. Apparently casual allusions turn out to be not at all innocent. Early in the narrative, for example, while TC is watching Addie and Jake together, the allusions are to mannerists like Edith Wharton (p. 87) and Jane Austen (p. 94). By the time the mystery heats up, the allusions are to the likes of Eric Amber (p. 105). After TC has left the scene for a while, another phone call takes him back—and, appropriately enough, it is Proust he reads (p. 120), the prime retrospective interpretive narrative that, as TC notes, is "rather like plunging into a tidal wave, destination unknown" (p. 120). The catastrophic imagery is justified, since Addie's life is swept away and, consistent with the imagery, by drowning. In other words, apparently inert allusions, always "justified" by the "realistic" context that cues them, are in fact a narrative line of literary frames that provide the appropriate sort of context within which to see these events taking place. To see them take place in such a context is not only to see them already interpreted in accordance with those frames, but to have one's responses plotted within the narrative by an all-but-omniscient narrator who exploits his knowledge of the materials, placing our responses in the sequence best suited to increasing their narrative impact upon us.

The imagery of the novel is no more crystalline in its treatment of fiction and nonfiction. In playing up the romance developing between Jake and Addie, a sort of sentimental subplot in this multiplotted novel, TC deploys some curious images. He says, for example, that "the style of the woman implied an erotic history complete with footnotes," a remarkably textual metaphor implying that either TC's perceptual framework or Addie's self-creation—or both—complies with specific narrative conventions. In the next sentence TC says that "the tension between them was as taut as the steel wire that had severed Clem Anderson's head" (pp. 86–87), a grotesque image conflating the desires of murder and sex, and prophetic of the consequences of the relationship fatal to both, though to Jake only metaphorically. Both metaphors invade reportage of objective facts with the interpretive figures of fiction.

The extent to which a mode of understanding preconstructs observation shows in passages like that in which TC notices Jake blowing smoke rings and decides that "the empty oval, floating through the air, seemed to carry with it an erotic message" (p. 89). Perhaps as another type of crystal lozenge this "empty oval" may be filled with whatever plot the narrator constructs, but it is clearly less a transparent window or neutral reflection than a flamboyant splash of rhetorical color upon the page. It is as heavy-handed as TC's parenthetical break away from Jake's vow to protect Addie to a scene he dreams up of wintry clumps of grass and "two spotted calves huddled side by side, lending each other comfort, protection: like Jake, like Addie" (pp. 107–8). Knowing when winter calves are sent to slaughter strengthens the reader's expectations that, come summer, Addie must die: after all, we have learned as well as Jake from Dickens and Trollope that plot resolutions conform to the miniature narrative epitomized in foreground imagery. It appears that when Capote combines the denotative language of journalism with the figurative language of fiction, he (inadvertently?) ends up clarifying how figures work in any discourse to betray the interpretive plots that writers-as-narrators impose upon whatever type of experience they set out to inscribe within their respective discursive orders. Badly put, language as figure points to discourse as fiction.

To turn to the substance of TC's relation to the mystery late in the novel is to see how much confusions come to fruition. Good novel reader that he is, TC keeps looking for the univocal "key" to Quinn-as-character, finding it finally—or perhaps constructing it finally—by identifying him with a character in his own private psychodrama, the traumatically austere Reverend Snow. Perhaps it is worth pointing out that snow is another crystal lozenge allowing the narrative projectionist full freedom. On the basis of this identification, TC finds Quinn guilty, seeing him as a sufficiently self-righteous monomaniac to perpetrate the crimes. He even constructs the scenario for us; he is again not quite sleeping, and tells us that "Images formed, faded; it was as though I were mentally editing a motion picture" (p. 129). We might take him to be simply an earnest editor of images that form themselves or are otherwise external if we had not already been disabused of such a naïve sense of the narrative act. What we are in fact doing is watching TC fit the images *he* has imagined to the criteria for causal coherence, character consistency, and the like that he inherits from the genre of film and, by extension, from the history of philosophical assumptions presupposed by that genre.

For a full page, TC elaborates his feature-length dream of the way it was, but then after daybreak had "lessened my enthusiasm for fevered fantasizing," concludes that "unless Jake had evolved a theory more convincing than my own imagination had managed, then I preferred to forget it; I was satisfied to fall asleep remembering the coroner's common-sense verdict: *Accidental death by drowning*" (p. 130). Having followed through the dream version Jake cues him to, TC finds it wavering in the illumination of daybreak, the light of common sense—that journalistic look at just the facts that presumably dispenses with imaginative reconstruction. A few pages later, however, he is angry to discover that his "fevered fantasizing" "*is* Jake's story," according to a colleague of Jake's, "give or take a lotta little details" (p. 132). TC is "angry at him [Jake] for not having produced a solid solution, crestfallen that his conjectures were no better than mine." Strangely enough, the narratives constructed by detective and novelist coincide, the plot lines of nonfiction and fiction cross. Movie editor, novelist, reporter, sleuth, metalinguistic hermeneutic theorist—they are all the same, it would seem.

The novel presses even further, however, in the way in which it subtly allies and even confounds the discourse of interpretive narrative with those of madness and religion. The figure of madness appears in a number of forms, some of them quite bizarre. Mrs. Parsons, for example, is a morphine addict whom Jake describes as "a woman who has already left life. She's looking back through a door—without regret" (p. 78). But she is nonetheless important to Jake because on first seeing the little coffin her husband receives, and without knowing of its presence in the other cases, she feels "a shadow" fall across their lives, and knows he has been murdered despite the lack of any evidence to that effect. That is, although a morphine-crazed recluse, she duplicates Jake's reasoning and conclusion.

This connection might seem far-fetched were there not other and closer ties established between the writer/detective and the madman. Juanita Quinn is another strange case with hair "too black to be true," a "narrow skull" with a face "like a fist" featuring "bored onyx eyes" (p. 112). More strange than her appearance is her drugged behavior; she sits regally in a chair that "may well have once decorated the throne room of an Iberian castle" (p. 111), with a shivering chihuahua and a guitar on her lap, watching a TV game show with the volume turned down: she is difficult to distract. But her case gets more curious when she explains herself to TC: "You asked why I have the sound off. The only time I have the sound on is to hear the weather report. Otherwise, I just watch and imagine what's being said. If I actually listen, it puts me right to sleep. But just imagining keeps me awake. And I have to stay awake—at least till midnight. Otherwise, I'd never get any sleep at all. Where do you live?" (p. 113). She, like TC, struggles in a confusing zone between sleeping and waking, she too has her trials with the night, and she too busies herself "imagining" plots in order to keep the demons at bay.

If we look at TC himself, we find not only these general parallels to Juanita's patterns, but passages like this one that more specifically ally him to the figure of madness: "Anxiety, as any expensive psychiatrist will tell you, is caused by depression; but depression, as the same psychiatrist will inform you on a second visit and for an additional fee, is caused by anxiety. I rotated around in that humdrum circle all afternoon. By nightfall the two demons had combined; while anxiety copulated with depression, I sat staring at Mr. Bell's controversial invention, fearing the moment when I would have to dial the Prairie Motel and hear Jake admit that the Bureau was taking him off the case" (p. 133). As it turns out, his plot no more fits the silent technology he stares at than Juanita's—Jake is not off the case, at least not yet. But in following the pattern he shares with Juanita of giving voice to the silent machine, a pattern peculiarly appropriate to the writer, he enacts the epistemological model in which one "explains" a silent truth supposedly within the material, voicing the presence of what had been only partly apparent before. But he also enacts the recurrent confusion of that model when its verbal account turns out to differ from the merely visible, nonverbal order we call "facts." He attempts, in other words, to reflect like a crystal lozenge though in fact he is painting like an ardent colorist. Moreover, he is doing all this within the context of neurosis, the low level rage of anxiety and its quiet intransigence as depression, each of which are to be "explained" by the other in a typically circular hermeneutic. It is only in these strange fringe states that he can give form to the material, it would seem, but the form derives not from within the material or even necessarily within him, but from the cultural imagination, which transpires in a mental space outlawed by the categorizing order of reason.

Perhaps Capote is simply being inconsistent in repeatedly conflating such contraries, but perhaps also the text demonstrates that the difference between them is illusory, a rhetorical strategy to make way for creativity. In keeping with this recurrent theme, the novel also places religion within the same philosophical template. Jake seems almost serious in attributing his continuation on the case to an answered prayer (p. 82), suggesting that a hermeneutic of prayer (the "help me?" answered by Addie) is at times an essential detail within the detective's picture. TC adds another analogical element to the religious and the detective hermeneutics when he, as writer, makes use of the connection between Quinn and the Reverend Snow to decide upon his characterization of Quinn. Dragged as a boy into the river during a revival, TC tells us that "I shut my eyes; I smelled the Jesus hair, felt the Reverend's arms carrying me downward into drowning blackness, then hours later lifting me into sunlight. My eyes, opening, looked into his grey, manic eyes. His face, broad but gaunt, moved closer, and he kissed my lips. I heard a loud laugh, an eruption like gunfire: 'Checkmate!'" (p. 118). The passage is like a Church Homecoming for our critical themes: blackness and sunlight as the two extremes, the strange grey zone where stable qualities like time become distorted, the fusion of the religious order and the "manic" rage, the identification of preacher and (presumed) murderer, the seepage of raging metaphoric gunfire into a "friendly" game of chess. The transubstantiation of Jesus, Reverend Snow, and Quinn is an example of a basic movement of logocentric logic, the however temporary effacement of difference in order to produce identity out of mere similarity, just as TC here effaces the distinctions among the three and transfers from Snow to Quinn the messianic ego. The point is not whether the process achieves a working insight, but that figurative displacement is its basis.

This would seem, however, to produce a problem for us. Up to this point we have been undoing the false dichotomy of fiction and nonfiction, created as a space-making strategy by which they can take place, and can take the place of the unnamable, dreamlike, inconsistently imaged state wherein they seem to originate. Now, it seems, there is a simultaneous countermovement in which the culture is accused of assimilating different entities into (deceptive) identities. How does one explain this? Perhaps by first seeing that it is not an isolated occurrence, that Capote apparently felt it an important enough gesture to repeat it, and in fact to let it stand as the end of his multiple hermeneutic venture—as sleuth, as novelist, as nonfiction chronicler, and as personally involved inquirer.

In a last, powerful scene, TC goes back to the Blue River after Addie's death and Jake's departure from the case. Drawn to Quinn as the center of the question—the party he must imagine guilty without knowing for sure—TC comes to him, appropriately enough, while

Quinn is wading in the river itself. Quinn laments that Jake had too many suspicions for them to have become friends, and that "'he even thought I drowned poor Addie Mason!' He laughed; then scowled. 'The way I look at it is: it was the hand of God.' He raised his own hand, and the river, viewed between his spread fingers, seemed to weave between them like a dark ribbon. 'God's work. His will.'" (p. 147). He invokes the novel's version of the hermeneutic issue (who-dunit?), and then in a manner more straightforward than that of other figures of the novel, makes explicit that what follows is *not* the way it is, but the "way I look at it." A narrator who affirms that his product is a fictive framework, a commentator upon nonfictional "realities," a monomaniac assuming cosmic knowledge, a possible murderer who may have chosen to appear before TC in the rubber suit that would provide the missing "how?" to TC's account of a death in those same waters, a religious believer who assigns causality to providence, Quinn here subsumes all the roles distributed throughout the novel to others. He becomes, were this one of Propp's folktales, all roles and functions. He even embodies in one sense the voice of TC, the actual narrator, for the river is a "dark ribbon," dark with the sinister themes of mass murder and hyperrational madness, and is figuratively woven as an implement in *his* fingers. It is a type of the writer's pen leaking its black flow of ink, and the final words of TC's narrative are the answer Quinn proposes. It is an appropriately theological answer: God's work, the Word embodied in fact.

A madman utters the culture's central, commanding image for order: all cases all differences, resolve themselves in the Word. Does it then require madness of a kind to affirm and maintain such an order, the order assumed by the kind of hermeneutic search that is reflected in this novel from the central cultural tradition? One notes the steady increase in TC's depressive anxieties and Jake's mania for evidence, even more intense the longer circumstances resist reduction to the univocal question their inquiry poses; one begins as a result to doubt their binary logic of madness and order, guilt and innocence, fiction and nonfiction, figure and fact. Quinn thus becomes a figure that threatens the very ground rules of the project's nonfiction dimension, for he handles the ancillary discourses as all the same kind of (fictional) ordering, and collapses them into a self-mystifying narrative delusion.

Hence one must turn back to the text itself, to the preface to the text, and recognize the implications for our thinking about literary genres. What Capote set out to do was to discover the "*really* true," and he set out with the classic logocentric dichotomies of fiction and nonfiction—that is to say, figurative and literal or referential language—with its attendant tools of inside-outside divisions and the hierarchical rankings of the two. Capote seems to have sought to bring the reality outside fiction into its inside, and thus make it more real; or, alternatively, he wanted to bring the fiction outside reality into the nonfiction, to increase its "energy and esthetic excitements," as he put it in the preface. As these dichotomies fold in on one another, we discover not the naïve realist's belief that fiction is adequate to reality, but the contrary, that nonfiction is never adequate to reality, that its distinction from fiction is one of the primary deceptive maneuvers of logocentric logic by which it hypothesizes the space in which it transpires. The "nonfiction novel" is thus a tautology, not an oxymoron.

Moreover, by talking of the "*really* true," Capote seems to have raised again the notion that truth is the indwelling meaning of events or entities themselves, and that the nonfictional discourses to which he resorts will give him privileged access: logical deduction solves the hermeneutic crisis. What we find, in fact, is a great deal of disorientation on TC's part as he tries to carry out this program. We see him deploying all manner of interpretive frames—both the fictional devices of allusion, figurative language, generic conventions, and the nonfictional devices of the assumptions implicit in these ancillary discourses. The "really true" inheres in the discursive order of intelligibility. It is outside the events, in the narrative covering them with the writer's colors, not in them; or, alternatively, it is not inside the "faithful" narrative version of events, but outside that order in the assumptions implicit in the language and the discursive conventions from which and by which and in which that narrative is cast. Either way, Capote's "inventive" of the nonfiction novel is both hoax and ingenious gathering of the full cultural resources into the act of narration, even if those resources have always been in fiction, if in slightly different guises, just as the fictional has always been there in alternative cultural discourses.

When Capote tells us that, after his conceptual breakthrough, "I set myself center stage, and reconstructed" experiences in his writing (p. xviii), he goes back to the necessarily egoistic positing of the frameworks within which those experiences are seen to take place. It doesn't matter whether such fictions are generated by creating binary myths to divide—and conquer—reality, or by assimilating that multifarious reality into an all but monomaniacal logocentric ego. The point in either case, as a tactician might put it, is to deploy your forces so that things begin happening.

Notes

1. *The Worlds of Truman Capote* (New York: Stein and Day, 1970), pp. 184, 178. Most commentaries on the novel follow Nance's lead, perhaps most explicitly John Hollowell in his *Fact & Fiction: The New Journalism and the Nonfiction Novel* (Chapel Hill: Univ. of North Carolina Press, 1977). Hollowell quotes Nance and Meyer Levin's definition of the "documentary novel" with approval. Jack De Bellis surveys some five thousand revisions Capote worked into the novel between its serialized and book forms, concluding that its factual accuracy is questionable and apparently subordinated to the subliminal goal of working out, novelistically, Capote's complex relationship to the South and to "the dual vision of his fiction" it gave him (p. 535), and he alludes to an earlier criticism of the novel's factual reliability by Phillip K. Tompkins in an article in *Esquire*. The De Bellis essay is "Visions and Revisions: Truman Capote's *In Cold Blood*," *Journal of Modern Literature*, 7 (1979), 519–36. Helen S. Garson talks of the way the novel is "mingling realism with novelistic imagination" (p. 143), an opposition that shows how completely within the fictional field she considers the type (in *Truman Capote* [New York: Frederick Ungar, 1980]). Kenneth T. Reed shows anxiety closer to the surface in emphasizing the "reordering and proportioning" of the orchestration but in seeing also no "distortion of fact" (in *Truman Capote* [Boston: Twayne Publishers, 1981], p. 112). See too Ronald Weber's *The Literature of Fact: Literary Nonfiction in American Writing* (Athens: Ohio Univ. Press, 1980); Weber admires the extent to which Capote draws us "into a world of meaning and inner coherence" (p. 73), "while remaining strictly within the historical record" (p. 80), a judgment perhaps too indulgent.

2. Mas'ud Zavarzadeh, *The Mythopoeic Reality: The Postwar American Nonfiction Novel* (Urbana: Univ. of Illinois Press, 1976), p. 68.

3. Alfred Kazin, in *Bright Book of Life: American Novelists and Storytellers from Hemingway to Mailer* (Notre Dame: Univ. of Notre Dame Press, 1980 [1973]), makes the same shift from quite a different perspective, summing up *In Cold Blood* as "a 'novel' in the form of fact" (p. 210). Both writers, in other words, feel the need for quotation marks around the same half of the nonfiction novel. Kazin, however, is more what Zavarzadeh would call a "liberal-humanist," with his concern for the tension between "our participation in the story [being] more narrow and helpless than [in] a real novel" (p. 218) and the book's aim "to give us this mental control over the frightening example of what is most uncontrolled in human nature" (p. 216). The trouble with the genre for Kazin is that the preoccupation with senseless crime "relieves the liberal

imagination of responsibility and keeps it a spectator" (p. 219) of reality, rather than achieving what Zavarzadeh disparages as the "totalizing" goals of "liberal-humanist" fiction.

4. Zavarzadeh, p. 68.

5. Perhaps a work like Derrida's *Writing and Difference* (trans. Alan Bass [Chicago: Univ. of Chicago Press, 1978]) is the most notorious demonstration of a basic cultural myth he calls "logocentrism" in a whole galaxy of discourses including mysticism, sociology, psychology, linguistics, anthropology, and so forth. But see also Wilson Snipes, "The Biographer as a Center of Reference," *biography* 5, No. 3 (1982), 215–25, for a study of that nonfictional genre as a version of the way relativity figures in history as well as in physics. One may think also of Thomas Kuhn's *The Structure of Scientific Revolutions* (2nd ed. [Chicago: Univ. of Chicago Press, 1970]) as a study of a kind of cultural fiction he calls "paradigms," imaginative orderings of the universe which shape even science, that bastion of supposedly objective nonfiction.

6. John Hellmann comes closer to this position than any commentator I know, in *Fables of Fact: The New Journalism as New Fiction* (Urbana: Univ. of Illinois Press, 1981). He argues the distinction between new journalism (and the nonfiction novel) and other forms of fiction as that between the contracts they establish with the reader: the latter "points outward toward the actual world without ever deviating from observations of that world except in forms—such as authorial speculation or fantasy—which are immediately obvious as such to the reader" (p. 27). As in all fiction, the focus is upon "a microcosmic selection, shaping, and interpretation of events of the macrocosm into a text, a construct representing not events, but an individual conscious-ness's experience of them" (pp. 25–26). Hellmann is acutely alert to the illusoriness of any direct, unmediated perception of actual events, pointing out that even an historical character like Hubert Humphrey "that the reader knows outside his experience of a text is an interpretively selected and ordered construct of impressions, as is the author's, whether arrived at through first-hand knowledge or (more typically) already interpreted as received from the mass media" (p. 31). But Hellmann is probably more inclined that I to accept that there is something called "external facts" with which a writer can begin. In actual practice, such "facts" are inevitably textual episodes from the moment they form in one's consciousness.

7. The quotations from the preface and the novel come from the paperback edition (New York: New American Library, 1981) and are noted parenthetically.

Chronology

1924   Truman Streckfus Persons, son of Lillie Mae (later Nina) Faulk Persons and Arch Persons, born 30 September, in New Orleans.

1931   Nina Faulk Persons and Arch Persons divorce.

1932   Nina Faulk marries Joseph Capote, 24 March.

1935   Joseph Capote legally adopts Truman, 14 February.

1942   Begins work as copyboy at the *New Yorker*.

1945   "Miriam" published in June issue of *Mademoiselle*; wins an O. Henry Memorial Award in 1946; "A Tree of Night" published in October issue of *Harper's Bazaar*; "Jug of Silver" published in December issue of *Mademoiselle*.

1947   "Shut a Final Door" published in August issue of the *Atlantic*; first-prize winner of the 1948 O. Henry Awards.

1948   *Other Voices, Other Rooms*.

1949   *A Tree of Night and Other Stories*.

1950   *Local Color*.

1951   *The Grass Harp*.

1952   Theatrical version of *The Grass Harp* opens on Broadway, 27 March, at the Martin Beck Theater.

1954   Nina Capote commits suicide, 4 January; theatrical version of "A House of Flowers" opens on Broadway, 30 December, at the Alvin Theater.

1956   *The Muses Are Heard*.

1958   *Breakfast at Tiffany's*.

1959   *Observations*; photos by Richard Avedon, commentary by Capote.

1963   *The Selected Writings of Truman Capote*.

1966   *In Cold Blood* and *A Christmas Memory*. The Black and White Ball, in honor of Katherine Graham, "The Party of the Decade," 28 November.

1967 Richard Brooks's film version of *In Cold Blood*.

1968 *The Thanksgiving Visitor*.

1973 *The Dogs Bark: Public People and Private Places*.

1975 "Mojave" published in *Esquire*, in June; "La Côte Basque, 1965" published in *Esquire*, in November.

1976 "Unspoiled Monsters" published in *Esquire*, in May; "Kate McCloud" published in *Esquire*, in December.

1977 Death of Arch Persons.

1980 *Music for Chameleons*.

1982 Death of Joseph Capote.

1983 *One Christmas*.

1984 Truman Capote dies, 25 August, in Los Angeles, at the home of Joanne Carson.

1985 *Three*.

1987 *Answered Prayers: The Unfinished Novel*.

Selected Bibliography

Primary Works

Books

Answered Prayers: The Unfinished Novel. New York: Random House, 1987. Contents: "Unspoiled Monsters," "Kate McCloud," "La Côte Basque."

Breakfast at Tiffany's: A Short Novel and Three Stories. New York: Random House, 1958. Contents: *Breakfast at Tiffany's*, "A Diamond Guitar," "House of Flowers," *A Christmas Memory*.

A Capote Reader. New York: Random House, 1987. Contents: Short Stories: "Miriam," "My Side of the Matter," "A Tree of Night," "Jug of Silver," "The Headless Hawk," "Shut a Final Door," "Master Misery," "Children on Their Birthdays," "A Diamond Guitar," "House of Flowers," "Among the Paths to Eden," "Mojave"; Novellas: *The Grass Harp*, *Breakfast at Tiffany's*; Travel Sketches: "New Orleans," "New York," "Brooklyn," "Hollywood," "Haiti," "To Europe," "Ischia," "Tangier," "A Ride Through Spain," "Fontana Vecchia," "Extreme Magic," "Greek Paragraphs," "Music for Chameleons"; Reportage: *The Muses Are Heard*, "Then It All Came Down"; *Handcarved Coffins*; Portraits: "The Duke in His Domain"; From *Observations*: "Richard Avedon," "John Huston," "Charlie Chaplin," "A Gathering of Swans," "Pablo Picasso," "Coco Chanel," "Marcel Duchamp," "Jean Cocteau and André Gide," "Mae West," "Louis Armstrong," "Humphry Bogart," "Ezra Pound," "Somerset Maugham," "Isak Dinesen," "Jane Bowles," "Cecil Beaton," "Elizabeth Taylor," "A Beautiful Child," "Remembering Tennessee"; Essays: "A House on the Heights," "Lola," "A Voice from a Cloud," "Ghosts in Sunlight: The Filming of *In Cold Blood*," "The White Rose," "Self-Portrait," "Preface to *The Dogs Bark*," "A Day's Work," "Dazzle," "Hidden Gardens," "Hello, Stranger," "Derring-do," "Nocturnal Turnings," "Mr. Jones," "A Lamp in the Window," "Hospitality," "Preface to *Music for Chameleons*."

A Christmas Memory. New York: Random House, 1966.

The Dogs Bark: Public People and Private Places. New York: Random House, 1973. Contents: "A Voice from a Cloud," "The White Rose," *Local Color*: "Fontana Vecchia," "Lola," "A House on the Heights," "Greek Paragraphs"; *The Muses Are Heard*; "The Duke in His Domain," "Style and the

Japanese," From *Observations*: "Isak Dinesen," "Mae West," "Louis Armstrong," "Jean Cocteau and André Gide," "Humphrey Bogart," "Ezra Pound," "Marilyn Monroe," "Jane Bowles," "Ghosts in Sunlight: The Filming of *In Cold Blood*," "Self-Portrait."

The Grass Harp. New York: Random House, 1951.

The Grass Harp: A Play. New York: Random House, 1952.

"The Grass Harp" and "A Tree of Night and Other Stories." New York: New American Library, 1956. Contents: *The Grass Harp*, "Master Misery," "Children on Their Birthdays," "Shut a Final Door," "Jug of Silver," "Miriam," "The Headless Hawk," "My Side of the Matter," "A Tree of Night."

House of Flowers. New York: Random House, 1966.

In Cold Blood. New York: Random House, 1966.

Local Color. New York: Random House, 1950. Contents: "New Orleans," "New York," "Brooklyn," "Hollywood," "Haiti," "To Europe," "Ischia," "Tangier," "A Ride through Spain."

The Muses Are Heard. New York: Random House, 1956.

Music for Chameleons. New York: Random House, 1980. Contents: "Music for Chameleons," "Mr. Jones," "A Lamp in the Window," "Mojave," "Hospitality," "Dazzle," *Handcarved Coffins*, "A Day's Work," "Hello, Stranger," "Hidden Gardens," "Derring-do," "Then It All Came Down," "A Beautiful Child," "Nocturnal Turnings."

Observations. New York: Simon and Schuster, 1959. Photographs by Richard Avedon, commentary by Truman Capote.

One Christmas. New York: Random House, 1983.

Other Voices, Other Rooms. New York: Random House, 1948.

Selected Writings of Truman Capote. New York: Random House, 1963. Contents: "A Tree of Night," "Miriam," "The Headless Hawk," "Shut a Final Door," "Children on Their Birthdays," "Master Misery," "A Diamond Guitar," "House of Flowers," *A Christmas Memory, Breakfast at Tiffany's*, "Among the Paths to Eden," "New Orleans," "Ischia," "A Ride through Spain," *The Muses Are Heard*, "The Duke in His Domain," "A House on the Heights."

The Thanksgiving Visitor. New York: Random House, 1966.

Three by Truman Capote. New York: Random House, 1985. Contents: *Other Voices, Other Rooms, Breakfast at Tiffany's, Music for Chameleons*.

A Tree of Night and Other Stories. New York: Random House, 1949. Contents: "Master Misery," "Children on Their Birthdays," "Shut a Final Door," "Jug of Silver," "Miriam," "The Headless Hawk," "My Side of the Matter," "A Tree of Night."

Trilogy: An Experiment in Multimedia. New York: Macmillan, 1969. With Eleanor Perry and Frank Perry.

Uncollected Stories

"Blind Items." *Ladies Home Journal,* January 1974, pp. 81, 122, 124.
"A Mink of One's Own." *Decade of Short Stories* 6 (Third Quarter 1944): 1–4.
"Preacher's Legend." *Prairie Schooner* 19 (December 1945): 265–74.
"The Shape of Things." *Decade of Short Stories* 6 (Fourth Quarter 1944): 21–23.
"The Walls Are Cold." *Decade of Short Stories* 4 (Fourth Quarter 1943): 27–30.

Secondary Works

Bibliographies and Checklists

Bryer, Jackson R. "Truman Capote: A Bibliography." In *In Cold Blood: A Critical Handbook*, ed. Irving Malin, 239–69. Belmont, Calif.: Wadsworth, 1968.
Stanton, Robert J. *Truman Capote: A Primary and Secondary Bibliography.* Boston: G. K. Hall, 1980.
Vanderwerken, David. "Truman Capote: 1943–1968. A Critical Bibliography." *Bulletin of Bibliography* 27 (1970): 57–60, 71.
Wall, Richard, and Carl Craycraft. "A Checklist of Works about Truman Capote." *Bulletin of the New York Public Library* 71 (March 1967): 165–72.

Interviews

Grobel, Lawrence. *Conversations with Capote.* New York: New American Library, 1985.
Inge, M. Thomas, ed. *Truman Capote: Conversations.* Jackson: University Press of Mississippi, 1987.
Ruas, Charles. "Truman Capote." In *Conversations with American Writers*, 37–56. New York: Knopf, 1985.

Books or Parts of Books

Aldridge, John. "Capote and Buechner: The Escape into Otherness." *After the Lost Generation: A Critical Study of the Writers of Two Wars.* New York: Noonday Press, 1951. Pages 194–230.
———. "The War Writers Ten Years Later." In *Time to Murder and Create: The Contemporary Novel in Crisis.* New York: David McKay, 1966. Pages 139–48.
Allen, Walter. *The Modern Novel in Britain and the United States.* New York: E. P. Dutton, 1964. Pages 301–3.
Blixen, Karen (Isak Dinesen). "Introduction" to *Holly* (*Breakfast at Tiffany's*). Translated by Jan Nordby Gretlund. Denmark: Gyldendal, 1960.

Bradbury, John. *Renaissance in the South: A Critical History of the Literature, 1920–1960*. Chapel Hill: University of North Carolina Press, 1963. Pages 132–33, 189, 197.

Brinnin, John Malcolm. *Dear Heart, Old Buddy*. New York: Delacorte Press/ Seymour Lawrence, 1986.

———. *Sextet: T. S. Eliot and Truman Capote and Others*. New York: Delacorte Press/Seymour Lawrence, 1981. Pages 3–96.

Clarke, Gerald. *Truman Capote: A Biography*. New York: Simon and Schuster, 1988.

Cowley, Malcolm. *The Literary Situation*. New York: Viking Press, 1954. Passim.

Dunphy, Jack. *Dear Genius . . . A Memoir of My Life with Truman Capote*. New York: McGraw-Hill, 1987.

Eisinger, Chester. *Fiction of the Forties*. Chicago: University of Chicago Press, 1963. Pages 237–43.

Friedman, Melvin. "Towards an Aesthetic: Truman Capote's Other Voices." In *Truman Capote's 'In Cold Blood': A Critical Handbook*, edited by Irving Malin, 163–76. Belmont, Calif. Wadsworth, 1968.

Garson, Helen S. *Truman Capote*. New York: Frederick Ungar, 1980.

———. "Truman Capote." In *Fifty Southern Writers after 1900*, edited by Joseph M. Flora and Robert Bain, 99–110. New York: Greenwood Press, 1987.

Goad, Craig M. *Daylight and Darkness, Dream and Delusion: The Works of Truman Capote*. Emporia, Kans. Emporia State Research Studies, 1967.

Gossett, Louise. *Violence in Recent Southern Fiction*. Durham, N.C.: Duke University Press, 1965. Pages 145–58.

Gray, Richard. *The Literature of Memory: Modern Writers of the American South*. Baltimore: Johns Hopkins University Press, 1977. Pages 257–65.

Hassan, Ihab. "Truman Capote: The Vanishing Image of Narcissus," in *Radical Innocence: Studies in the Contemporary American Novel*, Princeton N.J.: Princeton University Press, 1961. Pages 230–58.

Hays, Peter. *The Limping Hero: Grotesques in Literature*. New York: New York University Press, 1971. Passim.

Hoffman, Frederick J. *The Art of Southern Fiction: A Study of Some Modern Novelists*. Carbondale: Southern Illinois University Press, 1967. Passim.

Kazin, Alfred. *Bright Book of Life: American Novelists and Story-tellers from Hemingway to Mailer*, Boston: Little, Brown, 1973. Pages 209–19.

———, *Contemporaries*. Boston: Little, Brown, 1961. Pages 250–54.

———, *The Open Form: Essays for Our Time*. New York: Harcourt Brace and World, 1961. Pages 213–14.

Malin, Irving. *New American Gothic*. Carbondale: Southern Illinois University Press, 1962. Passim.

————, ed. *Truman Capote's "In Cold Blood": A Critical Handbook*. Belmont, Calif.: Wadsworth, 1968.

Morris, Robert K. "Capote's Imagery." In *Truman Capote's 'In Cold Blood': A Critical Handbook*, edited by Irving Malin, 176–86. Belmont, Calif.: Wadsworth, 1968.

Nance, William L. *The Worlds of Truman Capote*. New York: Stein and Day, 1970.

O'Connor, William Van. "The Grotesque: An American Genre." In *The Grotesque: An American Genre and Other Essays*, 3–19. Carbondale: Southern Illinois University Press, 1962.

Reed, Kenneth T. *Truman Capote*. Boston: Twayne, 1981.

Voss, Arthur. *The American Short Story: A Critical Survey*. Norman: University of Oklahoma Press, 1973. Pages 347–48.

West, Paul. *The Modern Novel*. London: Hutchison University Library, 1963. Passim.

West, Ray B., Jr. *The Short Story in America*. Chicago: Henry Regnery, 1952. Pages 110–11.

Windham, Donald. *Lost Friendships: A Memoir of Truman Capote, Tennessee Williams, and Others*. New York: Morrow, 1987.

Articles and Reviews

Aldridge, John W. "America's Young Novelists: Uneasy Inheritors of a Revolution." *Saturday Review of Literature*, 12 February 1949.

————. "The Metaphorical World of Truman Capote." *Western Review* 15 (Summer 1951): 247–60.

Allen, Walter. "New Short Stories." *New Statesman*, 20 December 1958.

Allmendinger, Blake. "The Room Was Locked, with the Key on the Inside: Female Influence in Truman Capote's 'My Side of the Matter.'" *Studies in Short Fiction* 24 (Summer 1987): 279–88.

Arvin, Newton. "The New American Writers." *Harper's Bazaar*, March 1947.

Baker, Carlos. "Nursery Tales from Jitter Manor." *New York Times Book Review*, 27 February 1949.

Balakian, Nona. "The Prophetic Vogue of the Anti-Heroine." *Southwest Review* 47 (Spring 1962): 134–41.

Barry, Iris. "Short Stories of Truman Capote." *New York Herald Tribune Weekly Book Review*, 27 February 1949.

Bentley, Eric. "On Capote's *Grass Harp*." *New Republic*, 14 April 1952.

Blake, Nancy. "*Other Voices, Other Rooms*: Southern Gothic or Medieval Quest?" *Delta* 11 (November 1980): 31–47.

Brown, Tina. "Goodbye to the Ladies Who Lunch." *New York Times Book Review*, 13 September 1987.

Brumm, Ursula. "Symbolism and the Modern Novel." *Partisan Review* 25 (Summer 1958): 329–42.

Bucco, Martin. "Truman Capote and the Country Below the Surface." *Four Quarters* 7 (November 1957): 22–25.

Clarke, Gerald. "Checking in with Truman Capote." *Esquire*, 78 (November 1972).

Cowley, Malcolm. "American Novels since the War." New Republic, (28 December 1953).

Curley, Thomas F. "The Quarrel with Time in American Fiction." *American Scholar* 29 (Autumn 1960): 552, 554, 556, 558, 560.

Davis, Robert C. "*Other Voices, Other Rooms* and the Ocularity of American Fiction." *Delta* (November 1980): 1–14.

Fiedler, Leslie. "Capote's Tales: A Tree of Night and Other Stories." *Nation*, (April 1949).

Fleming, Anne Taylor. "The Private World of Truman Capote." *New York Times Magazine*, 2 pts, 9 July 1978 and 16 July 1978.

Fowles, John. "Capote as Maupassant: *Music for Chameleons.*" *Saturday Review*, July 1980.

Hassan, Ihab. "The Character of Post-War Fiction in America." *English Journal* 51, no. 1 (January 1962): 1–8.

———. "The Victim: Images of Evil in Recent Fiction." *College English* 21 (December 1959): 140–46.

Hicks, Granville. "A World of Innocence." *New York Times Book Review*, 30 September 1951.

Hilton, James. "Travels of Truman Capote." *New York Herald Tribune Weekly Book Review*, 15 October 1950.

La Farge, Oliver. "Sunlit Gothic." *Saturday Review of Literature*, 20 October 1951.

Larsen, Michael. "Capote's 'Miriam' and the Literature of the Double." *International Fiction Review* 7, no.1 (1980): 53–54.

Levine, Paul. "*Breakfast at Tiffany's.*" *Georgia Review* 13 (Fall 1959): 350–52.

———. "Truman Capote: The Revelation of the Broken Image." *Virginia Quarterly Review* 34 (Autumn 1958): 600–617.

Lodge, David. "Getting at the Truth: *Music for Chameleons.*" (London) *Times Literary Supplement*, 20 February 1981.

Malin, Irving. "From Gothic to Camp." *Ramparts*, November 1964.

Moravia, Albert. "Truman Capote and the New Baroque," from "Two American Writers." *Sewanee Review* 68 (Summer 1960): 473–81.

Nance, William L. "Variations on a Dream: Katherine Anne Porter and Truman Capote." *Southern Humanities Review* 3 (Fall 1969): 338–45.

Richardson, John. "A Côté Capote." *New York Review of Books*, 17 December 1987.

Siegle, Robert. "Capote's *Handcarved Coffins* and the Nonfictional Novel." *Contemporary Literature* 25 (1984): 437–51.
Zacharias, Lee. "Living the American Dream: 'Children on Their Birthdays.'" *Studies in Short Fiction* 12 (Fall 1975): 343–50.

Index

The Author

Helen S. Garson is professor of English and professor of American studies at George Mason University in Fairfax, Virginia, where she teaches modern fiction. She writes and lectures in the United States and abroad about twentieth-century literature. Among her publications are numerous essays about Capote as well as an earlier book entitled *Truman Capote.*

The Editor

General Editor Gordon Weaver earned his B.A. in English at the University of Wisconsin-Milwaukee in 1961; his M.A. in English at the University of Illinois, where he studied as a Woodrow Wilson Fellow, in 1962; and his Ph.D. in English and creative writing at the University of Denver in 1970. He is author of several novels, including *Count a Lonely Cadence, Give Him a Stone, Circling Byzantium,* and most recently *The Eight Corners of the World* (1988). Many of his numerous short stories are collected in *The Entombed Man of Thule, Such Waltzing Was Not Easy, Getting Serious, Morality Play, A World Quite Round,* and *Men Who Would Be Good* (1991). Recognition of his fiction includes the St. Lawrence Award for Fiction (1973), two National Endowment for the Arts Fellowships (1974, 1989), and the O. Henry First Prize (1979). He edited *The American Short Story, 1945–1980: A Critical History,* and is currently editor of *Cimarron Review.* He is professor of English at Oklahoma State University and serves as an adjunct member of the faculty of the Vermont College Master of Fine Arts in Writing Program. Married, and the father of three daughters, he lives in Stillwater, Oklahoma.